Praise for *Reading Between the Signs* and Anna Mindess

"Anna Mindess has done it again. Her updates to *Reading Between the Signs* confront the challenges that cultural differences bring to interpreting between (Deaf) signers and (hearing) speakers, whether in face-to-face encounters or via video and computer. She proposes solutions, but don't expect simple rules: she and her acknowledged Deaf resources demand that interpreters use context, exercise judgment, and continue learning . . . a highly readable volume that will stay with you."

—Nancy Frishberg, Ph.D., Author of *Interpreting: An Introduction*

"*Reading Between the Signs* is the first text to identify, analyze and give practitioners some clues for successful communication across world views and the challenge of interpreting 'equivalent' meaning across the chasm of differences out of which individual meaning is created. This is a must-read for every interpreter or other professional attempting to communicate between the visual reality of deaf individuals and the auditory reality of hearing individuals. Bravo! The book is outstanding—well written, informative, and desperately needed in our field!"

—Jan Humphrey, Ed.D., Certified Interpreter, Interpreter Educator and Author of *So You Want to Be an Interpreter?*

"Adds a necessary dimension to understanding what sign language interpretation really entails—not the exchange of words for signs and vice versa but the translation of one view of life and all its meanings into another equally valid yet different view."

—William C. Stokoe, former Professor Emeritus, Gallaudet University

"A dazzling application of the tools of intercultural communication to illuminating Deaf and hearing cultures and their differences . . . This is a book for everyone interested in Deaf culture."

—Harlan Lane, Author of *When the Mind Hears* and *The Mask of Benevolence*

"A must-read! An enlightening book, *Reading Between the Signs* is a defining document in the literature of Deaf culture."

—Eileen Forestal, Professor, ASL Studies and Interpreting Training, Union County College

Reading Between the Signs

INTERCULTURAL COMMUNICATION FOR SIGN LANGUAGE INTERPRETERS

SECOND EDITION

Anna Mindess

with Thomas K. Holcomb,
Daniel Langholtz and Priscilla Moyers

Foreword by Sharon Neumann Solow

INTERCULTURAL PRESS
A Nicholas Brealey Publishing Company

BOSTON • LONDON

First published by Intercultural Press, a division of Nicholas Brealey Publishing, in 2006.

Intercultural Press,
a division of Nicholas Brealey Publishing
100 City Hall Plaza, Suite 501
Boston, MA 02108, USA
Tel: +617-523-3801
Fax: +617-523-3708
www.interculturalpress.com

Nicholas Brealey Publishing
3–5 Spafield Street, Clerkenwell
London, EC1R 4QB, UK
Tel: +44-(0)-207-239-0360
Fax: +44-(0)-207-239-0370
www.nbrealey-books.com

The author gratefully acknowledges permission to quote, paraphrase, and summarize material from El Paso Community College/National Multicultural Interpreting Project Curriculum (NMIP). Reprinted by permission of the NMIP.

Printed in the United States of America

10   09   08   07   06   1   2   3   4   5

ISBN-13: 978-1-931930-26-0
ISBN-10: 1-931930-26-0

Library of Congress Cataloging-in-Publication Data
Mindess, Anna.
     Reading between the signs : intercultural communication for sign language interpreters / Anna Mindess with Thomas K. Holcomb, Daniel Langholtz, and Priscilla Moyers; foreword by Sharon Neumann Solow.—2nd ed.
        p.   cm.
     Includes bibliographical references and index.
     ISBN-13: 978-1-931930-26-0
     ISBN-10: 1-931930-26-0
     1. Interpreters for the deaf—United States.   2. Communication and culture—United States.   3. Intercultural communication—United States.   4. Deaf—Means of communication—United States.   5. American Sign Language.   I. Title.
     HV2402.M56   2006
     419'.70802—dc22   2006012193

To my husband, who has always shared my fascination with culture,
and to my father, who inspired me to write about it.

Contents

Foreword

◆

This book provides us with a penetrating look at a subject that, up until its first publication in 1999, was rarely thought or written about. The community of interpreters and interpreter educators received the first edition of *Reading Between the Signs* with great enthusiasm and a tremendous hunger. It filled a gaping hole in the body of literature of interpretation. The original *Reading Between the Signs* was a groundbreaking text that provided interpreters and interpreting students with insight and greater comfort navigating the complex work we do. As we move into the new paradigm inspired by this book, this new edition will bring even greater inspiration with its updated information.

Ms. Mindess has made a significant contribution to the field of interpretation in her thoughtful and responsible journey into the heart of the world of interpreters. As a profession, we need to think together, and I am grateful for the opportunity to think about this topic provided within these pages.

Reading Between the Signs provides an excellent resource for many groups. Working interpreters, interpreter training programs, and interpreter educators are the most obvious beneficiaries. Others include colleges and universities, K-12 faculty, and administrators and staff involved in the education of Deaf people. Support personnel, such as counselors, vocational rehabilitation workers, and the like, will gain from reading this book, as will anyone else who happens to work with interpreters. Now, with updated information regarding VRS interpreting and multicultural influences, this new edition provides even greater resources to support our thinking and decision making.

This volume is carefully thought-out, well-resourced, and -researched. For years it was almost assumed that if one could sign, of course one could interpret. Then, as the model of the process of interpretation became more sophisticated, training in the art and science of interpretation became more or less the standard. Still, there was a sense of something missing, but that something was elusive. Interpreters were trained with vocabulary drills, ethics lectures, and, later, grammatical lessons. Cultural aspects were late additions to the curriculum. It is not until recently that the subject of cultural influence was viewed as critical to the success of interpretation. In an ever-changing world, Anna Mindess' book provides a framework for understanding culture as well as specific descriptions of the important elements of mainstream American and Deaf cultures, and offers suggestions for dealing with those elements in our work.

Today we realize that this kind of knowledge can be the very factor that heightens or decreases our effectiveness. My advice is: read these pages well, take notes, and think about the material presented. Any excitement, confusion, disagreement, or commentary should be taken to the profession in a public forum. Write an article, a monograph, or even a letter to the editor; or you may find some other outlet to think together, such as study groups, workshops, and the like. Dialogue can only help us to grow.

I am personally and professionally very grateful for the contribution Ms. Mindess has made to the field of sign language interpretation. It is a topic we are all striving to understand and explain. Within these pages is a fabulous resource.

—Sharon Neumann Solow
April 2006

Preface

"We live in a moment of history where change is so speeded up that we begin to see the present only when it is already disappearing."
— *R. D. Laing*

In the relatively brief span of seven years since *Reading Between the Signs* was first published, much has changed. Sign language interpreters have entered a new era: an increasing percentage of our work takes place via video camera. This would have been unimaginable 40 years ago at the "birth" of our profession. Until relatively recently, we did our work in examining rooms, offices, classrooms, churches, and courtrooms. Not being able to predict the future, we took our physical presence in these settings for granted. We failed to appreciate the contextual clues we received just by being in the same room with both clients.

Interpreters still travel to and work in all these same settings, but this may soon become a thing of the past, with the advent of Video Relay Services (VRS) and Video Remote Interpreting (VRI). We are living in a unique moment in time. Like a person standing in the middle of a racetrack where classic cars and futuristic vehicles zoom by, battling it out, we are not likely to have a clear perspective on our situation until the dust settles. Meanwhile, it would be useful to consider where we are now and examine the challenges brought on by these electronic advances. Personally, I am intrigued with the ways in which these new developments relate to cultural differences.

The Deaf world is another arena where recent technological innovations have had a huge impact. Deafness has often been characterized as a "communication handicap." For many Deaf people, however, the extensive use of text pagers, web cams, e-mail, and the Internet may temper that description. As with any technological breakthrough, there are things gained and things lost. When novel problems arise, fresh rules and conventions emerge to deal with them. We will examine how technology has affected Deaf culture, even though the specifics will surely have altered by the time these words are printed.

One fascinating aspect of cultural studies is the exploration of ways that cultures adapt to changing circumstances. Deaf culture is clearly not alone in adapting to modern technological devices. Before we examine some of the changes attributable to recent technology, we will take a look at other world cultures to see how their traditions and values have shifted in the wake of recent technological whirlwinds.

Another development, in the year 2000, was the long-awaited completion of the National Multicultural Interpreting Project (NMIP) at El Paso Community College. Five years of collaborative effort by dozens of dedicated team members produced a monumental 500-page work. Funded by a grant from the U.S. Department of Education, the final product was subtitled "Curriculum for Enhancing Interpreter Competencies for Working within Culturally and Linguistically Diverse Communities." Our interpreting community is privileged to have this resource in our midst, and I am grateful to be able to draw on the work of the multicultural team members who put it together.

No discussion of culture would be complete without the acknowledgment of perspectives from ethnic, cultural, and linguistic groups with whom we share our land. In the limited space available here, the entire range of material covered by the NMIP curriculum cannot be included. My endeavor, therefore, will be to highlight salient features of each group in order to understand those cultural characteristics that impact Deaf clients in interpreting situations. Related interpreting scenarios are included to get you thinking and inspire you to do further study either with the NMIP curriculum or on your own.

I am also delighted to include recent research that has increased our knowledge of issues mentioned in the first edition. Specifically, the work of Jack Hoza and Daniel Rousch in the area of politeness and non-manual markers will be discussed. In the last half-dozen years, I have also delved deeper into certain topics that demand more thought as they relate to our work. I present my latest perspectives on indirect versus direct communication and the linguistic necessity of back-channel feedback.

Has our work as sign language interpreters really changed that much in the last seven years? In the last decade of the twentieth century, freelance interpreters probably worked with one to four Deaf people from their local area in a single day. In a typical day as a video relay interpreter in the early years of the twenty-first century, however, it is not unusual to interpret for 50 Deaf people (albeit some for only a few seconds) from twenty different states plus several foreign countries. That we have rapidly adapted to this dizzying pace makes it all the more impressive. If it is true that as R.D. Laing stated, we can only see the present "when it is already disappearing," we had better not blink. If we do, we will certainly miss significant developments that are revolutionizing our world.

Acknowledgments

◆

I wish to thank my husband, Armand Volkas, for his loving support during the long labor of bringing this book into the world and for coming up with the perfect title; my daughter, Lila, for her patience with an often distracted mama; and my father, Harvey Mindess, for his calm voice of experience, his encouragement, and his help with the finer points of grammar.

My gratitude goes to the following sign language interpreters: Aaron Brace, Maureen Fitzgerald, Jewel Jauregui, Sheila Hall, Joyce Linden, Nikki Norton Rexroat, Bobbe Skiles, Sharon Neumann Solow, Daniel Veltri, and Anna Witter-Merithew for sharing their expertise and opinions with me and especially to Patricia Lessard for her wisdom, support, and unsurpassed skill.

I deeply appreciate the generosity of Thomas K. Holcomb, Daniel Langholtz, and Priscilla Moyers for acting as consultants on both editions of the book.

Thanks also go to the others I consulted with: Ella Mae Lentz, Ken Mikos, and Cheri Smith; Julie Johnson, Jacolyn Harmer, Holly Mikkelson, and Lynette Shi of the Monterey Institute; Claudia Bernard, Dr. Todd Imahori, Carl Kirchner, Paul Preston, Jurgen Schwing, Akio Shimuzu, Hans Stahlschmidt, and Laurie Swabey.

A debt of gratitude to L. Robert Kohls for his support and permission to refer to his as yet unpublished "Benchmarks in the Development of the Field of Intercultural Communication in the United States." And a deep bow to Theresa Smith for writing a brilliant dissertation and generously allowing me to quote from it.

A hearty cheer to all the librarians who have helped me over the years: Marti Goddard, Michael Callejas, Arden Wong, and Orkideh Sassouni of the Deaf Services Center at the San Francisco Main Library, who have always been willing to search for anything I needed at a moment's notice. And a big thank you to Peter Mann, librarian and friend, who helped me track down much of the information on new technologies in other countries.

Thanks to David Hoopes and Judy Carl-Hendrick of Intercultural Press for editing the original text and to Patricia O'Hare and Erika Heilman for making sure the second edition became a reality.

I owe a deep debt of gratitude to Mary Mooney, Project Director of the NMIP, for her gracious generosity in allowing me the freedom to quote and paraphrase from the magnificent curriculum that is the result of years of commitment and collaboration. My appreciation extends to the NMIP Team Leaders: Anthony Aramburo, Jeffrey Davis, Tupper Dunbar, Jonathan Hopkins, Jan Nishimura, and Angela Roth. Their dedication to this project has resulted in a significant resource for our field. My thanks also to the Senior Editors of the NMIP: Dr. Glenn Anderson, Dr. Douglas Watson, Dr. Howard Busby, Dr. Angel Ramos, and Dr. Steven Chough.

A sincere thank you to those I consulted with personally, Myisha Blackman, Marlene Elliott, Suzanne Garcia-Lightbourn, Jo Linda Greenfield, Holly Newstead, and Jan Nishimura, for sharing their thoughts and experience and for a careful reading of my text.

A big hug for last-minute moral and editorial support to Celene de Miranda, Marina McIntire, and Robin Mills.

And, as always, a special thank you to my dear friend and fellow interpreter, Margaret Dorfman, an astute cultural observer, for her continued encouragement and sensitive feedback given over countless sushi, paella, and seafood dinners.

PART ONE

Background

1

Introduction

*. . . a Foreign Service Institute linguist . . . while watching the evening news, discovered that a Vietnamese interpreter had simply given up when trying to bridge the gap between a CBS reporter and a Vietnamese villager. The TV audience watched the reporter ask a question, heard it go back and forth between the interpreter and the villager, and then heard the answer back in English. What the interpreter had done was simply ask the villager to count to ten, which he did. Then the interpreter reported what the villager **might** have said had he been able to understand the abstract ideas in the original question.*

—GLEN FISHER
International Negotiation

This incident from the Vietnam War era provides a striking example of the challenges interpreters confront daily. Why did the interpreter in this case abdicate responsibility for accurately conveying the message? Glen Fisher concludes that the interpreter "faced an impossible task. The life experiences of the reporter and the villager, and their languages as reflections of culture, presented too great a contrast" (Fisher 1980, 60–61).

As sign language interpreters, we can empathize with the interpreter described above, although it is hoped that we do not choose the same solution when faced with the challenge of large cultural differences. Cultural differences can be glaring enough to bring a meeting to a halt or so subtle that participants in a conversation do not even realize they are making erroneous judgments about each other. Why and how does culture affect our work, and what can we do when it seems to be at the core of communication difficulties? These are questions I hope to answer in this book.

How many of these situations have you encountered in your work as an interpreter?

+ The Deaf person makes a comment or asks a question that would
  be acceptable at a Deaf gathering but would seem rude to hearing
  people.
+ The hearing person, in an effort to soften a critical remark, speaks in
  an indirect manner that leaves the Deaf person unsure of the point
  being made.
+ The hearing person asks the Deaf person a question for which he or
  she anticipates a single-word answer (e.g., yes, no, a number). In
  response, the Deaf person commences a lengthy narrative, which to
  the hearing person does not seem to answer the original question.

Too often, we sign language interpreters work alone, running from one
challenge to another, without the benefit of others with whom to share our
ideas, frustrations, and triumphs. Even if we do have a partner and switch
off to give our arms and brains a break, rarely do we take the time to
debrief each other after the assignment, to discuss what worked and what
didn't. One reason may be a reluctance to share details with our colleagues, not only because our professional code of conduct requires us to
preserve the confidentiality of the parties involved but also because we
may be embarrassed to admit our uncertainties and errors. Yet without
this mutual sharing, we may fail to recognize crucial patterns that would
help us become better interpreters. Since many of us repeatedly interpret
similar interactions between hearing and Deaf people, it is inevitable that
we encounter similar cultural mismatches. We could greatly benefit,
therefore, from sharing our firsthand knowledge as a step in helping us
anticipate conflicts and brainstorm strategies to deal with them.

If we rarely share our experiences with other sign language interpreters, we almost never talk with professionals who work in the area of
cross-cultural communication. A few of us may be so isolated that we do
not even recognize that it is not only Deaf culture that has quirks and idio-
syncrasies. Every culture in the world has ways in which it appears strange
or wrong to others. By studying the characteristics of world cultures,
therefore, we will see that Deaf culture shares many features of Japanese,
Chinese, Israeli, French, and other cultures.

In order to successfully function as bicultural mediators, not only must
we be familiar with the elements of Deaf culture, but we must also pay
equal, if not greater, attention to the other half of the bilingual-bicultural
seesaw, American hearing, or mainstream, culture. Perhaps we have taken
a class or workshop in Deaf culture, but how many of us have made a

study of our own American culture? One's own cultural characteristics are hard to see because we are so accustomed to them; like our skin, they are a part of us.

Admittedly, it is an oversimplification to speak of the dichotomy between "American Deaf Culture" and "mainstream American Culture." The "bilingual-bicultural" model does not do justice to the complex society we live in. We are well aware that there are many cultural and linguistic groups with their own sets of values and behaviors who need to be recognized and respected. In chapter 6, we will examine in depth some of these perspectives. Any generalizations are employed for the sake of practicality, with no intent of exclusion or disrespect.

You may feel that you are already sensitive to the distinctions between Deaf and hearing cultures because you have been fascinated with them for many years. Those sign language interpreters who learned American Sign Language (ASL) as a first language in Deaf families have been dealing with their dual identity all their lives. Those of us who were not born into Deaf families and learned ASL later, by choice, probably did so because at some level we were aware that, as Edward T. Hall says in *The Silent Language*, "One of the most effective ways to learn about oneself is by taking seriously the cultures of others. It forces you to pay attention to those details of life which differentiate them from you" (Hall 1959, 32).

My Story

We all have our own stories of what drew us to the intersection of the Deaf and hearing worlds. I found sign language through theater. I was in my early twenties and trying to make it as an actress in the then-burgeoning experimental theater movement in Los Angeles. One night during the intermission of a mime show, I saw a couple of audience members signing and was intrigued. Later, after I went to a performance of NTD (the National Theater of the Deaf) and witnessed the expressiveness of sign language, I decided to study it to enlarge my acting repertoire. I was directed to CSUN (California State University, Northridge), where I was lucky to have as my first teacher Lou Fant, the undisputed master of our craft and one of the founders of our profession, who also shared my theatrical ambitions.

The moment I really got hooked, however, was on a hot, sticky night in a packed high school auditorium. I was still a novice signer. Another of my early sign language teachers, Joyce Linden, had heard that I occasionally performed mime pieces and had invited me to participate in a "Talent Show," where most of the performers and audience members would be Deaf. I had accepted, not realizing what august company I would be in. (One of the other performers that night was Dorothy Miles, the gifted poet and actress and former member of NTD.) When it was my turn to appear onstage, I began to perform my mime piece about a witch who changes herself into different forms. Almost immediately, I felt bathed in a wave of warm, appreciative energy coming from the audience. What struck me most was their responsiveness. It was as if they noticed every tiny movement, even the scrunching of my eyebrows!

After that I began to meet Deaf actors, like Julianna Fjeld, who were fighting for opportunities for Deaf performers in Hollywood. Opportunities to act in movies and TV were a lot less available in the 1970s than they are today. Although my signing skills were hardly fluent, I felt welcomed by the Deaf actors I met through our mutual love for theater. I acted in a few Deaf plays, then decided that since I wasn't making a living in theater and was becoming fascinated by sign language, I would try to become an interpreter.

After several years interpreting in colleges and universities in the Los Angeles area, I moved to the San Francisco Bay area and became a freelance interpreter, enjoying the variety of assignments plus the exciting, yet anxiety-provoking, element of the unknown, which freelance interpreters encounter daily. Years later, I successfully completed the six-week legal training program back at CSUN and now include legal interpreting in my freelance mix of medical, business, video relay, and occasional performing arts settings.

I have always been interested in different cultures. As far back as I can remember, I would gravitate to a voice with a foreign accent in order to gain some perspective on my world by looking through other eyes. I discovered intercultural communication while working on my master's degree at San Francisco State University. Prior to my first class in that subject, I had always assumed (as I believe some sign language interpreters still do) that our profession is so unique that no one else can empathize with the challenges we face. When I started studying the contrasts between world cultures, however, bells rang and lights flashed in my head. "Why, those are just the kinds of misunderstandings sign language interpreters deal with every day!" I concluded with excitement.

After graduating, I pursued additional training in intercultural communication and read everything I could find on the subject. I began to write articles and conduct workshops for other sign language interpreters to share my discoveries and my perspective. Then I was fortunate enough to live in France for a while, where I met some French Deaf people and began learning LSF *(Langue des Signes Française)*. I also observed my own process of culture shock and acculturation.

Over the years, in interactions with my Deaf friends, I have continued to rediscover that we have different ways of approaching certain things. Although it is fun to be able to discuss the aspects of "your way" compared to "my way," awareness itself does not inoculate us against emotional reactions. Even if I have a good intellectual understanding of the ways our cultures differ, I may still wince or feel taken aback by a direct personal comment, for example. When I jump to an emotional conclusion, my head has to explain to my gut what just happened, as I am sure my Deaf friends do with my behavior. Such is the power of cultural differences.

Audience

This book is aimed at a specific audience: sign language interpreters and those students who hope to become interpreters. It presupposes certain areas of awareness on the part of the reader: a fluent knowledge of ASL and a basic familiarity with the types of settings in which interpreters commonly work. It is assumed that the reader does not need to be convinced that ASL is a "real language" or that Deaf people are a linguistic/cultural minority.

Students who are still learning ASL may benefit from the general discussions of world cultures and the specific sections on American mainstream culture, American Deaf culture, and discussions of other cultural groups. They may also gain an understanding of how these differences are played out through the specific interpreting situations I describe. This book has a lot to say to other professionals who work at the intersection of the Deaf and hearing worlds, such as teachers, rehabilitation counselors, and telephone relay operators. Deaf readers are certainly welcome as well and may enjoy an inside look at how we interpreters approach our work.

Although readers from related fields such as intercultural studies or foreign language interpreting may find much of interest here, they may need to avail themselves of a more basic introduction to Deaf culture, which can be found in books such as *For Hearing People Only* by Matthew S. Moore and Linda Levitan (2003), *The Mask of Benevolence* by Harlan Lane (1992), *Inside Deaf Culture* (2005) and *Deaf in America* (1988) by

Carol Padden and Tom Humphries, *A Journey into the Deaf-World* by Harlan Lane, Robert Hoffmeister, and Ben Bahan (1996), and *Seeing Voices* by Oliver Sacks (1989).

Focus

The focus of this book will be primarily on the cultural aspects, rather than the linguistic challenges, of our work as sign language interpreters. Although it is never possible to disconnect language and culture, I will discuss neither the complexities of dealing with the passive voice in English nor the best way to translate classifier signs found in ASL. This book concerns itself with the differing worldviews and values found in Deaf and mainstream American cultures and how these affect interpreted situations.

Every interpreting situation is unique, consisting of specific people coming together in a specific setting for a specific purpose. There are general patterns, however, that one encounters repeatedly. When we study the cultural themes underlying certain behaviors, we begin to understand why this is so. Are these cultural differences relatively minor variations that only flavor the message with an alternate spice? Decidedly not. Research has shown that even subtle differences in communicative style between speakers from two different cultural backgrounds can radically affect the participants' perceptions of each other.

> This is a largely unrecognized type of communicative problem and most people, therefore, interpret the other person's way of speaking according to their own conventions. This means that a person may draw totally incorrect inferences about someone else. For example, s/he may conclude that someone is being rude, irrelevant, boring, or not talking sense at all. Or often hearers become lost in a maze of words or ideas that do not seem to cohere. (Gumperz and Cook-Gumperz 1982, 18)

To what can these types of misreadings of the other person's motives, personality, and intelligence lead?

> It is no exaggeration to say that continuous misperception, misinterpretation and misunderstanding in face-to-face linguistic encounters can develop into stereotypes that are reinforced over time. (Young 1982, 84)

As bilingual/bicultural interpreters we presumably have an understanding of both our Deaf and hearing clients' cultural presuppositions, worldviews, and the ways in which they structure their discourse in order to achieve their goals. This confers upon us a serious responsibility for seeing to it that mere cultural variations in communicative style do not escalate to the point of unfounded stereotypes. In a positive light, our role also accords us a wonderful opportunity to use our knowledge and skills subtly yet effectively to ensure that our clients' messages get through to each other, unhampered by erroneous judgments based on cultural differences.

To reemphasize, each interpreting situation is unique, and cultural factors are complex and multilayered; therefore, no book can offer all the possible solutions to our daily load of puzzles. What a work like this can do is stimulate thought and discussion and outline certain areas of special concern, where it would be wise to anticipate cultural differences. I also hope to convey the intercultural perspective, an open-minded flexibility that can help us to better adjust to any situation involving persons of cultural backgrounds different from our own.

Legal Interpreting

In the course of this book, we will examine several common interpreting situations that take place in medical, business, and educational settings. The principles discussed should then be applicable to other interpreting situations. A cautionary note is necessary, however: for the most part, I am intentionally not including legal interpreting situations. This is not to say that cultural factors are not important in the courtroom. On the contrary, it is in legal situations that culture most needs to be taken into consideration. While many of the same principles will apply (e.g., being sensitive to presuppositions on both sides, focusing on intent of the speakers), a multitude of complicating factors are also present: complex and specialized legal language, great power differences between the participants, assumptions about previous knowledge, the often unspoken, yet serious, implications of the proceedings and strategies for negotiating optimal interpreting conditions within the limitations of courtroom protocol. In short, the subject of how to handle conflicting cultural influences in the courtroom should be pursued in a separate book. My message is this: *do not try to apply the ideas in this book to legal situations without specific training in interpreting in such settings and many years of experience as an interpreter.* The consequences of one misjudgment can be too grave.

Scope of the Book

This book will proceed from the general to the specific, which is typical of hearing American discourse style, as we shall discover later. Part 1 will give you necessary background material. We will begin with the topic of culture. Then we will narrow our focus to the field of intercultural communication and look briefly at its history. Some of the many areas that fall under this domain will be examined. Chapter 3 will focus on four major topics in the field of intercultural communication: collectivism versus individualism, high-context versus low-context cultures, time orientations, and variations in rhetorical style. Not only are these some of the basic ways of categorizing world cultures, but they also constitute the major differences between the American Deaf and mainstream cultures.

In chapters 4 and 5 our attention will be drawn to specific features of American mainstream culture and American Deaf culture. Perhaps you resist the idea that many of your beliefs and actions are culturally influenced. We will examine this common American sentiment. Most people never take a class in their own culture because they learn it naturally. There are several reasons, however, why it is imperative that sign language interpreters explicitly study hearing American culture. First, we must be well versed in the assumptions and conventions of both groups we deal with in order to effectively identify when they are at odds with each other. Sometimes we may even be called upon to articulate to one participant or another why certain ways of doing things in Deaf culture clash with ways of doing things in hearing culture and vice versa.

Second, and perhaps even more important, is the ability to identify cultural influences in ourselves. That they go largely unnoticed makes them all the more powerful. Interpreters are supposed to be neutral facilitators of communication, but we are not blank slates. We come with our own biases, many of which were culturally formed. Without a thorough understanding of our own cultural assumptions, we cannot effectively perform our job as interpreters.

The subject of Deaf culture is clearly an indispensable one for sign language interpreters. Some of the topics in the chapter on Deaf culture will probably be familiar to readers who have spent years interacting with Deaf people. I believe, however, that the range of topics compiled here has not been presented in one place before. Chapter 5 was cowritten with distinguished Deaf educator Thomas K. Holcomb and benefits greatly from his many insights into his native culture. Dr. Holcomb also acted as a consultant in checking the accuracy of the rest of the book. In the Afterword, he speaks directly to interpreters.

Chapter 6 summarizes some of the work of the National Multicultural Interpreting Project and presents an examination of Asian American, African American/Black, Latino/Hispanic, and American Indian cultures. Recent innovations in technology and their effect on Deaf culture are the focus of chapter 7.

In Part 2 we will finally look at how all of these aforementioned cultural factors get played out in common interpreting situations. By examining in chapter 8 both parties' cultural presuppositions, we will be in a better position to predict where differences might lead to misjudgments between the parties. Chapter 9 will again borrow from the work of the NMIP and present multicultural interpreting scenarios. In chapter 10 we will examine how Deaf people view our role and contrast that to the way we as interpreters perceive our role (e.g., does "professional" connote coldness or competency?).

On the subject of role, we will consider the roles of professional mediators and spoken language interpreters in order to see if the commonalities between our tasks outweigh the differences and if we can benefit by modeling ourselves after these professions. We will then examine in depth what our role *should* be. Where does our responsibility begin and end? How do we differentiate the cultural factors we can adjust somewhat from other factors, which, although they affect communication, may be out of our control?

Specific suggestions of techniques with which to make cultural adjustments will be given in chapter 11 as well as a list of situations in which cultural adjustments would not be appropriate or necessary.

Chapter 12 is an introductory exploration into the uncharted land of video interpreting. Special focus will be given to the cultural challenges that accompany our odyssey into the world of two dimensions. Technology has brought us a new era of amazing gadgets and astounding communication access that has eliminated the need for many outmoded practices. The necessity of understanding the influence of culture, however, has not been eradicated. In fact, the accelerated rate of our contact with people from all over the world has made cultural sensitivity all the more indispensable.

In the last chapter, we will consider our relationships with Deaf people outside of our working hours to see how social relationships are also dependent on sensitivity to culture.

My Consultants

This book was not written alone. In the Acknowledgments section I have already listed the names of many fellow sign language interpreters and Deaf people who shared their thoughts, experiences, and opinions with me. At this point I would like to give special thanks to Daniel Langholtz and Priscilla Moyers, two Deaf friends and colleagues who acted as my consultants during the writing of this book. Along with Tom Holcomb, they read my drafts, made notes, and patiently answered my questions. Our discussions were not only enlightening but were also thoroughly enjoyable, as we compared our cultures and our feelings about them. Since both Daniel and Priscilla are superb relay interpreters (intermediary interpreters who work in legal and other settings to attain optimal interpretation*), I felt they had a deep understanding of the process and challenges of interpreting. In chapter 13 their thoughts and opinions regarding interpreters' relationship to the Deaf community will be expressed.

Conventions

Deaf/deaf

Following current convention I use capitalized *Deaf* to refer to features of Deaf culture and those individuals who identify themselves with the culture. The lowercase *deaf* is used to refer to the audiological condition of deafness. Since the focus of this book is about cultural differences between hearing Americans and Deaf Americans, the natural subject of this book will be the culturally Deaf. "Deaf people see themselves not as little 'd' deaf, a usage associated with the medical pathology, but as big 'D' Deaf, as members of a cultural group who have created their own language and who actively shape their lives and identity" (Rexroat 1997, 19).

Capital Letters for Gloss of SIGN

As a three-dimensional, multichannel language of movement, ASL is not easily captured on the printed page. For this reason, I try to avoid long

---

*Please see pages 203–04 for a more complete explanation of this role.

passages of transcribed ASL. When necessary, however, I use the convention of capitalization to represent the common gloss for a sign. I am only attempting to portray a rough sketch of which signs might be chosen. Since I make no effort to include nonmanual markers (eye gaze; mouth shape; movements of the eyebrows, head, body, etc.), this is in no way to be seen as a complete transcription of ASL.

Point of Reference

Let me stress again that this book is addressed to all sign language interpreters, those who learned ASL as a first language because their parents were Deaf (often referred to as "CODAs," children of Deaf adults) and those who learned it later by choice. Currently, the majority of sign language interpreters (including myself) grew up in American mainstream culture. Coming from that perspective, therefore, I often use *we* to mean hearing Americans as opposed to Deaf Americans. Those interpreters who grew up in Deaf families may, therefore, have to make some adjustments to the statements about "our" culture and "their" culture. Depending on their particular circumstances (e.g., presence or lack of hearing siblings or extended family or the extent of the family's involvement in the Deaf community), those with Deaf parents may find themselves with a mixture of values and perspectives from the two groups.

Similarly, I do not mean to discount interpreters who grew up in other than a white American environment. Interpreters of color or those who grew up in other cultures will have their own cultural influences to take into consideration. Chapters 6 and 9 include a wider array of perspectives. My basic message is that we all have to know where we are coming from so we can figuratively "check our cultural baggage at the door" while we are interpreting.

Our Profession

It is a rare profession that can pinpoint its origins, but ours can: the meeting at Ball State Teachers College in 1964, where the Registry of Interpreters for the Deaf (RID) was founded. As chronicled by Lou Fant in *Silver Threads*, the era preceding the establishment of the first professional organization of sign language interpreters was a far cry from the situation today.

No one worked full-time as an interpreter and to say that anyone worked part-time is misleading... [We] volunteered our services as our schedules permitted. If we received any compensation it was freely given and happily accepted but not expected... We earned our living as school people, rehabilitation counselors, religious workers, or were primarily housewives. We perceived our work as interpreters as just another way of helping deaf family members, friends, coworkers, or complete strangers. It was a way of contributing to the general welfare of deaf people, not a way to make money, much less earn a living. We did not expect to be paid, we did not ask to be paid, because we did not do it for the money. We felt it was our obligation, our duty to do it, and if we did not do it, the deaf person would suffer and we would feel responsible. (Fant 1990, 9–10)

Because of a shortage of competent interpreters, the deaf and hearing people present at the Ball State meeting formed an organization whose purpose was to recruit new members, promote training, assess competency, and compile a list of qualified interpreters for consumers to use. In the 1960s, ASL had not yet been widely recognized as a language, and although practitioners recognized that Deaf people had different ways of doing things than the hearing majority, the concept of "a Deaf culture" had not yet been widely disseminated.

A little more than forty years later, RID counts over eleven thousand members, most of whom consider themselves professional sign language interpreters and earn some, if not all, of their living from their work. The organization has numerous local chapters, holds biennial national conventions, has a testing system that awards various types of certification, requires its members to pursue continuing education, and is involved with lobbying and public awareness activities.

It is not surprising that a field as young as ours has not come to a consensus about exactly what our role entails. Fant explains that the first interpreters "grew up in an atmosphere suffused with patronization... So as adults we saw ourselves as helpers, available any time, day or night, to assist deaf people out of their difficulties" (Fant 12). Subsequently, the profession has used various labels to help interpreters grasp where the borders of their responsibility lie. In reaction to the "helper" model came the "machine" or "conduit" model, which greatly limited our responsibility for either party's understanding of the other's message. Like a tape recorder, we were only to transmit what we had received without altering its contents in any way. When a machine was judged to fall short of what was required in a complicated human interaction, we moved on to "communication facilitator" and "bicultural mediator." The latter acknowledged the fact that cultural influences on the messages we deliver must be taken into account. There has been talk recently about adopting a new model, "the ally," which interestingly seems to take us back in a circular path to include some of the features of the helper model. Although the term *ally* has not yet been adequately defined or debated, it seems to address Deaf people's desire that we be supportive without being patronizing. As our profession matures, we will undoubtedly redefine and refine our role many times.

As previously stated, our field has acknowledged that the image of the bilingual-bicultural relationship between Deaf and hearing cultures in America is an oversimplification. Deaf culture, as now perceived, is a complex mixture of all the elements present in American society at large. One way to increase cultural sensitivity is by encouraging the recruitment and training of more interpreters of color. Another avenue, which I believe would increase the cultural competence of the entire interpreting profession, is the study of intercultural communication. This field focuses on the ways individuals from various cultural backgrounds perceive events and express themselves differently. Just as we cannot assume that the hearing doctor will be a white middle-class male from the Midwest, so we must be prepared for Deaf clients coming from various cultural and ethnic backgrounds as well. Demographic studies predict that the multicultural influences within Deaf and hearing cultures will steadily increase in coming years.

This book serves as an introduction to the field of intercultural communication and examines some of the most common cultural challenges faced by sign language interpreters. It is not the final word on the subject. We can look forward to continuing research that will further describe interrelations between the multicolored threads that weave the cultural web in which we all live and work.

Why the Big Fuss about Culture?

Some of those in our field question the value of paying so much attention to culture. As one longtime interpreter told me, "Deaf people and hearing people aren't that different; we all want the same thing—nice friendly service, just like you get at McDonald's." Others feel that Deaf people are lucky to be living in the enlightened twenty-first century, where the Americans with Disabilities Act (ADA) guarantees them the right to have an interpreter who will translate English into sign and vice versa. Doesn't providing an interpreter solve the communication problem?

Theresa B. Smith, one of the most respected and skilled interpreters in the country, describes in her dissertation the struggle to convey not only the information contained in, but also the implications behind, Deaf discourse:

> As an interpreter I have noticed that simply translating the *language* (i.e., that which is explicitly stated) is insufficient. Not only do the listeners have difficulty understanding what is being said if discourse is unaccommodated, their perceptions of the speaker are often inaccurate. I found myself wanting to give the "real interpretation" to not only rephrase but restructure the argument just made to a more English-like discourse so the listeners would understand not only what had been said, but why. (1996, 221)

Smith concludes that

> hiring interpreters is certainly not enough to make most meetings or encounters "accessible." If nothing else is changed (e.g., timing, discourse style, underlying presuppositions, beliefs and values), providing interpretation is often form without content. (180)

Culture is the context in which the content may be truly understood. Interpreting without a thorough grounding and appreciation of the cultural implications is like trying to hang pictures in a house with no walls. Without building a cultural framework that holds the house together, the pictures—words and signs—will crash to the floor.

2

The Study of Culture

If we can accept the paradox that the real humanity of people is understood through cultural differences rather than cultural similarities, then we can make profound sense of our differences. It is possible that there is not one truth, but many; not one real experience, but many realities; not one history, but many different and valid ways of looking at events.

—JAMAKE HIGHWATER
The Primal Mind

Jamake Highwater's proposal represents a challenge to the popular, well-intentioned sentiment that down deep all people are basically the same. Actually it depends on how deep is "deep." Certainly we are all made of flesh and bones, we all need to eat and sleep, and we seek shelter and safety. After those similarities have been established, however, most of the rest of our beliefs, attitudes, and behaviors are at least to some degree culturally determined.

To ignore the reality of varying cultural perspectives is to discount the infinite variety of our humanness. To insist that we all share the same goals and desires is to refuse to humbly admit that our way is not the only way. Highwater, himself a Blackfoot Indian, gives an example of a Navajo family, who, when entering their newly built government house for the first time, may rip out the toilet. "[Anglo] people come away from the Navajo Reservation expressing their sorrow in finding that 'the poor Indians do not have indoor plumbing and live in terrible, primitive conditions unfit for human beings.'" From the traditional Navajo point of view, however, it is we Anglos who should be pitied for having bathrooms inside our houses; Navajos believe "it is disgusting to put a toilet under the roof of their living quarters rather than at a distance from the dwelling place" (Highwater 1981, 8).

Once we realize that there are vast differences between some of our beliefs and those of people from other cultures, we may feel a bit like the floor has dropped out from under us. If virtually all of our perceptions are mediated by culture, then what is really true and valid? Principles that we accept as universal truths because they are not questioned in our society, such as marrying for love and making decisions about our future based on our own individual desires, are nothing more than the particular thinking of our culture. Delving into cultural exploration may shake us out of our mental ruts. The insights we gain about what it means to be human, however, are well worth the momentary disequilibrium.

What Is Culture?

Since this book will focus on the influence of culture on our perceptions, thoughts, and behaviors, it would seem that the logical starting place would be a succinct, generally accepted definition of culture. Unfortunately, that is no simple task. Over a hundred definitions of culture have been offered. One way to begin may be, therefore, to eliminate what we do not mean by culture. Culture, in the context of this inquiry, is not something one acquires by attending the ballet, listening to classical music, or critiquing modern art. In fact, we don't have to make any special effort to attain it at all; we have already acquired it by virtue of being raised in human society.

Perhaps the earliest definition of culture, and one that is still serviceable was proposed in 1871 by Edward B. Tylor, known as the father of cultural anthropology, in *Primitive Culture.* "Culture . . . is that complex whole which includes knowledge, belief, art, morals, law, custom, and any other capabilities and habits acquired by man as a member of society" (Tylor 1958, 1). Tylor's phrase, "a complex whole," points out that culture is not a haphazard, arbitrary collection of behaviors but rather consists of parts that together make up an *integrated system.*

That culture is "acquired" differentiates it from the purely biological. The fact that we lose our baby teeth is not an element of culture, it is the beliefs and rituals we apply to the event that make it part of our cultural repertoire. As infants we begin to acquire our culture from those around us—our parents, siblings, relatives, friends, and teachers—who in turn learned it from their parents, siblings, relatives, friends, and teachers. Thus the wisdom of the group is passed down from generation to generation. Not only is culture *learned,* but also it is *shared* with a very large group. The quirks of our personality (our fear of snakes and our love of ham sandwiches) mark us as individuals and do not define our culture, although they exist within a cultural context. (In other cultural contexts, of course, the worship of snakes or a repugnance for eating ham might be more defining.)

As an integrated system, each culture is an apt set of adaptations that helps its members face the challenges of their environment. "Culture facilitates living by providing ready-made solutions to problems, by establishing patterns of relations and ways for preserving group cohesion and consensus" (Harris and Moran 1982, 65). Examples of such cultural adaptations are igloos, well suited for living in the arctic; afternoon siestas in tropical climates; and sign language as the natural mode of communication for those who cannot hear spoken language. Thus, culture is a means of "sharing successful results of choices made by others in the past" (Bohannan 1992, 13).

Most of our own culture is *out of our conscious awareness*. Like water to the fish or air to the bird, it surrounds us so completely that we may never notice it, and it may stay unnoticed until, like a fish plucked out of the water, we find ourselves in a new environment and begin to flounder. Or until we encounter a visitor from a different place who acts "strangely," as if the fish saw a bird drop into the ocean and wondered, "What kind of odd creature is this who moves his fins about so much and doesn't seem to know how things are done down here?"

Since culture is so omnipresent, it may help us to examine it indirectly through a few metaphors. Images that have been proposed to illuminate the impact of culture include computer software that regulates our actions, a tool kit that provides us with what we need to manage our physical environment, and a rainbow that we can only appreciate fully once we are standing out from under it.

My favorite metaphor for culture is an iceberg, only one-tenth of which is visible above the water. The tip of the cultural iceberg that one can see corresponds to those elements that visitors to a foreign country might readily notice: the different clothing, music, food, and architecture. What visitors might fail to perceive, however, is that a culture's notions of beauty, modesty, friendship, courtship, child raising, insanity, justice, and leadership may be vastly different from their own.

Ignorance of the unrecognized differences between cultures, like the unseen part of an iceberg, can have equally destructive consequences. The study of cultural variations, however, may provide us with maps to navigate these treacherous, yet fascinating, seas.

Culture and Communication

As sign language interpreters, we most often find ourselves untangling those aspects of culture that are related to communication.

> Culture and communication are inseparable because culture not only dictates who talks to whom, about what, and how the communication proceeds, but it also helps determine how people encode messages, the meanings they have for messages, and the conditions and circumstances under which various messages may or may not be sent, noticed, or interpreted. (Samovar and Porter 1982, 32)

The process of communication is often diagrammed as a sender encoding a message, which is then relayed to a receiver who must decode the message in order to understand the meaning the sender has intended. We engage in this complex process thousands of times a day, with relatively few glitches (e.g., "I'm sorry, I didn't quite get your point." "That's not what I meant!" "Huh?"). The introduction of a difference in cultures between the sender and receiver, however, greatly increases the likelihood that the original intent of the sender will not get through to the receiver.

> Our entire repertory of communicative behaviors is dependent largely on the culture in which we have been raised. Culture, consequently, is the foundation of communication. And when cultures vary, communication practices also vary. (32)

To take only one example, the author of *Culture and the Clinical Encounter* endeavors to sensitize health providers not to assume that communication strategies are universal. She points out that

> Silence and the word *yes* lead to numerous misunderstandings. Neither necessarily signifies agreement. Silence can mean "I do not agree with what you are saying, but I am too polite to say so." *Yes* can mean "I am listening but not promising or agreeing" [or] "I do not understand what you are saying, but I acknowledge you are trying to tell me something, and I am grateful for that . . ." (Gropper 1996, 2)

Until a few hundred years ago, only a very small percentage of the world's inhabitants had to contend with the challenges of communicating with representatives of another culture. Most people lived their entire lives in the same place where they grew up. Apart from a foray of marauding neighbors, a visit from a group of tourists, or a few missionaries dropping by, the bulk of communication took place between people who shared a common culture. Thanks to air travel, vast social and political changes, and the explosion of technology, those days of relative isolation are now gone forever.

> In the world of tomorrow we can expect to live—not merely vacation—in societies which seek different values and abide by different codes. There we will be surrounded by foreigners for long periods of time, working with others in the closest possible relationships. If people currently show little tolerance or talent for encounters with alien cultures, how can they learn to deal with constant and inescapable coexistence? (Barnlund 1989, 5)

The answer to this question may lie in a relatively young field, not much older than the profession of sign language interpreting, called intercultural communication. Let us examine its roots and the topics it considers, and see how the perspective it offers may provide a key to understanding not only the imminent global village but, closer to home, the challenges we face as sign language interpreters.

The Field of Intercultural Communication

When we think of studying cultures, the first discipline that comes to mind is anthropology. Intercultural communication is indeed an offshoot of anthropology and differs from it in certain significant ways. Traditional anthropologists focus on one culture at a time. During their fieldwork, they immerse themselves for several years in the culture of a group of people who often inhabit a remote, hitherto unexplored, region. There they learn the language of the group and observe their way of life, paying special attention to systems such as kinship, economy, and religion. Rarely, if ever, do they describe interactions between the group they are studying and members of other groups.

It is precisely these interactions, however, which most interest the interculturalists. The field of intercultural communication grew from a practical need that made itself felt in five different areas at about the same time. The time period was post–World War II, beginning in the early

1950s. The first area to demonstrate this need was our government, specif-ically the need to adequately train diplomats to be sent abroad.

The traditional approach to such training until that time had consisted of having diplomats attend language classes, then bringing in university professors from a variety of disciplines to lecture on their respective fields of study. This might include presentations on the history, geography, cli-mate, and political structure of the area in question. Once overseas, how-ever, the diplomats trained in what is now called "the university model" reported with dismay that they were unable to function effectively. As a result, the director of the Foreign Service Institute (FSI) hired a group of linguists and anthropologists to improve upon the previous training methods, among whom was a young anthropologist, Edward T. Hall, who had experience working with the Navajo and Hopi.

Hall concluded that the missing element in the diplomats' preparations was an examination of the daily interactions they could anticipate having in the host country. Hall recommended, therefore, that the emphasis in training shift from a cultural overview to the details of everyday life, which he termed "micro-cultural analysis." His first publication on the subject, an article entitled "The Anthropology of Manners," appeared in *Scientific American* in 1955. In it he stated:

> The role of the anthropologist in preparing people for service over-seas is to open their eyes and sensitize them to the subtle qualities of behavior—tone of voice, gestures, space and time relationships—that so often build up feelings of frustration and hostility in people with a different culture. (89)

Hall broke new ground with the publication of his first book on the subject of intercultural interaction, the first edition of *The Silent Language* (1959), which laid the foundation for the establishment of this new field. He later became the head of FSI and earned himself the sobriquet of Founding Father of Intercultural Communication.

The other four threads that, together with Hall's work at FSI, led to the emergence of this fledgling field were the large numbers of business exec-utives who were flung with their families onto distant shores, the influx of foreign students descending upon our college campuses, the establish-ment of the Peace Corps, and the Civil Rights movement of the 1960s.

In the decades following World War II, large American companies foresaw the potential benefits of establishing contacts, offices, and factories in Europe and Asia in order to take advantage of untapped markets. In their rush to achieve a competitive edge, however, they did not routinely provide their executives with even as much preparation for their interactions abroad as the early diplomats had received. Often completely forgotten were the adjustment needs of the executives' family members, who were plopped down in a foreign country with virtually no preparation and expected to carry on their lives for the next two or three years without complaint. The inability of his family to adjust to the new culture was often the impetus for the executive to abandon his post earlier than expected. Just as often, however, the frustrations stemmed from the executive himself as his expectations of progress and achievement seemed to be thwarted almost daily.

Although this high failure rate resulted in the loss of great sums of money invested in moving families abroad, these companies, rather than noticing a pattern and investigating its source, at first tended to ignore the problem, even going so far as to purposely not record these "failures" in their employees' files. After a while, however, this denial was deemed counterproductive. Attention, therefore, began to be paid to those business executives who were successful in their foreign ventures. What qualities did they possess that helped them meet the challenges of living in a different culture?

By contrast, one group of professionals who did share their frustrations with their colleagues was foreign student advisers on college campuses around the United States. With the influx of foreign students in the 1950s, 1960s, and 1970s, who came to the United States to study at the undergraduate and graduate levels, these advisers were struck by the cultural adjustment problems they perceived the students to be struggling with, both in regard to the American educational system and to society at large. They were responsive when a loose organization for exchanging ideas, the Intercultural Communication Network, was formed, with its center at the University of Pittsburgh. The Network sponsored exploratory intercultural communication workshops (ICWs) with foreign and American students that tackled cultural issues and became a model for many other programs around the country. It also led to the publication of a national newsletter, *Communiqué* (Dahlen 1997, 35–38).

Another important event that led to the development of the field of intercultural communication was the establishment of the Peace Corps in the early 1960s by President Kennedy. Much like the frustrations experienced by the ill-prepared diplomats, early Peace Corps volunteers registered complaints that their "university model" training was insufficient to prepare them for the realities of life in a different culture. Trainers soon realized that the missing piece was an orientation to the experiential aspects of crossing cultures. It was found, for example, that feelings of frustration and disorientation (now termed culture shock) can be anticipated and prepared for by giving volunteers a taste of these feelings before they ever leave home.

Peace Corps trainers tried different types of experiential training techniques, which mirrored the interest in experiential learning during the 1960s in general. Instead of relying solely on didactic lectures about the country to which volunteers would be sent, trainers adapted role-plays, simulation games, and other exercises borrowed from the newly popular "sensitivity training" movement. They stressed the importance of being sensitive to differences in cultural values and pointed out that people from other cultures may interpret our behavior in ways we did not intend. Creative thinking and problem-solving exercises, trainers and administrators believed, could help prospective volunteers learn to adapt to unfamiliar situations better than rote learning. So a combined method was adopted, one that included lectures, discussion, and experiential learning activities (Dahlen 33–34).

Also during the 1960s, the myth of the "melting pot" boiled over as the Civil Rights movement demanded social justice and equal opportunity for all Americans regardless of race or ethnic background. Rejecting the majority's belief that people could be boiled down into a generic American, activists marched peacefully or fought violently to garner respect for their own American identity. These social upheavals rocked the country and brought about needed change. Designations such as African American, Latino American, and Asian American began to gain acceptance, and colleges began to offer courses in ethnic studies. The new awareness of multiple cultural identities within the United States led to the demise of the "melting pot" and the birth of more pluralistic national images such as a "salad bowl" or a "mosaic," where the distinctive flavors or colors of each element combine to produce a rich and varied whole.

Despite some setbacks, there is growing acceptance that pluralism is the wave of the future. This has led the intercultural field to split its orientation into two divergent, yet complementary, directions. The international focus looks outward to our dealings with members of the global community, while the domestic focus is on multiculturalism outside of work and diversity within the workplace.

Today the field of intercultural communication includes "diversity training, cross-cultural counseling, intercultural negotiation, intercultural communications training, [and] cross-cultural sensitivity training" (Dahlen 9), and it has spawned books, videos, conferences, and national and international organizations as well as doctoral programs. It is finally widely recognized that the issue of cultural variation will not disappear and will only become more relevant to our daily interactions as the world becomes smaller through access to communications technology and our increasing ability to reach out and touch someone with a different worldview.*

Domains of Intercultural Communication

The field of intercultural communication includes *proxemics* (the study of social and personal space); *paralinguistics* (the study of the way something is said, including intonation, speech rate, and the use of silence); and *kinesics* (the study of body motions such as gestures, eye gaze, and facial expression). A basic tenet is that all these channels carry messages, whether intended or unintended. Underlying the study of the specific manifestations of any culture is the recognition that each culture has its own set of *values* that color its perceptions and behaviors. Our values pertain to everything from our connection to family and friends, our ideas about nature, our beliefs about the roles of the sexes, and our relationship to authority to our views on the meaning of life.

Proxemics

Just as animals aggressively defend their territory against perceived intruders, so do we bristle and hiss when we feel our personal space is being violated. Tailgaters make us agitated and lead some to display bumper stickers declaring, "If you can read this you're too close!" We feel strangely homeless when someone takes "our seat" in a class we have been attending. On a crowded elevator we try to hold ourselves in and become

---

*Many thanks to L. Robert Kohls for allowing me to review his notes for "Benchmarks in the Development of the Field of Intercultural Communication in the United States," based on an oral presentation.

extremely uncomfortable if a stranger touches us. We feel incensed when our seatmate on an airline flight takes possession of "our" armrest. And these invasions are perpetrated by people with whom we share a common culture!

Suppose you find yourself the only passenger on a bus. After riding for a while, you notice a new rider getting on board. What could be more unnerving than seeing him pick, of all the possible seats, the one right next to you? Yet this behavior would seem perfectly appropriate to most Arabs. In contrast to American patterns of personal space, where we try to maintain a bubble of space around us, Arabs prefer to position themselves close to others. "For Arabs the space which is comfortable for ordinary social conversation is approximately the same as that which Westerners reserve for intimate conversation" (Nydell 1996, 51). Part of the Arab preference for standing close to conversational partners stems from their desire to be able to smell each other's breath. To the Arab, "To smell one's friend is not only nice but desirable, for to deny him your breath is to act ashamed" (Hall 1966, 160).

One of the favorite areas of study in proxemics is the examination of the preferred conversational distance between people in different situations. An often-quoted example describes the "dance" that may take place when people from different cultures try to maintain their preferred conversational distance. An American may be slowly chased around the room and into a corner by an Arab or South American who keeps trying to lessen the feeling of coldness and distance between them. The American, meanwhile, backs away, resisting what feels like aggression or inappropriate intimacy communicated by the foreigner's coming ever closer.

Conversational distance in Deaf culture presents a fascinating contrast, yet one that, to my knowledge, has not been formally researched. A visual language has entirely different constraints on the distance between its interlocutors than a spoken one. Hall's distinctions of "shouting distance" and "whispering distance" (Hall 1966, 114) would obviously not apply to ASL. Signed conversations can take place comfortably at much greater distances than spoken ones. Signers may converse on opposite sides of a subway platform or busy street, through the windows while they are driving in different cars, or even from the edge of a theater balcony to its orchestra pit with only slight adjustment to signing style (making the signs a little bigger). On the intimate end of the spectrum, signing while closer than arm's length is hard on the eyes. Deaf skits and plays have poked fun at the necessity of interrupting an amorous embrace by having the lovers

jump back several feet in order to tell each other "I love you," then spring-
ing back together. When Deaf lovers are entwined in an embrace, they
find creative ways to communicate short remarks, some of which depend
more on touch than on sight.

Proxemics also looks at the design of public spaces (from a garden to an
entire town) and interior spaces (from offices to houses). Are the grassy
areas in parks designed to be romped on or roped off? Does the furniture
arrangement in a home hug the walls or draw everyone to the center of
the room? Where is the boss's office—in a protected corner or the accessible center of the office suite? If you are invited to someone's home, which
rooms will you be shown and which, if any, will be off-limits?

For Deaf people the arrangement of furniture in a room is always based
on ease of visual access to conversations. The chairs in a college classroom
that has both hearing and deaf classes, for example, may be continually
rearranged throughout the day: in conventional rows for the hearing
classes and in a visually accessible semicircle for the deaf classes.

A closed door in one culture may convey the message of an inviolable
boundary one does not dare open, while in another it represents only a
temporary barrier at which one knocks and enters at the same moment.
Many other aspects of culture can also be viewed either as protective
roadblocks or as invitations to further intimacy.

Paralinguistics

Although paralinguistics is frequently characterized as the study of the
way something is said as opposed to *what* is said, more often than not, how
something is said determines its meaning. Here are a few examples in the
areas of intonation, rate of speech, volume, and the use of silence.

Intonation. In many Asian and African languages, the tone determines the
meaning of a word. In the Thai language, for example, there are five contrasting tones: low, mid, high, falling, and rising. The same syllable, *naa*,
pronounced with different tones produces five different meanings: "nick-
name," "rice paddy," "younger maternal aunt or uncle," "face," and
"thick," respectively (Fromkin and Rodman 1983, 93).

Although English is not a tonal language, intonation still plays a large
role in determining meaning. Consider this simple sentence: "I will give
you an A." When spoken by a teacher to a student with the stress placed on
different words, the underlying message can vary greatly: *I* will give you

an A (as opposed to all your previous teachers who failed to recognize your intelligence) or I will *give* you an A (even though you haven't earned it). A sarcastic tone in English can even change a phrase to mean the opposite of what it says: "Oh, I get to stay home all day with three sick kids. *How fun!*"

Rate of Speech. Tempo is another aspect of paralanguage. When we are so enraged that we greatly slow down our delivery, we may say: "How . . . could . . . you . . . have . . . done . . . that?????" The underlying message is palpable: "Watch out, I am so angry I can barely control myself!"

Another instance when we may slowly overenunciate our words is when explaining something to children or to foreigners whom we assume would have difficulty understanding "normal everyday English." We may unknowingly, however, be sending a message of contempt to a foreigner who simply speaks competent English with a heavy accent.

Volume. People from certain cultures are notoriously soft-spoken to our American ears. Although it happens to be their way of showing respect, we may find it frustrating to have to strain to hear them. Americans often speak loudly to get someone's attention or be heard above the din, but a loud volume may serve other functions as well.

> Loud-talking in the Black community is used deliberately and publicly to divulge personal information that other individuals would not want to have known. The purpose of such loud-talking is usually to try to get such individuals to do something they have resisted or would in all likelihood not be inclined to do. Thus a young Black woman, bothered by the persistence of an older man at a party, loud-talked him . . . by saying, "Mr. Williams, you are old enough to be my father. You ought to be ashamed of yourself" . . . By loud-talking him, she hoped to use the public embarrassment produced as additional leverage to force him to leave her alone. (Kochman 1981, 101–102)

Silence. In America, skill at speaking is respected. We often judge our politicians by their speeches and relish our celebrities' talk-show revelations. To our ears, silence is just empty space, a waste of time, or it may be considered awkward or embarrassing. In many other cultures, by contrast, silence has a positive connotation and is seen as an awareness of being in the moment. In Japan, for example, talkativeness is mistrusted and seen as a symptom of a shallow character. As a Japanese proverb says, "One treats one's mouth as a guarded jar."

Even in our own culture, with its relatively low tolerance for quiet moments, we observe the silence associated with certain locations such as places of worship, libraries, courtrooms, and hospitals. Silence is also appropriate for events such as funerals, patriotic observances, appreciating nature, or a moment of intimacy. During conversation, we may use short silences to emphasize the words just spoken or about to be spoken, to signal our emotional reaction (by refusing to respond to an insult), to give us a moment to think, or to demonstrate our ignorance (by not answering a question).

Telephone culture, we are discovering, includes its own set of conventions about the lengths of silences permitted. Hearing Americans seem to have an extremely low tolerance for "empty air" in phone conversations between non-intimates. This subject will be addressed in more depth in chapter 12.

Kinesics

What could be more natural and easily understood than a friendly smile, a flirtatious wink, or a warm embrace? As it turns out, plenty! Many people assume that once we leave the verbal plane, rife with opportunities for misunderstanding, we enter the realm of universally understood gestures. Nothing could be further from the truth. For example, the "OK" hand gesture, with thumb and forefinger making a circle and three fingers extended, is used in much of the world; however, the meaning behind it varies considerably. In North America and much of Europe it signifies approval; in Japan its shape refers to money; and in France it means "zero, worthless, no good."* You had better be extra careful using this gesture in Greece or Turkey, however, where it is used insultingly to mean "You have a large (anal) orifice" (Morris et al. 1979, 100–18).

Besides the erroneous assumption of the universality of its meaning, there are several factors that complicate the study of nonverbal behavior.

---

*It would be interesting to trace the origins of the ASL sign TRIVIAL/INSIGNIFI-CANT, which uses this handshape, to see if it was directly adopted from LSF.

We have no dictionaries to consult. In your travels, for instance, if someone responds to your greeting with a head-tilt coupled with pursed lips,
you cannot look up its translation in a book. It is also extremely difficult to
ask for clarification, because the person who performed the head-tilt/lip-
pursing was probably not even aware of having done so (Condon and
Yousef 1975, 125–26).

Kinesics, then, is the study of nonverbal behavior and includes such
areas as eye gaze, facial expression, and gestures. Here are a few more
examples of these three aspects of kinesics to give you a sense of the wide
variation and the many possibilities for misinterpretation.

Eye Gaze. On a continuum depicting amount of eye gaze, American culture would be situated somewhere around the midpoint. We make eye
contact when we begin speaking, then usually look away and then check
back from time to time and again at the end of our statement. When we
experience more (or less) eye contact than usual, we may react emotionally, although we might not be aware of what is causing our discomfort at
the time.

When dealing with people from cultures such as Japan or Indonesia,
where respect is shown by downcast eyes, we may feel ignored or suspicious of what they are trying to hide. On the other hand, people from
cultures who prefer more eye contact than we are used to, such as Britons
or Arabs, may make us feel nervous as the object of their stare (Jensen
1982, 265).

Widening of the eyes is one behavior with numerous meanings in various cultures. To Anglo-Americans, it signifies surprise or wonder; to the
Chinese, it means anger; to the French, it demonstrates a challenge; to
Latinos, it is a call for help; and to African Americans, it can be a claim of
innocence. A teacher in a multicultural classroom, for example, may over-
look "a Spanish child's signal of distress" or misinterpret "a Black child's
mute plea of innocence as a display of insolence" (E. C. Condon 1982,
343).

Facial Expression. Contrary to the lyrics of a classic song, a smile is not
always just a smile.

> The Japanese smile and laugh does not necessarily mean happiness
> or friendship. As a carefully cultivated act of social duty and etiquette,

it is employed in a large number of circumstances and may, among other things, suggest shyness, embarrassment, discomfort, wonder, or surprise. In some areas of Asia and Africa laughing or smiling suggests weakness. Hence, teachers never smile in the classroom lest it impair discipline. (Jensen 265)

As some American women have learned, a friendly smile at a passing stranger may be erroneously interpreted as a sexual advance in many cultures. In fact, the United States is one of the few places where strangers exchange smiles, which are often reserved for intimates in other locales.

Gestures. If it is true that "actions speak louder than words," we had better be careful about the messages we are sending. One famous misunderstood gesture almost brought about an international crisis. When Prime Minister Khrushchev visited the United States on a supposed goodwill tour during the precarious Cold War period, he raised his arms above his head while clasping his hands. To many Americans this gesture resembled a boxer's arrogant sign of victory over an opponent. There was a widespread reaction of outrage to this gesture and the conceited swagger and presumption of the eventual triumph of Communism it seemed to convey. To Russians, however, this gesture has a very different connotation—it means friendship.

In another incident, an American diplomat was sent to negotiate with Arab leaders during a period of international tension. The diplomat unknowingly made an extremely insulting gesture when, while crossing his legs, he showed the sole of his shoe to the Arab contingent. An aide was discreetly sent over to the American side to inform him of his gaffe, and a crisis was averted. In Muslim countries, another potentially grave insult is to touch people or offer them food with the left hand, which is considered dirty. The "right hand has been glorified throughout the centuries" and is regarded as clean, while "a main function of the left hand is to aid in the process of elimination of bodily wastes" (Jensen 266).

Even the simple gesture of placing your hand at a certain level to describe someone's height can be cause for offense. In the United States, if you want to demonstrate how tall your daughter is, you would hold your hand out, with the palm facing downward and parallel to the floor at about the level of the top of her head. In parts of South America, however, that gesture is only employed for showing the height of animals. "To indicate the height of a human, one would keep the palm vertical" (267).

Some other gestures with cultural variations include beckoning, counting, hand/arm gestures of contempt, and pointing. In cultures where indicating with an outstretched finger is seen as rude, pointing may be accomplished with the nose, chin, or lips.

I remember an incident that showed me the potential pitfalls in assuming the universality of nonverbal behaviors. Interpreting at a meeting for a Deaf man who had recently moved to the United States from the Philippines, I became increasingly uncomfortable during the transaction because of what I assumed to be his strong flirtatious manner. After the meeting was over I confided to a friend of mine, an American Deaf woman who was also at the meeting, "Boy, did you see the way he came on to me! He kept seductively raising and lowering his eyebrows and making those kissy lips at me!" My friend, who happened to have worked in the Peace Corps with Deaf people in the Philippines, could barely contain her laughter. "Anna, he wasn't coming on to you at all," she explained. "In the Philippines, one shows understanding or agreement by that eyebrow movement, and because it is rude to point with the finger, they point with pursed lips instead."

Values

A sign seen in a Parisian hotel reads "Please leave your values at the front desk." This mistranslation actually offers some good advice, if it were only possible! The values that influence our behavior are so pervasive, yet unconscious, that if asked to enumerate them we would be hard-pressed to come up with even a few. Seen through an intercultural perspective, however, values are the underlying principles behind what may appear to be merely a collection of quirky mannerisms. They knit seemingly arbitrary acts into larger patterns and provide standards by which conduct can be evaluated by members of a culture.

Just as invisible ink is suddenly readable when the paper it is on is heated, we can obtain a momentary glimpse of our own values when we listen to ourselves instructing our children about what is expected in our society. For example, "You can be whatever you want when you grow up"; "When someone gives you something, say thank you"; "Always let the guest have the biggest cookie."

An engaging way to tease out values is to compare a single artifact and the values it reflects in two distinct cultures. Michael Rowland does this by comparing French and American travel guidebooks. In contrasting the approaches used in the two countries, Rowland finds that the French Michelin guides promote the French values of planning, respect for history, and a penchant for abstraction. The Mobil guides promote the American values of experiential learning, self-discovery, and saving money. The French guidebooks provide minutely detailed descriptions of the historical, geological, and architectural aspects of a region. "The principal object of traveling becomes confirming the truth of the guidebook, not discovering one's own truth" (Rowland 1991, 72). Extensive scheduling tips, including exact amounts of time to allot for viewing each church or castle, are supplied by the Michelin guidebooks, which support the French "compunction to shun the unplanned, to guard against the unexpected, to dominate the matter at hand" (63).

Americans, by contrast, are only encouraged to plan so as to save time and money. Exploring little-known byways and enjoying the unexpected surprises around the bend are encouraged, but the Mobil guidebook tries to discourage the American penchant for logging vast amounts of mileage and proudly boasting, "We covered 3,200 miles in four days." "Americans travel primarily for the vicarious pleasure of spending one's time on the open road, deriving satisfaction from moving through space and from exploring the sights as they may present themselves at random to the motorist" (73). "The French feel that the future is a realm of flux and uncertainty" and look to their guidebooks to provide them with a way of "imposing one's will on the unknown" (63).

Just as a travel guidebook or other cultural artifact may exemplify two different perspectives on the world, similar words may convey different meanings across languages, especially those related to value-laden concepts. In *An Introduction to Intercultural Communication* the authors offer the example of marriage:

> An excellent study among Americans, French, and Japanese conducted by a trilingual scholar revealed quite different reactions to the word "marriage" and its equivalents in French *(mariage)* and in Japanese *(kekkon)*. For the Americans marriage was associated with equality and sharing, togetherness, and love. For the French, sexuality and passion were highly salient, confirming some stereotypes, no doubt. For the Japanese, we find family and children at the heart, with a strong pessimistic undertone of obligations and "the end of the line." (Condon and Yousef 188)

Value Orientations: The Kluckhohn-Strodtbeck Model

No culture is made up of robots that uniformly respond to identical pro-gramming. Yet even though all societies contain competing values and alternative responses, it is still possible to make some generalizations regarding the overarching tendencies of the majority. One way of organiz-ing such major value orientations was devised by Florence R. Kluckhohn and Fred L. Strodtbeck (1961) and consists of a series of continua on which a culture's way of relating to fundamental value orientations can be plotted. For example, all societies have a basic attitude toward the way people relate to nature. The Kluckhohn-Strodtbeck continuum shows three alternatives:

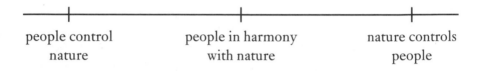

people control	people in harmony	nature controls
nature	with nature	people

The United States, which constructs dams to harness the power of rivers and builds spaceships to conquer the reaches of outer space, would be placed on the left side of the continuum. Traditional Hawaiian culture, where people felt the forces of nature to be so powerful that all they could do was make offerings to Pele, the Goddess of the Volcano, in the hope of appeasing her, would be placed on the right side of the continuum. A cul-ture that lives in harmony with nature, like the Taos Indians described in *The Silent Language*, would be in the middle. "In the spring the Taos believe that Mother Earth is pregnant. To protect the surface of the earth they do not drive their wagons to town, they take all the shoes off their horses, they refuse to wear hard-soled shoes themselves" (Hall 1959, 80–81).

The field of intercultural communication examines a culture's value orientations using such models in order to comprehend the goals and phi-losophy underlying its ways of living. "Not only do values pervade all the other topics, they also may provide the best guidance for understanding and adapting to other cultural patterns of communication" (Condon and Yousef 60).

The Intercultural Perspective

Intercultural sensitivity is not natural. It is not part of our primate past, nor has it characterized most of human history. Cross-cultural contact usually has been accompanied by bloodshed, oppression, or genocide. (Bennett 1993, 21)

Intercultural encounters can be likened to crossing minefields. The best advice when traversing them may be to carry a map, tread lightly, and be ready for surprises. Since our natural inclination is *not* to see things from another's perspective and to judge people negatively who are different from us, we may do well to double-check our initial reactions in intercultural situations. One way suggested by Elijah Lovejoy in *Experiential Activities for Intercultural Learning* (1996) is to be on guard for "negative red flags." We may catch ourselves internally castigating a group of people with a statement like "Those people are so _____!" This should tip us off that a cultural difference may very well be at the bottom of things (191–97). "Those people are so *rude!*" may be our immediate response when we are asked what is considered an impolite question in our culture. We might be stunned, for instance, on meeting a visiting graduate student from Thailand who proceeds to grill us on details of our personal life, such as how much money we earn and the reason for our recent divorce. "For people in Thai society, such questions would be appropriate and not considered too personal, let alone taboo" (Natadecha-Sponsel 1993, 48).

Lovejoy gives two examples of the rude red flag: first, a Moroccan living in France who is "shocked when French associates inquire about his wife. Such questions are a banal form of chitchat in France but may indicate to the Moroccan an improper interest in a private matter." And second,

> an Ethiopian girl visiting in the United States went to a swimming pool one day with friends. She was shocked and upset when someone asked her, "How do you stay so thin?" In the United States, this is not really a request for information, but a compliment on the fashionable state of a person's body. But plumpness is desirable for Ethiopian women ... [so] she perceived the questioner as being rude because the question would have been rude in her homeland. (194)

Other internal judgments to watch out for include "Those people are so dirty!" "Those people are so stupid!" "Those people are so cold!" "Those people are hypocrites!" If we catch ourselves making such negative judgments, we should see if we can rephrase our feeling of frustration in a more culturally relative form: "Something's going on here that seems stupid to me. I wonder if it seems stupid to them?" (Lovejoy 194–97).

In my own experience, I have found some areas ripe for this type of judgment: bureaucracy and time are two of my favorites. When I was living in Paris, there were a lot of things that would send me screaming into those charming cobblestoned streets, the worst of which was dealing with the bank. I had an account at a large French bank that, like my American bank at home, had its headquarters downtown and many small branch offices all over the city. While my American bank's branch offices seem as standardized and predictable as McDonald's, going to the bank in Paris felt like going to a casino—I never knew how much money I was going to walk away with. One branch office would cash my check, another would not. The rules seemed to change almost weekly. Even at my neighborhood branch, one teller would let me withdraw my money and another would refuse. Whenever I expressed dissatisfaction about the lack of standardization, they would coolly respond that Madame had better take her complaints to the downtown headquarters. Despite my intellectual understanding of the French pattern of centralization, I still reacted emotionally to the frustration of not being able to get my money. It was a struggle to keep a culturally relative outlook and tell myself, "Something is going on which seems stupid to me, but if these French people came to America they might be just as exasperated with our banking system as I am with theirs."

You do not have to visit another country, however, to experience the urge to judge others regarding their time-related behavior—all you need is to have friends, coworkers, or baby-sitters from another culture in order to inwardly denounce entire groups of people. When I find myself seething and thinking, "Why are they always late?" "Why do they always wait until the last minute to cancel or confirm appointments?" "Why does it take them so long to leave?" I try to remind myself that rules regarding time are culturally relative. And I might make my expectations explicit by telling my wonderful Ethiopian baby-sitter that I need her to come at "seven o'clock American time," because I really need to leave at seven, not 7:20.

Acknowledging our differences is the first step. The second is deciding who will do the cultural adjusting. The "When in Rome . . . " rule may work well while traveling, but what about encounters with our friends from other cultures here at home? And what constitutes "Deaf Rome"? A prime example is a conference organized and attended by a majority of Deaf people, such as the annual NAD conference. In 1999, I had the privilege of attending and presenting at the Deaf Studies VI Conference, a forum for Deaf professionals to share their research in Deaf art, history, culture, and education. After a co-presentation I made with Priscilla Moyers, a Deaf gentleman was kind enough to come up to me and inform me of a social gaffe I had made earlier. He told me he enjoyed our co-presentation and had changed his opinion of me. It seems that during the opening keynote speech by Carol Padden, a few days earlier, he had been sitting right behind me. He told me I had behaved very rudely at that event. Puzzled, I tried to recall what I had been doing that earned this criticism. I remembered being very absorbed by Carol's speech, which I could, of course, access in three channels, either by watching her signs, reading the projected real-time captions, or listening to the voice interpreter's words. I remembered that my friend Patricia Lessard had been doing an excellent job of voicing and I had glanced over to see if, despite her calm inflection, she appeared nervous in such a high-pressure role. I also recalled that Carol had used several ingroup acronyms and I had wondered whether the real-time captioner might not know them. I had looked over his way to see if maybe I should go and feed him their spelling. Then I had brought my attention back to watching Carol's elegant style of signing. "That was it!" the Deaf man informed me. "Your head was moving all over the place, it looked like you were not paying any attention to the wonderful speaker!"

If we attend a meeting of a Deaf organization, or a predominantly Deaf party, we may assume that Deaf cultural norms should be followed, but what about a one-to-one interaction or an ongoing friendship?

One way to approach such questions is to talk about them openly with our friends and associates and admit how far we are willing to go in adjusting our own behavior and what areas make us uncomfortable. At a meeting I attended recently, the facilitator asked the participants to introduce themselves by giving their name and occupation and by sharing one accomplishment that they were very proud of. This instruction was followed all the way around the room until it was the turn of a participant who was visiting from Holland. The Dutch woman gave her name and occupation, but when it came to accomplishments, she said in a friendly but firm manner, "You know, in my country we are taught not to say things like this about ourselves, so I will pass."

Some of the personal traits that have been identified with being successful in cross-cultural encounters include flexibility, a high tolerance for ambiguity, empathy, and the ability to communicate respect (Ruben 1982, 333). To me, these attributes add up to a mental stance of readiness. Athletes are taught to assume a position with knees bent and weight on the balls of the feet so they can instantly move in any direction in reaction to the play of the ball or the needs of their teammates. So should we be positioned in the intercultural arena. Cultural awareness, sensitivity, and the ability to laugh at our inevitable missteps will go a long way in helping us deal with the unexpected moves of our fellow players.

3

Selected Topics in Intercultural Communication

Collectivism and Individualism

Imagine the following scene: A group of white-coated psychiatrists in the country of Individuania circle around a seated, dazed patient. They are shaking their heads sadly and mumbling their observations to one another, "Patient passively submits to everyone else's wishes." "He stubbornly refuses to make known his preferences, desires, or opinions and acts as though he has no right to his own feelings." "Patient will only refer to the views of his family—obviously has not differentiated himself from the biological breeding unit." "A very serious case. We must keep him for further observation and recommend therapy in order to activate his underdeveloped sense of autonomy."

Now picture a group of psychiatrists in the country of Collectivestan. They are murmuring about their puzzled patient: "This woman is adamant and vociferous in her demands about *her* needs." "She refuses to recognize her obligations to her family or to any other group." "She dares to question our authority and refuses to accept our consensus." "Quite a serious case. She poses a threat to society and must remain in this protected environment." Although these scenarios are exaggerated, they serve to illustrate the fact that what is considered normal and desirable behavior in one culture can be deemed maladaptive, or even indicative of mental illness, in a different culture. They more specifically indicate that the differences between collectivist cultures and individualist cultures encompass such issues as identity, loyalty, obligation, and independence.

More than 70 percent of world cultures can be labeled collectivist, or group oriented. They include much of Africa, Asia, and Latin America. In all such cultures, members of a group (family, work group, tribe, caste, or even the entire country) help each other to survive. Individuals subordinate their personal goals to the goals of the group. American Deaf culture clearly qualifies as a collectivist culture with its emphasis on pooling resources, the duty to share information, the boundary between insiders and outsiders, and loyalty to and strong identification with the group.

> The Deaf Community... is a central part of life in a way that a neighborhood, township, or professional group is not for mainstream Americans... Deaf adults... feel a strong connection and obligation to the Deaf Community... and allocate more time and energy to it [than mainstream Americans do to theirs]. (Smith 1996, 88)

In collectivist cultures, rules for group membership are rigid, and one must essentially be born into and grow up within that culture to qualify as a member. For example, even if foreigners can speak perfect Japanese, it is said that they will never be able to think like the Japanese. The same feeling is found in Deaf culture.

> Deaf people seem to agree that a hearing person can never fully acquire that identity and become a full-fledged member of the deaf community. Even with deaf parents and a native command of ASL, the hearing person will have missed the experience of growing up deaf, including attending a deaf school, and is likely to have divided allegiances. (Lane 1992, 17)

Insider/outsider distinctions are crucial to determining behavior in collectivist cultures. The lines that are drawn around the center of the group show who is an insider. In some cases outsiders are not trusted; in others, they just don't qualify for membership because a certain attribute sets them apart. A hearing child growing up in a Deaf family, for example, may be fluent in ASL and the ways of Deaf culture, have many friends and relatives who are Deaf, and feel included in many Deaf activities. If he tries out for the local deaf boys' baseball team, however, he will be turned down.

Because identification with the group is of paramount importance, the worst punishment that can be meted out is ostracism from the group. An example is the story of a Zia, an Indian painter who in the 1920s was accused by his tribe of providing drawings of the sacred sun symbol of his Puebloan people to officials of the State of New Mexico, who subsequently adapted it as their . . . logo. [His] behavior was considered so outrageously individualistic . . . that he was cast out by his people . . . and he never again won reacceptance by his tribe . . . His fundamental "crime" was that he acted out of personal conviction. (Highwater 195)

In collectivist cultures, people identify with few groups, but those attachments become a highly defining feature of their identity and are long-term, if not permanent. One's status in such societies depends on one's connection to others through family, birthplace, friends, and the individuals and groups one associates with. In China, for example, the concept of self includes one's family. Therefore, anything that happens to the family or to anyone within it happens to every member of the family. Collectivists place a high value on group harmony and face-saving, so cooperation is encouraged and confrontation avoided. In Japan, a primary goal is to understand and share the attitudes of others.

Another illustration of collectivism is the preference of members of such a culture to engage in many activities together, rather than to go off alone. The Israeli custom of all the workers at a job site taking their coffee break at the same time can be viewed by Americans as an inefficient waste of time. However, as an Israeli secretary explained to an impatient American, in this situation efficiency is not the priority. "They'd never agree to go on their break in shifts. What's the point of having a break if you can't sit around and talk to friends?" (Shahar and Kurz 1995, 102). As collectivists, Deaf people feel strong ties to the Deaf community. "Most . . . work at regular non-Deaf jobs, but spend virtually all their social time with Deaf friends and at community events" (Smith 1996, 88).

In individualist cultures, such as the United States, Australia, and most of northwest Europe, the basic unit of survival is the individual. One is repeatedly encouraged to be independent, self-reliant, and always ready to take responsibility for one's own actions. Heavy emphasis is placed on personal choices, opinions, and creativity. Group membership is flexible, and one can be a member of many groups simultaneously. Identification with these groups is relatively weak, however, and no one group completely defines its members' identities. Here in the United States, for example, one may be a part of a book club, a church choir, and a hiking club, but any of these may easily change if one's interests change or one moves to a different city. We engage in a continual process of joining and leaving a series of groups, and we identify with a group not because we must, but because of the (temporary) benefits it offers.

We are mistrustful of becoming too strongly attached to any one group, seeing this as surrendering our personal identity. Many Americans' lives appear to be a quest to find their personal identity. This often includes a purposeful breaking away from their family and birthplace. Sayings such as "Look out for #1" or "God helps those who help themselves" underscore the autonomous nature of individualist societies. Status in cultures like ours depends largely on personal achievement.

An interesting way to capture the essence of cultural values is to look at proverbs and aphorisms. Compare the American saying "The squeaky wheel gets the grease" with a Japanese proverb that translates as "The nail that sticks out gets hammered down." In the Japanese proverb, being noticed as separate from the group is dangerous, whether one is singled out for positive or negative reasons. In contrast, American culture admires and rewards those who dare to call attention to themselves.

A Deaf "hero," as seen in folktales and stories, is admired because he or she helped other Deaf people. In Deaf culture, the most respected leaders are "felt to be responsible for other Deaf people, in a personal way. They must not only work for the betterment of the community but are expected to be open to all its members, giving them time, attention and help" (Smith 1996, 30–31). Success in Deaf culture is applauded with the proviso that one must not distance oneself from the Deaf community.

> Marlee Matlin, the actor awarded an Oscar for her role in *Children of a Lesser God*, took advantage of her ascribed deafness to get the role but later, when she accepted the Oscar, rejected the primary marker of a Deaf identity, ASL/Sign, by speaking with her voice . . . thus, intentionally or not, shaming and alienating the Deaf Community. Some Deaf people began using a name for her indicating her outsider status. She has subsequently chosen to adopt a more Deaf stance in public. (29)

Loyalty to the group is an important characteristic of collectivism. One does not behave in a way that would bring disgrace to the family. Nor does one betray or embarrass other members of the group. "Deaf leaders rarely confront others directly in public. If they are friends or care about the person, they do so in private" (94–95).

In collectivist cultures (and minority groups) one is expected to devote time and energy to promoting the welfare of the group.

> The ideal Deaf person contributes to and supports the community; they hold parties or sponsor events to bring people together, to entertain, enlighten and to create solidarity—spending much time socializing. They put the welfare of the community higher than their own immediate needs. (107)

Decision Making

Many cultural behaviors can be linked to and explained by the collectivist/individualist divide, for example, decision making. In individualist cultures, each person in a group is supposed to have a separate and equal voice and is supposed to make up his or her own mind independently when decisions are to be made. In collectivist cultures like Japan, on the other hand, the group often caucuses or negotiates before a formal vote is taken and agrees by consensus upon a course of action that is in the best interest of the group as a whole. Then a united front is presented at the formal meeting. At a meeting of an organization with both Deaf and hearing members, the Deaf members may tend to caucus to decide together what position is best for the Deaf community at large and then vote as a bloc. Hearing members of this group, if not aware of the cultural dynamics, may judge such behavior as weak-minded or collusive.

Reciprocity

Reciprocity, or giving to and taking from the collective pool of skills in the group, can be a feature of collectivist cultures as well. In comparison, members of individualist cultures do not like to feel obligated beyond the present moment and operate more on a quid pro quo basis. Therefore, if a member of a collectivist culture needs help to repair a car, move to a new apartment, or paint a house, he or she has a network of friends and relatives upon whom to rely, while one from an individualist culture might have to hire a stranger. In Deaf culture, there is an unspoken system of reciprocity, which we will examine in depth in chapter 5. Even though no one keeps a tally of what each person gives or takes from the collective pool, the members of the community censure those who fail to do their share in assisting others.

Names as a Reflection of Group-Oriented Culture

In "Cross-Cultural Training across the Individualism-Collectivism Divide," authors Harry C. Triandis, Richard Brislin, and C. Harry Hui (1988) make an interesting point about names and how they illustrate cultural values: "In Individualistic cultures we put the person's [given] name first (e.g., *Harry* Triandis); in many collectivist cultures the family name comes first (e.g., *Hui* Chi-chiu)." In Deaf culture, too, names, or more specifically name signs, are subject to the preeminence of the group. Name signs, which will be described in depth in chapter 5, are used mostly to refer to a person when he or she is not present and thus *belong* more to the group than to the person being referred to. Although Deaf people cherish their own name signs, it is the group's prerogative to change a person's name sign. This is not done lightly but happens most often when a name sign is physically uncomfortable to make or duplicates another person's existing sign and is therefore confusing to the group (Mindess 1990; Supalla 1992).

Crossing the Individualist/Collectivist Divide

Though Triandis, Brislin, and Hui make no mention of Deaf culture and may not have even been aware of its existence, their points are quite valid across the hearing-Deaf divide. For example, collectivists who interact with individualists are cautioned that the written word carries great importance in individualist cultures. They are also warned that individualists take pride in their own accomplishments and expect to be complimented on them, while placing less importance on activities that occur within the group.

For Deaf people, who spend a great deal of their lives coping with the hearing world, the above advice could alert them, say, to be sure they understand the small print before affixing their signatures to a contract. It might also explain why some sign language interpreters end an interpreting assignment by asking the Deaf consumer, "Was that okay?" What the interpreter may be looking for is validation of his or her work in the form of a compliment. The Deaf person may be puzzled at this request and matter-of-factly state, "If there was anything wrong, I would have told you."

From the opposite vantage point, individualists are told what to expect when they deal with collectivists, who are deeply involved with the events in their group. Collectivists have social duties and obligations that carry great weight in their lives. Individualists are admonished, therefore, to be patient, spend a lot of time chatting, develop long-term relationships, and be willing to answer personal questions. Things change as individualists move from outsider to insider status within the collectivist culture: they are then expected to sacrifice for and contribute to the group. Those individualists who develop even closer ties by marrying someone from a collective culture are put on notice that they may become "annoyed with the time, energy, and resources which the collectivist puts into the extended ingroup" (Triandis, Brislin, and Hui 285).

These pieces of advice seem especially appropriate for sign language interpreters who, although they are hearing, occupy a special place in the Deaf community. Those interpreters who are not from Deaf families learned ASL and Deaf culture from associating with Deaf people and now earn their living from their signing skills. Although it seems natural to interpreters to compartmentalize their work life and social life, in collective Deaf culture these things are not so easily separable.

To return to our opening example of the misunderstood visitors to the countries of Individuania and Collectivestan, unfamiliarity with the opposing worldviews inherent in individualist and collectivist cultures may not, of course, result in a stay at a psychiatric hospital. It is entirely possible, however, that a student adviser at an American college may see Asian students, who refuse to state personal preferences for a major but are resigned to following their parents' wishes, as passive to the point of being clinically depressed. In the same way, collectivist members of the Deaf community may label an interpreter with a "9 to 5 attitude," who makes money from the community but gives nothing back, as terminally self-centered.

High Context and Low Context

Suppose you are sitting in a busy cafe, sipping coffee and chatting with a friend. All around you are others doing the same. Because you are a curious person, you happen to overhear bits of other conversations. (All right, admit it—you love to eavesdrop!) On your right are two women planning a trip to Europe. On your left, a man is complaining about a coworker. Then your friend notices a Deaf couple who are chatting too, but of course in sign language. Your friend says, "Hey, you know sign language, what are they saying?" So you look and look but you can't figure out exactly what they are talking about. Something about a party. Was it in the past or in the future? It's hard to tell. And to whom are they referring? Men? Women? Something is missing here. "So," pesters your friend, "what are they saying?" You mumble a vague reply and change the subject. Had you been familiar with the difference between high-context and low-context cultures, you might have been able to explain to your friend the ineffectiveness of your eavesdropping.

The terms *high context* and *low context* were coined by Edward T. Hall in his groundbreaking book, *Beyond Culture* (1976), and summarized concisely some years later in *Understanding Cultural Differences*, coauthored with Mildred Reed Hall (1990). These terms deal with the question of how much information must be made explicit in a given culture compared with how much is already understood implicitly because of shared experience. It helps to keep in mind that a high-context culture has a high dependence on context; in other words, if you do not share the same cultural experience as everyone else, you might not understand what is going on in any given conversation. Low-context cultures have a low dependence on context, so it is not assumed that you have as much shared background and experience; therefore, things will be explained more. Think of the difference between the economical conversational style of twins who have grown up together compared with the amount of explanation, clarification, and reiteration needed by opposing lawyers presenting their case in court. Hall says that "The level of context determines everything about the nature of the communication and is the foundation on which all subsequent behavior rests ..." (Hall 1976, 92). He also observes, "A high-context (HC) communication or message is one in which most of the information is either in the physical context or internalized in the person, while very little is in the coded, explicit, transmitted part of the message" (91). "In high-context cultures," Hall says elsewhere, "interpersonal contact takes precedence over everything else ... information flows freely" (Hall and Hall 23). Conversely, people in low-context cultures "... compartmentalize their personal relationships, their work, and many aspects of day-to-day life" (7). When they communicate, "most of the information must be in the transmitted message in order to make up for what is missing in the context" (Hall 1976, 101).

Clearly, American Deaf culture would be placed on the high-context end of the continuum, while mainstream American culture would be found on the low-context side. As the student workbook for the acclaimed ASL course, *Signing Naturally,* explains, "Among Deaf people there is a great deal of shared knowledge, common experiences, goals and beliefs, common friends and acquaintances, a common way of talking; that is, their lives share a common context" (Smith, Lentz, and Mikos 1988, 79). We can also appreciate the characteristic way Deaf discourse describes certain events in great detail with another observation from Hall:

> In general, HC communication, in contrast to LC, is economical, fast, efficient, and satisfying; however, *time must be devoted to programming. If this programming does not take place, the communication is incomplete* [italics added]. (Hall 1976, 101)

If we return to our eavesdropping example (and put aside the commonality that both cultures consider such behavior rude), we can see how the basic difference between high and low context affects our perceptions on various levels. On the grammatical level, English fits the mold of a low-context language by its redundancy in comparison with high-context ASL. Every verb in an English sentence shows its tense, while, in ASL, tense may be set at the beginning of an utterance and then carried implicitly until a change of tense is noted. English repeats the same subject throughout the conversation by using proper names or gender-specific pronouns, while in ASL there are several possibilities such as mentioning the subject at the beginning of a conversation and then carrying it along implicitly until it is changed, incorporating it into directional verbs, or representing it by name signs or gender-neutral pronouns. What this means is that if you miss the beginning of an ASL conversation, you may be lost as to which person is being talked about and in what tense. In English conversations, on the other hand, even if you miss the beginning, there will be repeated clues along the way to help you fill in the blanks.

Equally, if not more, important is the cultural level of context. Hearing Americans, in general, come from a diverse set of backgrounds, including differences in socioeconomic class, education, and religion. Although Deaf Americans may be born into families of equal diversity, their ensuing experiences of growing up deaf in a hearing world, attending the same types of schools, and being part of the same community result in a shared context that fosters mutual understanding.

Introductions

Let's see how this contrast between hearing and Deaf Americans is played
out in personal introductions. Hall says that in introductions a high-
context culture focuses on questions regarding social background and
group membership, while a low-context culture seeks out data that emphasize personal background. This is borne out in Deaf and hearing introductions. When two Deaf people meet, they ask each other what schools
they attended, to whom they are related, and which friends they have in
common in order to place each other in a known social context. In contrast, hearing Americans ask each other what they do for a living, where
they live, what hobbies they enjoy, and so on to get an idea of their personal identity.

Sharing Information

Another variant between high- and low-context cultures is how information is managed in a society and how it is shared: which topics are discussed, with whom, and in what situations. In a low-context culture,
information is shared with only a few people; it is compartmentalized and
its flow is restricted. In a high-context culture, on the other hand, information flows rapidly and is freely shared. This could be likened to the flow of
water in a series of canals compared with a free-flowing system of rivers
and tributaries. An excellent example can be found in Stephanie Hall's
article, "Train Gone Sorry" (1989), about communication etiquette at a
Deaf club. She explains that

> hearing people often comment that Deaf people do not keep secrets
> among themselves—although they may keep their secrets from
> hearing people! Yet it should not be surprising that among people for
> whom all information is precious, even sacred, secrecy is considered
> antisocial. Sharing information is an affirmation of the unity of the
> Deaf community. Deaf people in turn often think a hearing person's
> attitude toward privacy [is] infuriating and perplexing. (S. Hall 99)

Context in the Legal Arena

One final example of differences in levels of context can be found in the
legal arena. This aspect of American culture is even farther out on the

low-context end of the continuum. Edward T. Hall (1976) describes the American legal system as so decontexted that "... it is extraordinarily difficult to guarantee that the proceedings can be linked to real life" (106). The inadmissibility of hearsay, personal opinion, and background information as well as the heavy usage of yes-no questions "... reveal the U.S. courts as the epitome of low-context systems" (107). In comparison, Hall describes the French courts, which are higher context and which "... allow great leeway in the testimony admitted as evidence. The court wants to find out as much as possible about the circumstances behind the surface acts ... Everything is heard—facts, hearsay, gossip" (108).

Hall goes on to say that low-context legal systems view the participants as adversaries, while high-context cultures such as Japan put "the accused, the. court, the public, and those who are the injured parties on the same side, where, ideally, they can work together to settle things" (111). Another example of this high-context justice system is found in American Indian "sentencing circles," which are community-based tribunals that are composed of tribal leaders, the victim, the defendant, friends, and families; at times a judge presides and there are lawyers present. After a long process—sometimes several days—of discussion and consensus building, participants arrive at a sentence (Turner 1996).

It would be quite interesting if the Deaf community had a formal system of justice to compare with those described above. In its absence, it would seem that the closest parallel would probably be to look at an exclusively Deaf organization like the Deaf club still found in a few cities and see how those who break the rules are handled. In a classic example, a treasurer (such as the one depicted in the Deaf play *Tales from a Clubroom* by Bernard Bragg and Eugene Bergman [1981]) who absconds with the treasury may be punished by temporary ostracism from the group. This practice fits the collectivist principle of ostracism as punishment. After a suitable period of time has passed, the ex-treasurer can then be allowed back into the club and may even hold another position of responsibility (but not the post of treasurer).

We Are Not Imprisoned in a Low-Context World

Although American culture is by and large low context, we all have many moments of high-context communication with those people we know well: spouse, mate, partner, family, closest friends. In these relationships we share a great deal of information about each other, memories of past experiences, details of our daily routines, and common jargon. We do not need to spell everything out. Sometimes one word or a quick "How'd it go?" will suffice when both of you know that what you are referring to is the first day of a new job, an afternoon at the zoo with six kids, or a long-dreaded root canal.

Conversely, we all have experienced the frustration of being the only one who does not understand what is going on in a high-context situation. A good example is interpreting at a staff meeting of a business corporation, especially if it is your first time there. All of the staff members present, including the Deaf workers, share a common vocabulary of acronyms, jargon, and technical terms they don't bother to explain to you because they forget that the interpreter is not privy to this specific terminology. If it happens to be a computer-oriented workplace, you may wonder if there is any English being spoken at all.

Now that we know we have the ability to function in either a high- or low-context mode, despite our cultural tendencies, we can be more sensitive in matching our behavior to the situation at hand, whether that be eavesdropping in a cafe, sharing news with a Deaf friend, or interpreting in the courtroom.

Time Orientation

Imagine that you are a businessperson and have just gotten off a plane after flying halfway around the world. You find yourself suffering from jet lag in a new country. You walk out into blinding morning sunlight, while every cell in your body begs you to find a nice dark bedroom and succumb to slumber. Instead, you stumble bleary-eyed into a busy bakery, hoping that some sweet pastry can convince your brain it is really morning. You search for a semblance of a line or a comforting red metal box that dispenses numbers. How will you know when it is your turn? The counter person seems to be helping several people at once. But as you stare at the confusion of milling bodies, you finally notice that somehow everyone eventually gets served.

Glancing at your watch, you realize you must hurry to your important business meeting so as to arrive on time and not insult your host. Weary yet proud, you arrive on the stroke of the hour but are dismayed to find that nothing is set up and no one else has arrived. After what seems like an eternity, the meeting is finally convened. Trying to hide your irritation, you use up your last ounce of energy to focus on the agenda at hand—making plans for future business endeavors. Then, the last straw: all the other participants in the meeting insist on talking only about the past accomplishments of their company. Your eyes glaze over and you wonder, "What is wrong with these people?"

Time, clearly, organizes our lives in many ways, and we can view these from a cultural perspective. We can look, for example, at the pace of a culture. If it has a comparatively slow pace, people will walk, talk, and eat slowly, unhurriedly relishing the moment. If, on the other hand, it is a fast-paced culture, its members will move and converse more quickly and may be spotted scarfing down their food, to their digestive detriment. This distinction is not only applicable to other countries, but may be observed in different regions of our own (e.g., New York City and Atlanta).

Another way to compare time orientation is to study a culture's degree of precision. Does the 2:03 train always arrive at 2:03? In Switzerland it does. When the plumber in Mexico says he will come to fix your drip "mañana," does that mean he will assuredly be at your house tomorrow? Probably not.

What Is Late?

Attitudes about time include the definition of what is considered "late," which also varies from culture to culture. One could characterize the stages of reaction to being late as follows:

Stage 1: I am only a tiny bit late. No one will even notice, so I don't have to comment on it.

Stage 2: I am a little late so I will mumble a vague apology and let it drop, as it probably bothered no one.

Stage 3: I am definitely late. I hope no one has been too inconvenienced. I will make a clear apology and explain the reasons for my tardiness.

Possible Stage 4: This is awful! I am terribly late. I am sure everyone is angry with me. How can I ever make it up to them? I will put myself at their mercy and beg their forgiveness.

In the United States we are at stage 1 from 0 to about 5 minutes, stage 2 from 5 to 10 minutes, and stage 3 from 10 to 15 minutes. After 15 minutes, there is an optional switch to stage 4 depending on the circumstances. In Germany, stage 1 is shorter, perhaps only until 2 minutes after the appointed time. Then all the stages get moved up accordingly. In Latin America and Arab countries, however, stage 1 may last as long as 20 minutes and stage 2 may last 45 minutes. Obviously, this is fertile ground for intercultural conflict.

Americans seem to be particularly obsessed with time, viewing it as a commodity. We see it as something precious that we can save, waste, buy, spend, find, lose, make, pass, take, spare, run out of, and kill. Not every culture shares this perspective.

Deaf and Hearing Differences Related to Time

Many subcultures in the United States refer to their own variant of the accepted time system half-jokingly as Black People's Time or Jewish Standard Time, and so on. But they are only half-joking, because there really are differences in behavior and attitude toward time in different cultures. This category would include DST, or Deaf Standard Time, as well. Perhaps all of these "standard time" references are only glorified excuses for being late. Or, to their credit, some subcultures may recognize that in their group punctuality is not always next to godliness.

Besides arriving at events late, another element of Deaf time is staying late at gatherings such as parties. In Deaf-only parties, this behavior goes unremarked upon because it is expected. In a mixed party of Deaf and hearing, people often joke that the party really gets started after all the hearing people go home (early). If there is an event at a public location such as a theater, it often happens that the Deaf people in attendance must be shooed out at closing time, and they sometimes continue the conversation on the front steps outside the theater. At a restaurant, a group of Deaf patrons may be deep in conversation as the restaurant staff stacks the chairs upside down on the tables and turns off the lights. If Deaf people are involved in a discussion, cutting it off arbitrarily because the clock says it's getting late is almost unheard of. These moments of face-to-face communication with fellow Deaf people are so precious that "there is minimal value placed on being 'on time' to the next appointment, getting home to sleep, or even finishing the immediate business at hand" (Smith 1996, 190).

Although DST is often used as the reason that meetings start late, there are some instances where punctuality and even showing up early are common in order to get a good seat. This is linked to the importance of sight lines and having a good view of the signing. It may apply, therefore, to signed or interpreted plays or lectures.

There is also a cultural difference in timing between Deaf culture and hearing culture with regard to greetings and leave-taking. Hearing Americans practice a greeting ritual that precedes our getting to the point: "Hi." "Hello." "How are you?" "Fine thanks, and you?" "Not too bad." And then on to the matter at hand. Hearing leave-taking is more abrupt: "Great party. Bye." Deaf culture reverses the pacing of these two interactions. After the hello, they get right to the point without the warm-up and save the long ritual for leave-taking. At a party or other large event, hugs, good-byes, agreeing when to meet again, more hugs, a last bit of news, and so forth can easily continue for half an hour.

Polychronic versus Monochronic

Polychronic and *monochronic* are terms coined by Edward T. Hall to describe another distinction regarding time. In monochronic cultures like the United States, Germany, Switzerland, and countries in Scandinavia, time is segmented linearly, and people tend to focus on one thing or person at a time (witness our ever-present date books or PDAs neatly divided into hourly or smaller units that we often assign one by one until our days are fully booked.) By scheduling our time so rigidly, we compartmentalize our life, trying to make it manageable by concentrating on only one thing at a time. This process has the side effect of reducing context as we separate business from pleasure, family from friends, exercise from daily chores, and so on. So deeply ingrained is our system of dealing with time that we forget it is not universal. It seems the only logical way to organize our lives in order to make sure that time is not lost or wasted.

In polychronic cultures, such as those of Latin American countries and France, people and relationships take precedence over agendas and schedules. People may carry on several conversations at the same time. This means that if an American is meeting with a businessperson in a polychronic culture, he or she will probably become upset when the business counterpart's brother "intrudes," the phone rings, the secretary comes in with another matter, and the businessperson deals with all of these occurrences simultaneously. The American literally wants one-on-one attention and feels discounted, or even insulted, if he or she doesn't get it.

This difference is also apparent in business meetings, where the monochronic members want to follow the agenda strictly as it was planned. The polychronic members may feel that doing so is too rigid and leaves no room for personal interactions, which are really more important than agendas anyway. In the Deaf community, "Groups move toward goals rather than complete checklists and move on. The process, the mutual feeling and perception of progress is more important than the completion of specific tasks or outward signs of 'progress'" (Smith 1996, 192). As Hall states in *The Dance of Life*, "Polychronic people are so deeply immersed in each other's business that they feel a compulsion to keep in touch. Any stray scrap of a story is gathered in and stored away. Their involvement in people is the very core of their existence" (1983, 50). For Deaf people who depend upon communication with each other for so much of their information about the world, the polychronic description also seems to fit. Being involved in others' lives takes time—time to share the news and time to listen. When interpreters do not include this "human time" to chat after the work part of the assignment is over, they may be characterized as rude hearing people who continually glance at their watches and then rush off without even a good-bye.

Because we cannot always predict exactly how long things will take, our monochronic time system has some unforeseen consequences. Time runs out before things are finished; money runs out before a research project is completed; the allotted appointment time runs out before we finish describing our complaints to the doctor. For freelance sign language interpreters, this is a particularly relevant dilemma. In order to make a living, we must often schedule several appointments back-to-back and so are constantly trying to predict the impossible: how long a "routine checkup" or a deposition will last. Even when we are not responsible for the erroneous prognostication, we are stuck in the middle. Our excuse as we run out the door, "They told me this would only last till three and I have another assignment at four," does not assuage the Deaf client who is in the middle of an important meeting or a tooth extraction.

Past versus Future Orientation

Yet another way to compare time among cultures is through the continuum of past, present, and future orientation. Past-oriented cultures such as those of Iran, India, and most nations of Asia are connected to their history, respect their ancestors, keep traditions, and look back with reverence on a "golden age." Future-oriented cultures, of which the United States is a good example, are more focused on change and progress. According to Edward C. Stewart and Milton J. Bennett in *American Cultural Patterns*

(1991), people with a past or present orientation may assume a fatalistic outlook toward the future and be upset by aggressive attempts to structure the unknowable.

In some ways American Deaf culture can be considered a past-oriented culture. It treasures its sign language and cherishes those Deaf pioneers who fought for basic rights for their fellow Deaf citizens. One of the most significant of these is the right to a good education for all Deaf children. In this context, one could say that Deaf culture looks back on a "golden age" in the nineteenth century when more than twenty state schools for the Deaf were founded by Deaf people. Nine of the schools had Deaf principals or superintendents, and sign language was the language of instruction in all of these schools. There were also many more Deaf teachers during this "golden age" than there are today. At its height in 1858, 40 percent of the teachers at the state schools for the deaf were Deaf themselves, compared to only 14 percent today (Gannon 1981). (This dramatic drop can be traced to the infamous Congress of Milan, 1880, when oralism became the official policy in both European and American deaf schools. One result was the firing of Deaf teachers [Lane 1984].)

Unfortunately, many Deaf people are not taught about their heritage in school.

> While community memory is long, Deaf people's awareness of their history [and] their heritage is vincible and often fragmented. Its continuity depends on community and the memory of elders. Yet while many details have been lost the sense remains. Deaf history exists not in books, but in stories, in events at the residential schools. (Smith 1996, 194)

An interesting anecdote that points up the past orientation of Deaf culture is the following story, which was told to me by a well-respected leader in the Deaf community. A meeting was held at a Deaf-run service agency that had applied for and received a large grant of money from the state. Various leaders in the Deaf community were invited by the head of this agency to contribute ideas for the five-year plan, which was required by the grant. It seems that the Deaf community members had a difficult time coming up with plans for the future. When pressed by the agency director, their ideas all seemed to relate to the past—things that they didn't want to repeat or projects in the past that proved successful.

Of course the Deaf community wants change and progress in the areas of equal rights and improved communication and technological access for its members, but that is change in the context of the majority hearing culture. Within the Deaf culture, traditions are cherished. This includes traditional forms of folklore such as jokes and storytelling as well as the Traditional Name Sign System (see chapter 5 for a fuller description).

Hearing Americans, by and large, are future oriented. We believe we can always improve on the present through action and hard work. Any attempt of futurists to try to effect changes on a past-oriented culture, however, will be met with puzzled dismay if not angry resistance. This is why American Deaf culture does not look kindly on attempts by outsiders to invent new ASL signs, new traditions, or new name signs.

An interesting internal struggle with change has been evident in the recent shift in signs for countries. Many signs in ASL have iconic roots. It is no surprise, therefore, that the traditional signs for certain countries referred to perceived physical features of their citizens (e.g., JAPAN and CHINA were made with twisting movements at the eye). In about the last twenty years, however, parallel to the American mainstream movement of showing respect to diverse cultures by using "politically correct" terms, Deaf people from different countries have chosen to demonstrate mutual respect by adopting the sign used in the country itself. For example, the traditional ASL sign for *Sweden* was made with an initialized "S" at the forehead, but now many people have adopted the Swedish sign for *Sweden* made on the back of the hand. Nevertheless, there are competing feelings that pull in two directions. Although it is more polite to refer to Japan with the Japanese sign for *Japan*, where the two hands outline the shape of the country, many older Deaf people resist changing traditional signs and continue to make the old sign for Japan at the eye.

The Perennial Now

To further enlarge our perspective on time, we find it interesting to note that not all cultures perceive of time as a line leading from the past through the present toward the future. Time is experienced in yet another way by many native peoples. Australian aborigines, for example, divide time into two types: the ordinary time of daily life and the sacred state of "dreamtime," which includes "not only the events of our sleeping state, but also those things we anticipate, envision, imagine, intuit and conceive" (Highwater 89). Things are not always divided neatly into the realm of the objective, defined by sequences of cause and effect, and the realm of subjective feelings about those facts. It is the interweaving of these two seeming opposites that determines reality to many native peoples. The focus is more on eternal recurring cycles than on a linear time that moves ever forward in predictable progression (90–91).

In fact, the Hopi language, studied in depth by Benjamin Whorf, seems to contain no words or grammatical constructions that refer to what we think of as "time," including no references to the past, present, or future. To our Western minds, used to seeing time as a concrete commodity that is measured by clocks and calendars, this way of relating to the world seems completely alien if not mystical—something out of this world.

Reasoning and Rhetoric

Suppose you read in the newspaper that there is to be a lecture on the question, "Can Chocolate Really Increase Your Intelligence?" Sounds interesting, so you decide to attend. Driving over to the lecture hall, you might anticipate the shape the lecture could take: after a short introduction to the topics of chocolate and intelligence, the speaker, you might expect, will quote studies, cite statistics, and refer to expert opinion. The discussion will most likely include charts, graphs, and scientific terminology. The speaker, you imagine, will probably conclude with a summation of her points in a logical sequence to convince you of the validity of her position.

What if, to your surprise, instead of beginning with general comments, the speaker starts by describing the history of chocolate since the Renaissance and the many ways intelligence has been viewed throughout the ages. You might squirm a little in your seat and try to suppress a yawn. What if the speaker then tells detailed personal stories about people she knows who have eaten a lot of chocolate and become a lot brighter? You might feel confused or doubtful and wonder, "Where's your proof?" And what if, rather than a cool objective discussion of test scores and chemical analyses, the speaker recites poetic analogies in a loud voice, gesturing broadly? What if she repeats herself in an exaggerated fashion and appears quite emotional? You would probably judge her immature. When, instead of facts and evidence, she quotes the ancient writings of the holy prophets and talks of fate, you might get up, disgusted, and leave, wondering how in the world this speaker thought she could convince anyone of anything.

If we are determined, we can manage to achieve some objective insight into the way our culture handles group membership, information sharing, and time, but the topic we are now considering is much harder to see with a dispassionate eye. It covers the way we think, how we organize our thoughts, what we trust as evidence, and how we try to persuade others.

An enlightening discussion of this topic can be found in the chapter "Thinking about Thinking" in John C. Condon and Fathi Yousef's *An Introduction to Intercultural Communication*. These authors characterize cultural rhetoric as "acquired habits, widely shared by speakers within a particular society, influencing both the speaker and his own cultural audience and *extremely difficult to translate satisfactorily into another society . . . without some loss or awkwardness*" (emphasis added) (235–36). Clearly, for interpreters working between any two languages, one of the major challenges will not only be to find equivalent words, phrases, and idioms, but also to present them in a familiar structure and in a convincing manner.

Organizing Information

Of course, each language has its little quirks in the way it organizes information. Condon and Yousef cite as an example the numerous ways American English uses patterns of threes to describe things, as in the following phrases: "tall, dark, and handsome," "wine, women, and song," "hook, line, and sinker." We break things down into a beginning, middle, and end, and we award three basic college degrees. Many children's stories follow this pattern as well: "Three Blind Mice," "The Three Little Pigs," "Three Billy Goats Gruff." We tell people, "If at first you don't succeed, try, try again" and "Third time's a charm," and many of our jokes end with the punch line, "And then the third guy says . . ." and so on.

Since reality doesn't really come in threes, it is possible that as Condon and Yousef suggest, ". . . our culturally influenced rhetorical forms themselves help shape our worldview, our thoughts, and our actions" (233). We can see this in ourselves: in writing a sentence we come up with two adjectives and then feel compelled to find a third one to make it feel right.

Another aspect of cultural rhetoric is the way we organize and present our thoughts. It includes "where to begin, where to stop, how to move from point to point, how many and which points to stress . . ." (240). Hearing American children learn in elementary school a basic form of organization: topic sentence, three clarifying examples, and conclusion, and they are instructed to line up their points in a logical progression.

Our style of communicating, however, is not by any means universal. German communicative style, for instance, differs from American style in several important ways. As described by Hall and Hall, Americans prefer a "headline style"—short and to the point; we often open a presentation by divulging what it will be about (e.g., today I will discuss the three reasons why you should vote for X). In contrast, according to Hall and Hall, "Just as the verb often comes at the end of a German sentence, it takes a while for Germans to get to the point." Germans also place great value on history and often commence a presentation with a discussion of the historical background of the subject at hand (49).

Chinese (as well as other Southeast Asian languages *and ASL*), is a *topic-comment* language. This term refers to the grammatical structure of its sentences. In contrast with English, which most often uses a subject-predicate style, 50 percent of Chinese utterances describe the topic first, which "sets the spatial, temporal or personal framework for the following assertion" (Young 74). In other words, the topic gives the background information and the context needed to appreciate the new information or argument contained in the comment. An example is the sentence "Blue surf board, giant squid ate" cited by Linda Wai Ling Young in her essay "Inscrutability Revisited," where she discusses the implications of this difference.

In her study, Young went beyond the sentence level and noted how this same organizational framework applied to chunks of discourse expressed by native Chinese speakers *when speaking English*. She found that when the Chinese speakers were attempting to persuade others, they would start with the background and then make their main point at the end. The most striking finding in this study, which carries deep implications for sign language interpreters, is the strong negative reactions native English speakers expressed upon hearing a tape of Chinese speakers utilizing the topic-comment structure in English. Without the introductory thesis statement common in English, "the main point was initially lost on them because it lay buried in a mass of information" (79). The indirectness characterized by "the absence of a preview statement and the mere item-by-item listing of justifications" (80) may lead English speakers to view the Chinese discourse as "imprecise, unwieldy, and downright inept" (81). Young asserts that "a basic unawareness of alternative linguistic structures and discourse conventions can shade into doubts concerning the reasoning abilities of the Chinese mind" (79).

Interestingly, when the Chinese speakers were questioned about their discourse strategy, they expressed a strong distaste for the American style of beginning with a thesis statement. One person said he would stop listening after that first sentence, since it gives away the whole point. Others characterized such a direct approach as "pushy," "inconsiderate," and "rude." In later chapters we will examine what happens when Deaf ASL users, like the Chinese speakers in this study, begin their discourse with an explanation of the background needed to view the present situation and not with the introductory statement that the hearing English speaker expects.

Aside from typically starting with an introductory statement, English presentational style usually proceeds from the general to the specific. American Sign Language, on the other hand, proceeds from the specific to the general. As an illustration of this point, I recently attended a lecture that Dr. Samuel J. Supalla gave on the subject of name signs in ASL. It happens that I wrote my master's thesis on name signs and have lectured on it myself, so I am familiar with the subject. As Dr. Supalla (who is Deaf) lectured, my attention became drawn to the way he organized his presentation. It seemed to be a complete reversal of the approach I would take. I would probably start my lecture as follows: "Today we are going to talk about name signs in ASL. There are two major categories of name signs, descriptive and arbitrary. Here are some examples . . . Are there any comments or questions?" Sam, however, started like this: "My name is Sam Supalla. Does anyone in the audience know my name sign? It looks like this. Let me tell you the story of my name sign . . . Do people in the audience want to share the story of their name signs . . . ? By the way, we have been talking about two kinds of name signs, descriptive and arbitrary."

My approach proceeds from the general to the specific, while Sam's went from the specific to the general. In addition, in my structure the lecture is separated from any questions or comments from the audience. Sam, however, used the stories and examples elicited from the audience members as threads with which he wove a collective lecture.

Persuasion

How do we go about convincing others? Americans prefer expert opinion, hard evidence, and facts that translate into numbers, statistics, and percentages. We even like imaginary numbers such as projected yields and the 2.3 children that the average family is supposed to have. We see no role for emotions in the thinking process. Other cultures, such as those of France, Russia, or Latin America, prefer deductive to inductive reasoning. In this more abstract approach, they begin with a discussion of theory and principles and put less emphasis on data and evidence. In addition to the inductive and deductive approaches, there is a third one called relational thinking, which characterizes Chinese and Japanese thought patterns. In this mode, one pays more attention to context, relationships, and issues of group membership and identity. The person's experience of the event is the fact that matters, not the so-called objective fact in itself (Stewart and Bennett 42–44).

A particularly strong contrast with the American focus on objectivity is found in Arab culture, where one persuades not by logical arguments and facts but through an emotional presentation that exploits the beauty and vividness of stories and analogies. In terms of their speech mannerisms, Arabs shout when excited, for it signifies sincerity. They repeat themselves, exaggerate, and gesture a great deal. They quote as authorities the Prophet or the Koran and often make use of oaths such as "I swear by God. . . ." Arabs utilize personalized arguments that may put personal pressure on the listeners to adopt their point of view, and they view discussions as arenas in which to display their verbal skills and personal charm (Nydell 44).

Advertisements are mini lessons in persuasion. Hall and Hall contrast German, French, and American styles of attracting potential buyers with their print ads. The low-context German shoppers rely on a recitation of the facts (which incidentally are monitored for accuracy), so their ads are full of technical details, description, and analyses. French high-context culture expects shoppers to be already familiar with the product and so gives more focus to aesthetics, design, and the evocation of the appropriate feeling in the viewer. Print ads may consist of nothing more than one word—the name of the product—over a provocatively sexy photograph. One may see this ad plastered hundreds of times in Metro stations, on billboards, and in magazines, until the effect of so much aesthetic repetition triumphs. American ads, in contrast, often resort to exaggerated claims to persuade the consumer that their product is the best, the newest, or (in recent years) the lowest in fat or carbs.

Communicative Style in ASL

Let us look at rhetorical style and persuasion from a Deaf cultural viewpoint. What are some of the rhetorical forms of ASL? Besides the topic-comment structure and beginning with the specific, another common structure is the time-sequenced and detailed narration that describes in chronological order the events of the day, week, and so forth, from the first to the last. A Deaf person arriving late for work, for example, would probably describe the reasons for being tardy in an extremely detailed, step-by-step fashion, beginning with getting up, what happened when she tried to start the car, why the bus didn't arrive on time, and so on—all leading up to her late arrival. In a similar situation, a hearing person would tend to give a shorter statement summarizing the cause of the tardiness.

Shelley Lawrence, an instructor at Ohlone College in California, at an "Expansion Workshop" at an RID Region 5 conference in San Jose in 1996, identified seven characteristics of native ASL discourse, which she terms "expansion features":

1. "contrasting feature"—used for emphasis, where the contrasting information states what something is as well as what it isn't
2. "faceting" or descriptive elaboration—the use of several synonyms placed sequentially in order to more specifically define the subject
3. "reiteration" of the same signs either side by side or at the beginning and end of the utterance
4. "utilizing 3D space" in which objects or scenes are described from more than one perspective
5. "explaining by examples" rather than by giving a definition
6. "couching" or "nesting"—to identify an object or phenomenon by description, analogy, or function, instead of by label
7. "describe, then do," which uses role shift to describe the manner in which an action was done (Smith 1996, 220).

In her article "Features of Discourse in an American Sign Language Lecture," Cynthia Roy discusses several characteristics of ASL that relate to rhetorical style. One feature of ASL is the use of reported speech. Instead of reporting a dialogue between two people in the third person (i.e., he said . . . then she said . . .), the speaker/signer constructs a first-person dialogue by assuming the roles of the people involved to make it more dramatic and interesting (Roy 1989). There are of course many more elements of rhetorical style in ASL that take advantage of its being a visual language.

What Persuades Deaf People?

Whom do Deaf people rely on as authorities? "Truths learned from personal experience take precedence over objective evidence. Deaf people . . . are unimpressed by abstract findings published in books or taught in universities *unless* they have personal experience consistent with it" (Smith 1996, 232). Interpreting a typical medical appointment, we sometimes run across a certain behavior that can illuminate this point. In discussion with the doctor about their medical condition, Deaf people will often relate stories about their friends. If the deaf patient is suffering from some type of heart ailment, for example, he or she might tell the doctor about another Deaf person who had a similar condition and then go on to describe in detail what type of medication the friend took and with what results. Lacking the understanding that in Deaf culture the peer group serves as the trusted authority, the hearing doctor will usually dismiss this seeming digression and try to go back to the point without ever answering the patient's implicit question regarding an alternative medication. If a hearing patient, however, were to bring up the same concern about a new blood pressure medication but cite a magazine article or a television news report as the source of the information, it is likely that the doctor would respond to that patient's concerns directly.

Guilty or Innocent?

Another aspect of reasoning which is subject to cultural variation is the assignment of guilt or innocence. In *Black and White Styles in Conflict,* Thomas Kochman contrasts the ways whites and Blacks handle accusations and assert their innocence. Whites, if they hear a general accusation aimed at all whites or all men and consider themselves innocent of the charge, will demand some kind of qualification of apology from the accuser. Blacks, on the other hand, use the "individual exclusion rule" or, in everyday parlance, they think, "He ain't talkin' to me" and do not react. Whites observing this may misinterpret Blacks' failure to react defensively as a tacit admission of guilt. The reverse also holds true: when Blacks see whites "issue a vigorous and defensive denial—the kind that whites often use when they feel *falsely* accused—Blacks consider this a confirmation of guilt, since they believe that only the truth would have been able to produce a protest of such intensity" (92).

It is interesting to note that even though the white style of asserting one's innocence is characterized as "vigorous and defensive" compared with the Blacks' way in the passage above, to the (white) hearing majority, Deaf rhetorical style could be seen as even more vehement. Because of the intense facial expression and strong body movements used in expressing a denial of guilt in ASL, police or court personnel may be all the more convinced that someone who "doth protest too much" is really guilty.

What constitutes proof of guilt in Deaf culture? Not surprisingly in such a visual culture, what the eye can see is of prime significance. For example, this story was related by an interpreter trainer who is an experienced legal interpreter. She was interpreting for a Deaf man who had been accused of a serious crime. During the trial, as expert witnesses testified to the large amount of circumstantial evidence that seemed to connect him to the crime, the defendant seemed unconcerned. When his lawyer later took him aside to inform him that his case did not seem hopeful, he was shocked. And when the lawyer reminded him of the circumstantial evidence, such as hair samples recovered from the carpet on which the crime had been committed and microscopic threads from the victim's clothing found on the bottom of his shoe, he exclaimed, "So what? No one saw me do it!"

In this chapter we have examined in depth four major topics of study in the field of intercultural communication. As part of this examination, we have also identified several clear contrasts between mainstream American culture, which is by and large individualistic, low context, monochromic, and future oriented, and American Deaf culture, which can be characterized as collectivist, high context, polychronic, and past oriented. In addition, we have touched on some of the variations in communicative style among cultures.

My purpose has been to give you a sampling of the many different flavors that make up the smorgasbord of human experience. If sign language interpreters, like trained chefs, are familiar with the range of tastes shaped by cultural expectations, then we can blend our interpretations to suit the preferences of particular palates.

4

Do Americans Really
Have a Culture?

I remember the moment well. It was during my first semester studying intercultural communication at San Francisco State University. As Professor Dean C. Barnlund enumerated various American cultural values and behaviors, I found myself fidgeting in my seat. "Excuse me," I interrupted, "something is really bothering me. You keep saying that these are typical American values, but I don't consider myself a typical American." Professor Barnlund eyed me calmly, "That," he replied, "is a typically American thing to say."

If you feel that you do not particularly identify with American culture, you are not alone. We Americans are notorious for our unwillingness to acknowledge that our perceptions and behaviors are culturally influenced. To many Americans, culture is something that other countries have which makes them either interesting to visit or in need of our aid. Many of us don't realize that we, too, have a culture. Like most of the world's inhabitants, we feel that the way we do things in our country is the right way to do them. Members of certain nationalities insist that their superior culture has passed down the proper ways of behaving (think of the French pride in their language, art, and cuisine). Many Americans, on the other hand, assume that any values they hold, they have individually selected.

Another trait that leads us to minimize cultural influence is our tendency to focus more on similarities than on differences. In contrast to cultures like France and Russia, where a lively dinner-table debate is enjoyed as sport, in American conversation we more often seek to find accord. Many heated discussions are concluded by someone pointing out, "Well, at least we can all agree that . . . ." In the nation that came up with the mind-numbing refrain "It's a small world after all . . ." it is not surprising to hear the comment, "Basically we're all the same" when the subject of cultural difference is raised—the unspoken subtext is, of course, "Basically we're all like me."

As sign language interpreters, however, we cannot afford the luxury of denial. In order to view both our hearing and Deaf clients' cultural points of view objectively, it is important to assess our own cultural characteristics and biases. Mainstream American culture consists of much more than a handful of customs or isolated cultural characteristics that can be used to point out contrasts with other cultures; it constitutes an entire system of values, beliefs, and patterns of behavior.* I know that the term "mainstream American culture" is an imprecise generalization. Americans who belong to other cultural groups, therefore, may not identify with some of the following cultural values. I hope their views will be represented in chapter 6. My aim in this chapter is not to discount or disrespect, but to compare in broad terms, Deaf and hearing American cultural tendencies.

Self-Reliance and Independence

Self-reliance is a preeminent value among Americans. We can find its seeds in beliefs about childhood. Children are supposed to dress themselves by the age of three or four and are encouraged, as they grow, to behave more and more independently so they will be ready to make a complete break and move out of their parents' home at eighteen. We reproach those who are still hanging around the house in their twenties, regardless of their economic difficulties. In modern psychological jargon, we speak of a family that is overly close as "enmeshed" or having "separation-individuation problems."

At the other end of the life span, the ideal for seniors is to stay as independent and active as possible until their very last day, thereby avoiding the worst possible fate: becoming a burden on their children. Of all the aspects of American life that surprise and dismay foreigners, the status of the elderly is probably the most shocking. While they may shudder at

---

*If you want a more thorough discussion of this topic, I refer you to two excellent sources. *American Ways* by Gary Althen presents a lively description of our values, style of communication, patterns of thinking, and customary behaviors. Although it is written as a guide for foreigners living in the United States, it is clear, concise, and perceptive, and it can give you a quick overview of our American style of relating. Stewart and Bennett in *American Cultural Patterns* deliver a more in-depth analysis of American patterns of thinking, attitudes toward language, social relations, and perception of the world and the self.

what appears to be abandonment of our older citizens, we see it as respecting them by not undermining their prized independence.

In many other cultures, dependence, far from being a sign of weakness, is seen as a desirable quality. "Chinese parents, for instance, take pride in being dependent on their children and being supported by them. In Japan, to be self-reliant ... is to be without an identity.... For the Japanese, dependence is a virtue" (Stewart and Bennett 138).

In American Deaf culture, mutual dependence is a survival tactic that has become an integral part of daily life. To pick only one example, in a lecture class at a college where several Deaf students watch the interpreter, if one student misses a point or needs a little extra explanation, he or she turns to the other Deaf students, who immediately take their eyes off the interpreter, thereby missing out on the next chunk of lecture in order to supply their classmate with the needed information. There is neither a feeling of stigma associated with having asked the question nor any recognition of the individual's right to refuse to help, for in Deaf culture the sharing of information is an almost sacred obligation or duty that takes precedence over individual concerns.

Hearing Americans, on the other hand, are uncomfortable with being obligated to others and therefore may try to avoid too much personal commitment. If a friend is going through a hard time and we want to help, we take pains not to offer insult by implying that our friend is not completely capable of taking care of him- or herself. Dropping by unexpectedly, we might stretch the truth by saying that it was on our way home, as if admitting that we had gone out of our way to help would demand too great a reciprocal gesture. This attitude is the exception among many of the world's cultures, where systems of mutual obligation define relations, often down through generations. "... [In] all of the world outside of the United States, a relationship without obligation is simply not significant" (95).

Egalitarianism

Interestingly, egalitarian sentiments are strong among both Deaf and hearing Americans. While there are glaring inequalities in American life, egalitarian behavior—in such things as associating with people who would be considered lower in class in other cultures (for instance, inviting your servants to have dinner with you, as Americans often do abroad, to the consternation of their host nationals), readily engaging in manual labor, and chatting with waiters and thanking them for their services—can be surprising if not shocking to people from more hierarchical societies.

Deaf people are similarly egalitarian; for them the value originates from belonging to a linguistic/cultural minority. In the Deaf community, one type of hierarchy that can be identified is a college education (usually at Gallaudet) versus "grass roots" or working class. Yet the shared experience of being Deaf forms a bond of equality that cuts across social class. The goal of the community is not to dwell on differences but to work together for the good of all Deaf people. On a personal level, it is not unusual for Deaf individuals of different "classes" to have a great deal in common. At a state residential school for the deaf, for example, an administrator and a groundskeeper may have much to chat about because they both attended the same school where they now work, share many friends, and are on the same Deaf baseball team. Their shared language, ASL, is a powerful equalizer, and it transcends the variations in the details of their daily lives.

Personal Choice

As we stand in the breakfast cereal aisle of the supermarket trying to decide which of the more than one hundred varieties to buy, it may be hard to believe that many people in the world actually eat the same thing for their breakfast every day. Freedom of choice—which we have come to feel is an inalienable right—fuels our entire economy, providing us with jobs to make more (and we hope better) versions of products that we have plenty of already.

The same freedom applies to our selection of occupation. This perhaps is one of our society's greatest achievements—that the sons and daughters of a farmer or factory line worker may pick any field for which their aptitude qualifies them. Nor are we limited to a single career choice in our lifetime. We have the opportunity to switch from art to business or from medicine to acting at any time during our lives.

Deaf people in the United States do not enjoy the same freedoms that hearing Americans take for granted. When it comes to employment, for example, their options are much more limited. Despite the passage of the Americans with Disabilities Act, the reality is that most employers are reluctant to hire deaf employees. Consequently, it is not unusual for deaf workers to stay in a position—as a postal worker for instance—for thirty or more years, whether or not they enjoy their work or feel challenged by it, for the security of having a job. Even Deaf teachers have a much more limited pool of potential schools to pick from, and if we go all the way up the ladder, a deaf school administrator who aspires to be a college president has basically only one choice: Gallaudet.

Choice seems to be an intrinsic feature of American life. Perhaps this is so because, historically speaking, the first Europeans to settle this land came here by choice. It feels so natural for most of us to choose almost every facet of our lives from our hair color to our marriage partner that it strikes us as peculiar that in other places around the world people's lives are largely out of their personal control.

Doing and Achievement

The inevitable icebreaker when getting to know someone is "What do you do for a living?" And our first question after running into an old friend or acquaintance is often "What are you doing these days?" Our fixation on *doing* seems to pervade our every waking moment, because what we do provides a large part of our identity and helps define who we are. No doubt tracing back to our Puritan roots, we believe that "idle hands are the devil's workshop." Although we are supposed to work toward the big reward of retirement, some new retirees are shocked to discover the sense of uselessness that accompanies having "nothing to do."

Because success in American life is measured by external accomplishments, we feel compelled to keep accomplishing more and more. While we may complain to those closest to us that we are always too busy, who among us would care to be the opposite—as defined in Webster's—"idle, lazy, indolent"? Activities valued in other cultures but assessed by many of us as unproductive—meditating, standing around chatting, or sitting and relaxing and doing nothing—tend to make us nervous, as if they represent lost moments in which we could have been doing something useful. We even have a hard time "letting go" on vacations, which some of us only regard as another opportunity for performing (doing) different activities such as skiing, sightseeing, antique collecting, or even making house repairs. People from other countries often comment on the frenzied pace of Americans who are obsessively "on the go."

In our mainstream culture, we feel pressured to prove our self-worth through new accomplishments (and more material goods). Haven't you found yourself thinking, "If only I could achieve that—academic degree, interpreting certificate, athletic feat, salary increase—then I would feel like a success"? And most of us notice that having accomplished our goal, we feel we must set our sights on another milestone. In many non-Western cultures, by comparison, it is peoples' traditional roles in their family or community that define their identities, and their personal relationships are more important than their measurable achievements.

In Deaf culture, a person's achievements are more likely to be viewed as the group's accomplishment than as the individual's. A toast at a party for a Deaf woman who had recently passed the State Bar was "Hurray! One of *us* became a lawyer," and a comment from a prominent Deaf leader to a Deaf social worker who achieved his license was "I'm happy for *us*." However, if a Deaf person fails to share his or her accomplishments with the community (by giving credit to those who made it possible and by donating time, energy, and skills to help others), then the "crab theory" operates, whereby the group pulls down those who try to get ahead.

Work and Compartmentalization

Why are we not surprised to hear that a man who recently won many millions of dollars in his state lottery continues to work at his old job as a garbage collector? Because, as we know, work in the United States is more than simply a means to make money. "Work constitutes a practical ideal of activity and character that makes a person's work morally inseparable from his or her life" (Bellah et al. 1985, 66). We take pride in our industriousness and are pleased to have a reputation as hard workers. This leads some "workaholics" to put in sixty or even eighty hours of labor a week. It is common for Americans to take only one or two weeks of vacation a year, while many Europeans are guaranteed four to six weeks annually. Although the work incentive has weakened in recent decades, our attitudes are still strongly influenced by the Puritan work ethic, that the most meaningful activity in life is work.

Americans think of work as a serious occupation and prefer not to "mix business with pleasure." We conceive of separate realms for work and play. Although some people derive great satisfaction from their chosen careers, many of us grumble and grouse when we have to get up and go to work in the morning. Play, on the other hand, is what we do on weekends and during vacations as a relief from the drudgery we face at the office. In other cultures the boundaries that contain the workday are more elastic. Latin Americans, for example, do not see work and play as mutually exclusive. A meeting in a Latin American workplace may turn into a social event.

In a workplace with many Deaf employees and clients, such as a school or Deaf agency, work and play are not as compartmentalized. Deaf people's lives inevitably overlap too much for that. This may lead to some confusion. When, for example, a Deaf social worker goes to the local Deaf club and is greeted by her clients with tales of their latest problems, she has to remind them that she is on her off-time now.

Informality and Friendliness

Although most of us could forego the insufferable tableside greeting "Hi, I'm Chris and I'll be your server tonight," we Americans usually appreciate friendly, down-to-earth interpersonal relations. This aspect of our culture is frequently the first thing foreign visitors notice (although they may later refer to it disparagingly as "superficial friendliness").

Following our egalitarian beliefs, we feel that everyone should be treated in the same way. Our monosyllabic one-size-fits-all greeting, "Hi," is extended to friends, salespeople, and sometimes even strangers we pass on the street (though definitely not in New York City). Foreigners, depending on their own predilections, may find this behavior refreshing, disconcerting, or rude. "Whereas the average American tends to consider formality, style, and protocol as somewhat pompous or arrogant, in other cultures these elements provide the context within which dependable expectations for the behavior of others is established" (Stewart and Bennett 99).

Many languages have built-in distinctions of formality. Japanese, Thai, and other Asian languages have complex systems of personal pronouns that express the relative status of the speakers. Most European languages also make a distinction between a formal and informal relationship in their second-person pronouns: *vous* and *tu* in French, *Sie* and *du* in German. In Germany, this division is taken seriously. One must be invited to switch to the informal *du*. In a lovely old custom no longer in vogue, the shift to the more intimate style of address was formally acknowledged by the new "du" friends hooking arms, taking sips from the same glass, and announcing their first names to each other (Hall and Hall 48–49). English, on the other hand, has only one form: *you*. We also tend to use first names with the vast majority of people we address out of a belief that we are showing respect through equal treatment. What leads to some foreigners' disappointment in this regard is their assumption that our friendliness equals the initiation of a friendship, while we never feel that our easy greetings obligate us to anything beyond the moment. When we use phrases such as "Let's get together sometime" or "Don't hesitate to call me," a foreigner may read into them an offer of a relationship much deeper than anything we had in mind.

On a scale of formality, Deaf Americans rank as even more informal than hearing Americans. Conversations get to the point faster and intimate details are quickly shared with Deaf strangers. Maybe the point is that another Deaf person is never really a stranger. While some hearing Americans may share details of their lives with someone standing next to them in the checkout line, it is with a security that they will probably never see them again. In a similar exchange between two Deaf strangers, one may .very well bump into the other person next week or next month. Perhaps the sharing of personal stories carries a different point than just passing the time; its aim is to share valuable information or pool resources.

Friendship

Many Americans have deep, close personal ties with friends, which last over long years if not a lifetime. But close friendships are often difficult for Americans to maintain because of the extreme mobility of the American lifestyle. We, therefore, also tend to have a wide circle of acquaintances we call "friends," who are simply people whose company we enjoy. For large numbers of Americans, in fact, these are the only friends they have, and it is this friendship pattern that is most evident—and often disturbing—to people from other cultures. Over the course of our lives, we may easily count a hundred people as friends in a sort of revolving door of friendships. Friends come into our lives when we have something in common—the same school, job, hobby, or the same-age children, but when one of us moves or our interests change, we tend to drift apart. Although we enjoy entertaining our friends and are willing to do them small favors from time to time, we generally avoid imposing on each other. We expect our friends to be supportive, cheer us up if we are down, and accept us as we are, but if a friend is seen as too needy, we may soon pull away.

This pattern of mainstream American friendship, however, refers mostly to modern urban relationships. In smaller towns and in times gone by, it was more common that one's school chums would become one's life-long companions. Nowadays, on the other hand, we tend to choose our friends to fit our present circumstances, creating a "support system" to call on in times of need.

In other cultures, friendship is defined differently and is limited to fewer people. It is also more lasting and intimate; in fact it may deeply obligate the participants to one another for life. The Russians' experience of friendship, for example, involves heavy obligations and a nearly constant companionship where no secrets are allowed. In contrast to our compartmentalized practice of having certain friends or acquaintances with whom we play tennis and others to whom we pour out our problems, Russians pursue closeness in its entirety (Stewart and Bennett 102). In Japan, the concept of friendship also involves a complex set of ideas about "obligation, duty and ritualized interaction," which is in direct contrast with the American emphasis on spontaneity in friendships (101).

Having lifelong friendships is the norm in Deaf culture. Even though miles and years separate old school classmates, the informal Deaf information network spreads the news of marriage, children, and other life events so that friends keep up on each other's lives and can immediately renew their relationship if they happen to be in the same place at the same time.

The way we deal with difficulties that arise in our friendships also has cross-cultural overtones. In the United States, if a problem arises, we might choose to drift apart, knowing there will be other friendships to take the place of this one. Russian friends, on the other hand, will pursue a quick resolution to the problem through a highly emotional exchange. A French friendship that breaks down will likely be put on hold, though if either of the parties suffers a terrible calamity, the other will immediately come to his or her aid (102).

Since the Deaf world is so small, troubles with friends are cause for great concern. One is likely to bump into that person at some community gathering and news of the spat will get around. Since friendships are expected to be lifelong, a problem between friends can become a lifelong one. Sometimes the disputing friends go through a cooling-off period before they deal with the conflict. Often friends of the squabbling friends will get involved, giving advice for ironing out their differences or even acting as mediators. Although not all such quarrels are resolved, in the small world of the Deaf community there is great motivation to settle personal feuds.

Problem Solving

"Where there's a will, there's a way." "Necessity is the mother of invention." Americans love to solve problems. As part of our focus on the pragmatic, we see a problem as something negative that needs immediate action in order to be resolved. We are impatient with discussions of principle and theory and want to roll up our sleeves and get right to work. In business, the steps involved in problem solving have been formally set out: (1) define the problem, (2) identify the obstacles, (3) draw up a list of possible options, (4) choose the best one, (5) make an action plan.

While this process seems logical and straightforward to us, it is based on cultural assumptions that are by no means universally shared. One assumption is that change is positive and will lead to an improvement in whatever is changed. Another is that humans have the ability and the right to dominate their environment. Other cultures take a more fatalistic view, their primary goal being to endure the hardship rather than eradicate it.

In Deaf culture there seem to be two opposite responses when a problem arises: "just accept it" or organize a group to solve it. I observed an instance of the former while interpreting for a Deaf woman's orientation week in an executive corporate position. One day she told me about the rude treatment she had received from a bus driver that morning. When she showed him her disabled discount card, he refused to believe she was entitled to a discount. She wrote him a note explaining that she was deaf. In response, he confiscated her card, made her pay the full price, and humiliated her before a bus full of passengers. After hearing her story, I became so incensed that I suggested we call the bus company immediately to lodge a complaint. The Deaf woman declined my offer, saying that these things happen and it's not worth trying to do anything about it.

It may be that joining together empowers Deaf people to solve their problems. When the need arose for a program to distribute TTYs (telecommunications devices) and administer a telephone relay system in California, Deaf organizations pooled their efforts and successfully lobbied for new legislation mandating these needed services.

The American predilection for solving problems may be one of the factors involved in the pervasive view of deafness as pathological. The "problem," as it is too often defined, is that deaf people cannot hear and speak. Therefore, we hearing people will solve their problem with a range of options: hearing aids, lipreading and speech training, cochlear implant surgery, and so forth. The error in this line of reasoning is that most culturally Deaf individuals do not view their deafness as a problem and therefore see no reason why it needs to be fixed. When asked if she would rather be hearing, Roslyn Rosen, the daughter of Deaf parents and mother of Deaf children, shakes her head vehemently "No!" This past president of the National Association of the Deaf (NAD) goes on to assert,

I'm happy with who I am and I don't want to be "fixed." Would an Italian-American rather be a WASP? In our society everyone agrees that whites have an easier time than Blacks. But do you think a Black person would undergo operations to be white? (Dolnick 1993)

A Balanced Picture of American Culture

Although it can be enlightening to hear foreigners' observations about American culture, we may initially feel put off when the bulk of their comments appear to be negative. When pressed, however, most foreign visitors will admit that many of the aspects of American culture they enjoy would not be possible without those that are less desirable; for example, it is our rapid pace of life that allows us to accomplish so much. The important thing for us as Americans is to recognize that we do, indeed, have a culture and that every culture is a mixed bag and cannot, for the most part, be ranked as better or worse than any other.

It has been the intent of this chapter to help make our American cultural selves a little more visible in the mirror. We are ready now to look with a clearer perspective at the details of American Deaf culture.

5

American Deaf Culture

This chapter is written from two perspectives, one from the inside and one from the outside. The insider to Deaf culture and coauthor of this chapter is Dr. Thomas K. Holcomb, a distinguished educator from a respected and well-known Deaf family. Not only has he taught Deaf culture to both deaf and hearing students, but he has also lived it. Having learned it from his parents and grandparents, he now passes it on to his own children. I, on the other hand, am an outside observer who has been studying Deaf culture for more than twenty-five years. Consequently, my focus may be drawn to aspects of Deaf culture that are most at odds with my own mainstream way of doing things. If Deaf culture were a house, Tom would examine its familiar contours from residing within its walls, while I, as a visitor, would notice this piece of furniture or comment on that structural element—items that strike me as unique. Yet all the while, we would both be describing the same house.

When one speaks of French culture or Japanese culture, it is relatively easy to pinpoint the central locus from which the culture springs. Not so with Deaf culture. Since it is not based on a geographical location, what then constitutes its boundaries? Who are the insiders? What is the basis for its cohesiveness? What values does it promote?

The following elements are often identified as the core of Deaf culture: fluency in ASL, residential school experience, and Deaf parents. It must be noted, however, that most deaf children have hearing parents, do not acquire ASL at an early age, and are nowadays increasingly educated in mainstream settings. Despite their lack of roots in Deaf culture, however, deaf people seem to gravitate toward the cultural values of the Deaf community. It is the assimilation of these values that then determines a person's place in the Deaf community.

Carol Padden has noted the following cultural values: respect for and use of ASL, sacredness of the hands, disassociation from speech, the passing on of cultural values through stories, and the importance of social activities (Padden 1980, 95–98). Barbara Kannapell has described several reasons why Deaf people feel comfortable relating to each other within the Deaf community: 100 percent access to communication; a common language; a strong sense of bonding in their relationships, which stems from common experiences; and a feeling of equality (Kannapell 1989, 22–25). And most recently, Theresa B. Smith has defined the center of Deaf culture as consisting of (1) audiological deafness, (2) identification with, affiliation to, and participation in the Deaf community, (3) ASL as a primary language, and (4) adherence to core cultural values (Smith 1996, 31–32).

Acquisition of Deaf Culture: Insiders and Visitors

Most deaf children with Deaf parents automatically acquire these values and sidestep any painful roadblocks to a culturally grounded identity. Deaf children of hearing parents who learn ASL early on and attend a program with a large number of Deaf students and staff may also take on a Deaf identity with relative ease. For those whose parents refuse to let them learn ASL or attend a Deaf program, however, it may be a long and difficult road to development of a healthy identity as a Deaf person (Holcomb 1997).

In past generations, most deaf children attended residential schools, where they became enculturated into the "Deaf way" of life. Despite the policy of oralism that was prevalent prior to the 1970s as the method of instruction in the primary grades, a sense of bonding developed among the children in the residential schools through the use of the forbidden signs with each other, behind the teacher's back.

This survival tactic, in which children helped each other to understand what was going on, resulted in an "us" versus "them" attitude toward the hearing teachers and staff. Often the few children from Deaf families who had already learned ASL at home acted as language models for the other students. In other cases, children who had more intelligible speech, better lipreading skills, or some residual hearing assisted the others in understanding the teacher or vice versa. These students were accepted as part of the group despite a possibly smaller decibel loss. Conversely, if students used their hearing or speech skills to advance their own standing with the teachers to the detriment of their peers, they were often shunned. This is one example of the fact that it is not the extent of hearing loss that defines a member of the Deaf community but the individual's own sense of identity and resultant actions.

When the children entered the upper grades of some residential schools, they were finally allowed to sign in the classroom and gained greater exposure to Deaf adults among the school staff. As their mastery of ASL grew, so did their involvement in the Deaf community. Thus did their identity as being Deaf become more solidified.

Recent Developments

During the 1970s, the popularity of oralism waned as it was gradually replaced in school settings by one of the forms of manually coded English (systems whereby signs that represent English words are used in an English grammatical order, often referred to as SEE signs). "Many Deaf people feel that it [SEE] is an unnatural, stiff way to communicate" (Rexroat 1997, 21). In addition, mainstreaming became the preferred option for parents who wished to keep their deaf child living at home. Instead of being sent away to a residential school with its large population of deaf students, a mainstreamed deaf student may be the only deaf person in the entire school. Although signing is usually permitted, for some deaf students their classroom interpreter may be their only language model. Others may sign at school, with their teachers, or at home with their hearing parents, an increasing number of whom have learned SEE to communicate with their deaf children. On the surface, this may seem like an improvement over past oppression and isolation, but in reality ASL and Deaf culture are rejected in favor of English-like signing and integration. As a result, the values dear to the Deaf community (ASL, traditional folklore, participation in social events, and group identity) are lost to these children.

Despite these new developments, Deaf culture has not disappeared. In fact, the need for Deaf culture may be even stronger than in previous generations because, with the closing of many state residential schools, the opportunities for enculturation are now either gone or delayed for many deaf people. Our human hunger to connect, to relate to people like ourselves, however, will never be eradicated. For this reason a large majority of deaf people eventually gravitate to the Deaf community, regardless of educational background or communication mode used by their parents or school.

There are certain periods when deaf people tend to become enculturated: at birth (for those with Deaf parents); when placed in a Deaf school at an early age; upon transfer from an oral or SEE program to a Deaf school; and at young adulthood, either in a college program with other Deaf students or when on their own they seek out the Deaf community.

At whatever point the enculturation takes place, it must be noted that Deaf culture is not a set of rules that deaf people must formally learn, nor is it a mandate that all deaf people must follow. As Padden and Humphries point out in *Deaf in America*, culture provides people with access to historically created solutions. While the condition of being unable to hear may be extremely disabling, the solutions devised by Deaf people over the years to remedy this condition have resulted in the creation of a culture. This culture has enabled them to lead full, rich, meaningful lives in spite of the obstacles presented by hearing society. Deaf culture, then, is a compilation of experiences and solutions that Deaf people have found to be effective in providing them with productive lives.

Every culture is made up of individuals, and within each culture there exist variations shaped by the background and personality of its members. So, too, there is not just one homogeneous Deaf culture. Although most of the elements mentioned in this chapter should be easily recognizable to Deaf community members from California to New York, regional variations do exist, as do individual differences. There are also certain groups within the Deaf community that may have a distinctive kind of Deaf culture (e.g., African American Deaf, Gay Deaf). The next chapter will explore these issues in greater depth. And just as in other cultures, differences in education and socioeconomic level may produce corresponding variations.

At the beginning of this chapter, we cited Japanese and French cultures as instances where geographical perimeters define the cultures' boundaries. Another way in which Deaf culture differs from this traditional conception of culture is that the Deaf culture in any country exists totally within the boundaries of the majority hearing culture. Although Deaf people tend to move to large metropolitan areas in order to find others like themselves and may even migrate to a certain neighborhood and form a residential school community, by and large Deaf people live, work, and play surrounded by hearing people. "Members of the Deaf Community are influenced culturally, politically and practically, individually and collectively by ideas and movements in the surrounding culture" (Smith 1996, 31). Since they do not live on a "deaf island" in the middle of a "hearing sea," they cannot cut themselves off from the products of hearing culture, nor would they want to. Books, TV, magazines, newspapers, movies, advertisements, and the Internet can be enjoyed, although some, like TV and movies, need to be made accessible through captioning.

What, then, is the relationship between the Deaf and hearing cultures? Deaf culture is actually a relatively new concept. Prior to 1980 the term was largely unknown. In ASL, one used the term "DEAF WORLD" to describe the unique experiences and distinctive ways of Deaf people. As the study of the Deaf experience has become more formalized and academic, scholars have employed an ethnological perspective, which has introduced the idea of culture. More complex than two intersecting circles, the relationship of the Deaf and hearing worlds varies from individual to individual depending on such factors as family background, educational level, and personal curiosity about the hearing majority. Probably each Deaf person's identity is a distinctive tapestry made up of threads of several cultures woven together in a unique way. Nevertheless, some generalizations can be made.

The insider/outsider distinction appears to be very strongly felt. In the past this was a simple deaf/hearing dichotomy. In recent years, however, as sign language has "come out of the closet" and onto TV and movie screens and into classrooms and lecture halls, large numbers of hearing people with no particular family ties to deafness are learning sign language for their personal enrichment. Most Deaf people welcome this development, as it leads to the possibility that one can find waiters, bank tellers, and police officers with whom one can communicate in sign. For many Deaf people there is now a new dichotomy: signers/nonsigners. It is as if Deaf people live in a castle surrounded by a communication moat which protects them yet makes it difficult to interact with the majority of people in their land. They can see the other people in their kingdom and exchange a few gestures with them but cannot engage in a deep exchange of thoughts and feelings. If someone stands outside the moat, however, showing an interest in learning sign language, the drawbridge is let down and the new signers are welcomed to the castle (although perhaps only to its public rooms, its inner chambers being reserved for longtime residents).

Where Do Interpreters Fit?

All of us "nonnative" signers began our journey into the Deaf world as welcomed visitors when we first learned sign language. The welcomed-visitor status may change, however, when one becomes an interpreter, meaning when one gets paid for the sign language abilities gained through interaction with the Deaf community.

> Interpreters are "half-breeds" somewhere in the middle, between Deaf and Hearing... Their status is somewhat problematic and suspect... In some ways interpreters are closer to the core of the Community: in language, customs and ease at being together. Yet interpreters, by virtue of their privileged status within the majority culture, their access to mainstream jobs and outside information coupled with their inside information, are to some extent too powerful. (Smith 1996, 27–28)

Interpreters, it seems, do not fit easily into the categories of insider or outsider. There are mixed feelings about them. On the one hand, they are appreciated for being able to sign and making accessible many areas of life that were hitherto impenetrable for many Deaf people. On the other hand, as hearing Americans, interpreters often do not follow the cultural conventions of Deaf culture.

> Interpreters... maintain a cool impersonal "professional" relationship. They "DRAW-A-LINE-BETWEEN-US." They are overly concerned with "role" in the abstract, the rules and codes of conduct prescribed by their profession rather than "HAVING-HEART," an understanding of the "role" within the current context (which includes people's feelings), in other words, the Deaf definition of the role. (111–12)

We will return to the interpreter's special relationship to the Deaf community in the last chapter of this book. Let us now go on to describe some of the elements of Deaf culture, keeping in mind that each deaf person may be at a different stage of cultural awareness (see Holcomb). It would be a mistake to assume that the following elements of Deaf culture are fully embraced by all deaf people. The information presented below describes the core of Deaf culture and the characteristics of many Deaf people who are actively involved in the Deaf community. As deaf people become more and more enculturated into the Deaf way of life, these values will emerge as being more central to their lives.

Communication and Information Sharing

> Deaf people do not wish to be Hearing. Rather than mourning the "loss" of hearing, or wishing they were like the majority, they are frustrated at the lack of access and opportunity. The Deaf fantasy is not that they could hear, but that the world would be Deaf. (Smith 1996, 80)

Being deaf is a communication handicap only when deaf people are around hearing people. As it happens, the world is full of hearing people, so deaf people are compelled to communicate with nonsigners on a daily basis. In the hearing world, communication and gaining access to information is often a struggle, which at its worst can lead to loneliness and isolation. This may be true even at home, where, if their relatives do not sign well or at all, deaf people may miss out on everything from dinner-table gossip to a feeling of being truly understood and accepted by their family.

Those few deaf people born into Deaf families are lucky enough to have full and easy communication at home, but they still face many situations daily where communication will be slow, awkward, and frustrating, and one is never sure if one has understood completely. With nonsigners, deaf people need to resort to lipreading (which is a challenge even to the most skilled lipreaders), to writing (requiring the use of English, which is difficult for many deaf people for a complex set of reasons examined in Harlan Lane's *The Mask of Benevolence* 1992), to gesturing (with a limited repertoire of iconic signs), to using interpreters (who are not always available or well trained).

After using such cumbersome methods to communicate with nonsigners, deaf people, not surprisingly, have little tolerance for ambiguity with each other, hence the value of direct and clear communication in Deaf culture. In addition, ASL, as a visual language which evolved as a natural cultural solution, is perfectly suited for precision in explicitly describing the appearance of a person or object, the directions to a location, the relationship of objects to each other in space, and countless other language acts, leaving little room for confusion or misunderstanding.

As well as facing daily communication struggles, deaf people also miss out on the constant barrage of bits of ambient information that hearing people take for granted: the radio talk show about the dangers of lead that we hear while waiting for our car to be repaired, the overheard conversation on the bus about a recent movie, the whispered office gossip in the coffee room about a coworker's messy divorce. These unintentional avenues of acquiring information supply hearing people with options, warnings, good ideas, and entertainment. As hearing people, we do not even notice how much information we pick up without trying until we have an extended stay in a country where we do not speak the language.

Information, because of its relative scarcity, is a precious commodity in the Deaf community, and its value is demonstrated by sharing it with others. If one acquires a piece of information, one feels obligated to pass it on. This applies to practically everything from the latest news to one's own and others' medical conditions and marital problems; to movie plots, warnings about dangers, recommendations of restaurants where the waitress signs, names of Deaf friends where one can stay when out of town, stores with good bargains, and stories of the ups and downs of the lives of mutual acquaintances.

Let us now examine five elements of Deaf culture that demonstrate the high value accorded to clear communication and the preciousness of information: "straight talk," direct personal comments, keeping others informed, sharing personal information, and access to communication. Although these features of Deaf culture are not practiced to the same extent by every member, to an outsider's eye they represent a striking departure from mainstream American culture.

"Straight Talk"

The degree of direct or indirect communication a culture tends to employ can be plotted along a continuum for purposes of comparison, just as we have noted variations along the collectivist/individualist, high-context/ low-context, polychronic/monochronic continua. It is interesting to note that in most of the cross-cultural literature, mainstream American culture is treated as if it were located on the "direct" end point of the continuum. "America shows a preference for direct, accurate, clear, and explicit communication" (Zaharna, 1995). A common comparison pits direct American communication against Japanese communication, which is seen as representing the epitome of indirectness. If graphed on a continuum, it would look like this:

Indirect   **Direct**

Japanese   American

If cross-cultural scholars describe American discourse style as direct, it should be no surprise that ordinary Americans pride themselves on their forthrightness and square dealing and believe that "honesty is the best policy." We *think* we "lay our cards on the table," "shoot from the hip," and "tell it like it is." This somewhat inaccurate self-evaluation can lead to the following misjudgment. Assume, for a moment, that another culture (we can call it "X") practices a style of communication that is considerably more direct than the American variety. Suppose that a member of Culture X delivers a critical remark to an American in a blunt manner. Since Americans already consider themselves to be straight shooters, any comments that appear even more direct than their own may be viewed as "just plain rude." The following graph depicts the way it might feel to many Americans.

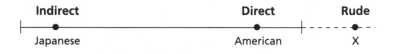

In actuality, there are several world cultures that practice a much more direct style of communication than hearing Americans and whose members would characterize the typical American style as "beating around the bush." In Germany, for example, "speaking plainly when it's for another person's own good . . . will be seen as a sign of consideration" (Storti, 2001 241–42). American Deaf culture also practices a direct form of discourse in certain situations. A third example is Israeli mainstream culture, which we will briefly discuss to help shed light on the way the direct style of communication functions. A more accurate representation of the indirect/direct continuum might look like this:

Israeli culture has been likened to sandpaper because it is "rough, grating, devoid of a smooth finish" (Shahar and Kurz 78). For example, if someone disagrees with you in the United States, he or she might say, "Excuse me, I have a problem with what you've just said." In Israel, you are much more likely to hear, "You're wrong!" "In informal Israel, 'smooth' is

often suspect. It is equated with being artificial, insincere, and hypocriti-
cal. Rough is real; ... honest, authentic" (78–79). Israelis get right to the
point, even if they have a negative comment. In a business situation where
Americans might preface a criticism with a softening phrase such as "It
seems to me that..." or "You might want to consider..." many Israelis
would say directly, "This part of your project is impractical" or "These
dates on your timeline are impossible" (123–27).

In *Talking Straight: Dugri Speech in Israeli Sabra Culture*, author Tamar
Katriel describes directness as "the most central element in the Sabra's
[native-born Israeli's] expressive repertoire" (Katriel 1986, 48). *Dugri*
refers to a truthful, clear-cut, unambiguous expression of feelings or opinions. Despite the fact that such Israeli speech does not make use of politeness formulas, it "is associated with the expression of respect rather than
disrespect" (116). The social framework in which directness demonstrates
courtesy is one of "intimacy and solidarity." This "way of speaking...
challenges the common assumption that all interaction is grounded in a
rule of considerateness. ..." (38). In other words, linguists and sociologists
have assumed that face-saving behaviors are a universal way of expressing
politeness. What straight talk in Israeli culture proves is that the concept
of politeness is culturally relative. Sometimes it is the very absence of
"crooked talk" (elaborate ways of saying or avoiding the truth) that is seen
as most polite and respectful.

It is a stereotype to say that Deaf people are always blunt. However,
many English-speaking Americans are struck by the fact that American
Deaf culture tends to employ a direct mode of expression in certain specific situations, such as remarks about a change in another's appearance,
warnings and advice, and the expression of personal opinions and complaints (Roush, 1999, 7). "Hinting and vague talk in an effort to be polite
are inappropriate and even offensive" (Lane 1992, 16). Among themselves,
Deaf people have no patience for ambiguity. As in Israeli culture, straight
talk is an expression of intimacy and solidarity among the Deaf. As Tom
Holcomb puts it, "It's the way you would talk to your siblings."

Another function of straight talk in both Deaf and Israeli cultures is
that it is "a way of providing social information that would be either
unavailable or difficult to accept under less favorable conditions" (Katriel
39). As many Deaf people have explained to me, "If other Deaf people
don't tell you the truth, who will?" In Deaf culture, with the high value
placed on sharing information, straight talk puts one's thoughts and feelings

out on the communal table, or as Katriel describes it in Israel, "... *dugri* speech is seen as facilitating the circulation of social information, especially in contexts in which this may be problematic: when negative valuations are involved" (39).

In certain types of speech acts, it should be noted, such as asking someone for a favor or refusing another's request, ASL utilizes many of the same politeness strategies as English, (e.g., hedges, minimizing impositions, apologizing, and "conventional indirectness" (Hoza, forthcoming). See "Polite Behaviors" later in this chapter for more discussion on this topic.

Before we discuss a specific type of negative valuation in Deaf culture, one that hearing Americans have an especially hard time accepting, let us speculate for a moment about why there exist these similarities between Deaf and Israeli cultures. One thing members of Israeli and Deaf cultures have in common is that a great number of them are from another place: from other cultures all over the world (in the case of Israeli culture) and from the majority hearing culture (in the case of Deaf culture). Both groups are or have had the experience of being minorities, aware of their tenuous position as outsiders to the vast majority of the world, which leads to a feeling of solidarity within their own society. In Israel, the almost universal experience of military service reinforces that solidarity, tending to homogenize differences in background. "When they leave the army, soldiers often transfer army norms, values, and behavior patterns to civilian life" (Shahar and Kurz 19). Although deaf residential school experience is not as widespread as it once was, like Israeli military service it produced a cohesive leveling that is still passed down as part of Deaf culture.

The other factor is called "the situation" in Israel, which "refers to a state of perpetual tension brought on by a daily blend of threats and surprises" (25). "Because everyone is affected by 'the situation,' it produces a common mindset" (26). Although Deaf people are not in danger of physical harm from terrorist bombs or imminent war, many experience a similar tension from being on guard against the oppressors/outsiders by whom they are surrounded (e.g., the push for oralism, cochlear implants, SEE, and mainstream schools). It should not be surprising, therefore, that a fantasy they share is of a Deaf country within the boundaries of which they could all feel secure. As the residents of Israel have learned, however, even having a country of one's own does not guarantee a feeling of security.

Direct Personal Comments

Although this topic could be discussed under the general heading of "Straight Talk," I believe it deserves special attention because it may be the hardest part of Deaf culture for hearing people to accept. I have heard several skilled interpreters say, regarding this behavior, "That's not culture, that's just rude!" What kind of remark can provoke such "insensitive" criticism? Probably being greeted by a Deaf person with a remark about one's appearance such as, "Boy, you've put on a lot of weight!" or "Oh, you dyed your hair, it's not a good color. It looked better before," or "Wow! You are getting bald so fast!" Deaf people maintain that such comments demonstrate closeness, connection, loyalty, sincerity, and friendship.

In American mainstream culture, by contrast, such forthright personal remarks are considered rude. Peggy Post, author of *Emily Post's Etiquette*, likens such remarks to "rubbing salt into an open wound." If you tell someone they don't look well, they "will only be depressed that it shows" (Carroll 1997).

In Deaf culture, these direct personal comments often come right after the "Hi" and can be positive, negative, or mixed. For example, "You got a new haircut. It looks good" (positive); "You got a new hairstyle. It's too short. It makes you look fat" (negative); "You got a new hairstyle. It looks great! Much better than your old one" (mixed). There is, of course, a lot of room for individual variation within these statements. For example, whereas a particularly blunt Deaf person may greet you with, "Oh, new glasses. Ugh! Really ugly," another Deaf person might put it, "Oh, you got new glasses. Hmmm, I think I prefer the old ones. They fit your face better. Made you look younger."

Let us informally analyze one of the most insulting things one can say to a hearing American: "Boy, have you gotten fat!" Priscilla (one of my Deaf consultants on this book) and I compared how our cultures might interpret this statement and the different ways we would handle the situation. Priscilla says that in Deaf culture it is better to acknowledge the fact that one's friend has put on weight than to try to ignore it. It shows you care. In hearing culture, on the other hand (as I perceive it), it is polite to pretend not to notice the extra pounds. I think to myself, "My friend has clearly put on weight. She probably feels bad about it. She knows that I can tell, but if I pretend I don't notice, it will make her feel better—like it's not so obvious. So I will compliment her on something else (e.g., her dress, hair, or earrings) and avoid the subject of weight altogether. I am saving her embarrassment by not mentioning it."

In response to my inner monologue, Priscilla says that coming from a Deaf perspective, she would not appreciate my attempt to be polite. If there were some obvious physical change in her appearance (either positive or negative) and it was not noticed by a friend, she would feel insulted. And if her friend chose to comment on an insignificant detail, like her earrings, in the face of some larger obvious change, it would make her even more upset.

It is quite possible that not all hearing people would behave as I described in the situation above and that not all Deaf people would feel the same way as Priscilla did (perhaps our imagined inner monologues are more a feature of female discourse style). This conflict, however, highlights two fundamental aspects of Deaf culture: first, that the value accorded the sharing of information may take priority over other considerations; and second, that Deaf people feel a familial closeness with each other and can therefore tell each other things in a way that presupposes an intimate relationship.

A couple of times, in talking with some Deaf people about this manifestation of straight talk, I was assured that while it was true that *other* Deaf people do use straight talk, they themselves considered it to be rude behavior and would never engage in it. Ironically, I have bumped into these very same Deaf people on several occasions when they have greeted me with statements such as, "Oh, you're looking good now, not like after you had your baby and put on so much weight" or "Hi, I know I look terrible. I didn't put on any makeup because I didn't think I'd run into anyone I knew and then here you are. But it's okay. You don't have any makeup on either. You look as bad as I do."

Besides the feeling of intimacy with other Deaf people, another factor that may contribute to comments on people's physical appearance is that ASL is a visual language and Deaf people live in a visual world. Anything that is visually observed is open for comment. If one needs to refer to another person and does not know his or her name, a set of physical attributes (usually two or three in number, such as "short, curly hair, glasses") is used to describe that person. Many Deaf people are keen observers of physical traits and mannerisms. In residential schools a favorite pastime was for the most gifted mimics to imitate the posture, facial expression, and mannerisms of their teachers, which kept their classmates in stitches.

Tom Holcomb says that it is hearing people's easier access to communication that allows them to satisfy their curiosity more indirectly and thus avoid direct confrontation. Suppose I see an acquaintance of mine named Mary at a large gathering and notice that she is not wearing her wedding ring. I am curious and a little worried about her, so I might talk to a mutual friend or a neighbor, or call up her sister (if I know her) and see if she knows what's going on. In contrast, if Tom was curious about Mary's missing ring, he would probably ask her to her face if she was separated or getting a divorce. Because Mary's family and neighbors might all be hearing and thus more awkward to communicate with, it's just easier and more direct to ask Mary herself.

Keeping Others Informed

The expectation in Deaf culture that one needs to keep others informed operates on several levels. One is the practical reality that in a family situation or group meeting, if a deaf person leaves the room, no one can call to the person to find out where he or she went. Consequently, it is polite and expected that one inform at least one other person that one is, for instance, on one's way to the restroom. Then, if that person's absence is questioned, someone can enlighten the rest of the group. "Even temporary unexplained departures are unacceptable" (Lane 1992, 18). Unlike the hearing, deaf people do not have access to the noises that clue us in to what others are doing when out of view (e.g., using the computer, mowing the lawn, flushing the toilet). Holcomb recalls when his children were young that his household resembled Grand Central Station as his three children continually zoomed by their parents with information about their next destination: "I'm going upstairs now," "I'm going outside," or "I'm going to take a shower." They knew this was something they had to do so that their parents could locate them if necessary.

"Sharing information is the norm in the Deaf community. Especially when there is a change in the routine or expectations, an explanation is warranted" (Smith, Lentz, and Mikos 35). Deaf people tend to describe in greater detail than hearing people the reasons why they are late or must leave early for an appointment. Given the narrative mode of discourse, these explanations often take the form of a recitation of a chain of events instead of a summary. In a classroom situation, for example, most hearing students arriving late will try to slip quietly into their seats unnoticed, while Deaf students arriving late would more likely bring the classroom discussion to a temporary halt to explain the cause of their tardiness (e.g., a car accident, a malfunctioning alarm clock, or unexpected traffic).

On a broader level, Deaf people feel obligated to tell other Deaf people pertinent information about their health, relationships, work, travel plans, and other significant aspects of life. To have a great change in one's life and keep it to oneself would be perceived as an insult. As in a small town or a large family, news travels fast in the Deaf community by what some people ruefully refer to as the "deaf grapevine." Since Deaf people often have contacts all over the country, it is not surprising that word of one's serious illness or troubled marriage can spread fast. With the increasing popularity of pagers, videophones, and e-mail, the circulation of news is even more efficient. Although some Deaf people complain about the lack of privacy, others feel comforted knowing that news of their troubles will be disseminated to their acquaintances without much effort on their part. Because of the Deaf community's preferred direct style of communication, it is far more likely that one will receive an e-mail that says, "Heard you have cancer, I'm so sorry" than a seemingly polite but irritatingly ingenuous, "So . . . how are things?"

In American hearing culture we are not supposed to gossip or talk about others behind their backs, but of course, almost everyone does anyway. The trick is not to admit it. This leads to a cultural quandary for me. Since in Deaf culture it is expected that people will talk about what's happening in other people's lives, "talking behind one's back" does not carry a negative connotation. In fact, if there were a major development in someone's life and it were *not* discussed, that would be even more insulting. My quandary occurs when I bump into a Deaf friend who is looking glum. I ask her, "What's wrong?" and she replies, "I'm getting a divorce, *haven't you heard*?" To be polite in Deaf culture, I should answer yes, but it is hard for me to get over the hearing taboo against gossiping. It feels more polite to say no and let her tell me all about it; but then my Deaf friend might assume (since we share the same circle of friends) that it would have been impossible for me not to have heard the news. Therefore, she might surmise that what I heard were negative comments about her. In order to avoid this erroneous assumption, I should answer honestly. If I truly have not heard the news when it seems that I should have, an explanation would be in order, for example, "No. I didn't hear about it. Sorry. I've been so busy lately, I haven't socialized much."

If there is value in sharing information, it follows that withholding information is considered rude. If a Deaf person who works as a relay or intermediary interpreter in the courts (see pages 203-04 for a full description of this role) happens to notice two Deaf people at a party having a disagreement about the procedures followed in traffic court, it would be appropriate to let them know that that person has some knowledge of the subject. The ticklish issue is that in conveying such information one must not appear to put oneself above others because of having it. If a graduate of Gallaudet University, for example, attends a meeting of a community organization and is struck by the lengthy and seemingly inefficient manner in which the meeting is run, he or she will have to weigh carefully the decision whether to interrupt and offer advice. A statement such as "At Gallaudet we ran much better meetings, let me show you how" will probably be met with more hostility than openness. Recent graduates of Gallaudet have a reputation for their "know-it-all" attitude. Older Gallaudet grads seem to have learned that discretion is the better part of wisdom.

To withhold the very fact that one can sign may also be seen as rude. It is impolite to watch a signed conversation if the people conversing assume there is no one around who knows sign language. One time I was sitting at a table in a busy restaurant having a meeting with two Deaf people. A man who had been standing in line for a while came over and signed, "Hi, just wanted tell you I'm Deaf, visiting from another state, and I wasn't really watching your conversation, but thought I should let you know that I sign."

Formerly, public places such as restaurants and subway trains were assumed to be safe spots for Deaf people to discuss any topic in sign language in relative obscurity. One of the downsides to hearing people's increasing interest in learning sign language, however, is that this assumption of privacy in public no longer holds true. Although, as a visual language, it is impossible to completely shield an ASL conversation from curious eyes, there are conventions and adjustments that make it harder for an onlooker to figure out exactly who and what is being discussed. Previously, these precautions were taken mainly at Deaf events, but now one can never be sure who understands sign. As hearing signers, it is our duty to inform people carrying on an ASL conversation that we know how to sign. Either that or we should have the courtesy not to watch.

While Deaf people expect information to be shared within the community, if that information is gleaned by a professional (e.g., lawyer, therapist) during their working hours, then Deaf people have the expectation that the professional will keep such information confidential. The assumption that stories about others will be shared makes it difficult for some Deaf people to trust that interpreters will not spread the confidential information they are privy to in their professional role. If so challenged, many interpreters would point to the RID Code of Professional Conduct prohibition against breaking confidentiality. For low-context hearing Americans a written rule carries great weight, but it may not appear so convincing to some Deaf people. One woman told me that the only CODA interpreter she would accept would be one whose parents were no longer living, because cultural conventions about sharing information would compel other CODAs to tell their parents about any significant occurrence in the Deaf community. Interestingly, when interpreters socialize with Deaf people on their off-time, they are expected to share any news heard during non-working hours.

Sharing Personal Information

Certain topics are taboo in American hearing culture. I am not only referring here to the famous threesome that polite people are supposed to refrain from discussing at the dinner table: politics, sex, and religion. I am also thinking of such topics as money, the graphic details of sickness and death, and bathroom habits. None of these seem to carry a similar prohibition in Deaf culture. On the contrary, perhaps it is the general reticence of the hearing majority to discuss these aspects of life, coupled with the value placed on clear and direct communication in Deaf culture, that makes these topics seem to crop up so often in Deaf conversations.

Mainstream Americans are very circumspect when it comes to talking about money. Many other cultures (Israeli, Thai, and Filipino, for example) find nothing wrong in asking people how much money they earn a year or how much they paid for their dress, TV, car, or house. In Deaf culture, too, such questions are another way to gather important information. How can one get a good deal on a car if one has no basis for comparison? Probably more than advertisements, magazine articles, or expert opinion, Deaf people look to each other for input about what to buy and where to buy it. There are also tales of warning to be shared: how not to get taken advantage of by unscrupulous salespersons and accounts of Deaf people who were unwittingly pressured into signing on the dotted line without realizing what the small print on the contract committed them to pay.

Clear descriptions of bodily functions do not seem to embarrass Deaf people the way they do hearing Americans. A touching example is the story of a high school sex education teacher who traveled to different schools in her district. She noticed a distinct difference in reaction when she lectured on the subject of circumcision to Deaf and hearing classes of high school boys. In hearing schools, the boys would become very quiet, while eyeing each other in embarrassment. In the Deaf school, by contrast, the boys would immediately address each other directly on the subject: "I am. Are you?"

I have heard complaints from Deaf people who think that interpreters allow their own reluctance to describe things graphically to interfere with clear communication. If a doctor, for example, inquires about a Deaf patient's recent bowel movements, ASL provides many ways to unequivo-cally depict the various possibilities. If the interpreter, however, chooses to use a generic sign such as "BM" out of his or her own embarrassment, both parties may suffer from the inadequate communication. Similarly, while statements related to sexual behavior may be comfortably vague in English (e.g., "Do you practice safe sex?"), to accurately convey the infor-mation in ASL, interpreters may have to overcome their natural reticence to explicitly describe sexual activity.

Clear Access to Visual Communication

Since the eye and the ear process information differently on its way to the brain, a visual language poses different requirements than a spoken one. Non-deaf people can hear several things at the same time without expending any effort: the TV blaring, birds chirping outside, and the teenager talking on the phone in the next room. The flip side of hearing things without having to listen, however, is that we do not have complete control over our hearing. In fact, we are often bothered by noises we wish we could shut out, especially when we are trying to sleep.

Eyes, on the other hand, can only focus on one thing at a time. Seeing necessitates watching, and a prolonged effort can make the eyes tired. Such is the importance of access to communication in the Deaf world that neither intimate conversations nor large meetings begin before partici-pants make sure that everyone has a clear and comfortable view.

For conversations in a visual language, certain conditions are neces-sary: enough light in the right place and an absence of visual distractions. In many Deaf homes, furniture is arranged in a semicircular setting to allow clear visual access. The kitchen is often the most popular spot in the house because of its bright lights and round table. With this in mind, interpreters should never position themselves in front of an unshuttered window, as back lighting produces a glare that is hard to endure for long periods. Sometimes Deaf speakers or interpreters are asked by the group to stand on a chair so they may be more visible. Deaf banquet planners also know that even low centerpieces may end up on the floor so that conversations across tables are not hindered.

In a world where communication is highly valued, refusing to look at a person who is telling you something is one of the rudest possible behaviors. In the middle of a signed argument, it is probably more of a rejection for Deaf participants to close their eyes or go into another room than for hearing people in a similar situation to put their hands over their ears or shut the door, because if a hearing quarreler's partner yells loudly enough, he or she can still be heard.

While Deaf people who deliberately close their eyes in the midst of an argument are guilty of intentional rudeness, an unintentional rudeness occurs more frequently in conversations between Deaf and hearing signers. If there is an unexpected loud noise in the vicinity (e.g., the screech of brakes, a scream, or a crash), it is an automatic reflex for hearing people's eyes to dart away in the direction of the noise. We are probably not even aware of this behavior when we are talking to another hearing person. However, if this eye-darting happens repeatedly while we are engaged in conversation with a Deaf person, it can be very distracting, especially if we never explain what drew our attention away. Fortunately, we can train ourselves to control this instinct most of the time. Meanwhile, the most polite solution is to inform the Deaf person (before we look away) what we have just heard. If this is not possible, then we need to explain after the fact the reason that our eyes strayed ("Sorry, I heard a siren over there"). And if our attention is drawn away for a moment by someone else in the room speaking to us, it is polite to hold up one finger, which indicates "Excuse me, my attention will be back with you in a moment." If this annoying interruption occurs more than once, it may prompt the Deaf person to wonder why it seems that he or she never gets priority. Why don't we hold up one finger to the hearing person and make him or her wait instead?

Connectedness:
The Deaf Community as Family

Deaf people often refer to their schoolmates as their sisters and brothers. This may be due in part to growing up together in a residential school setting. It may also be due to the fact that their Deaf friends are closer to them than their own hearing siblings who do not sign or appreciate Deaf culture. The experiences of growing up deaf in a hearing world, the frustrations of daily communication struggles with the hearing majority, and the ease and delight of communicating in a visual language give Deaf people a lot in common before they even meet. This is one reason why Deaf people from different countries, even with different sign languages, can find a way to converse much more quickly than two hearing people who do not share a spoken language.

This family-like connection helps explain many things about Deaf culture. Because of their familial sentiments, topics that might be inappropriate for casual friends in hearing American culture would not be considered off-limits in the Deaf community. People are more involved in each other's lives—a state of affairs that can have both positive and negative effects. In times of trouble, for example, Deaf people will rush to aid a fellow Deaf person. Some Deaf people complain, however, that everyone knows the intimate details of everyone else's lives. As we know, it's hard to keep a secret in a family.

There is also a "small world" aspect to the Deaf community. It is almost always possible to find some connection between any two Deaf people. Usually one can find a mutual acquaintance acquired through residential school, attendance at universities such as Gallaudet, CSUN, National Technical Institute for the Deaf (NTID), or a Deaf sports organization. This leads us to our next topic.

Introductions

In Deaf culture, introductions can be viewed as a search for connection. When the introduction involves a hearing person, however, the focus is more on that person's attitude and invisible "set of references." In this section, three categories of introductions will be discussed: when two Deaf people introduce themselves to each other, when one Deaf person introduces two Deaf people to each other, and when the introduction involves a hearing person.

Introductions in American hearing culture typically focus on occupation, as I noted earlier. Essentially, you are what you do. By comparison, in Deaf culture, you are who you know. When two Deaf people introduce themselves to each other without the benefit of a third person who would try to locate a connection for them, the two will exchange information through a series of statements about themselves and questions posed to each other that will continue until one or more connection(s) have been established. At the point when a mutual friend is identified, however, the conversation may shift to catch each other up on recent developments in the friend's life or to share old stories about him or her.

Certain pieces of information will aid in this process. Others are considered extraneous and thus inappropriate during introductions. If they do not further the search for a mutual connection, these statements are just dead ends and seen as a waste of time.

Person-to-Person Introductions. In unmediated introductions, names are exchanged. The two people usually spell out their first and last names plus a maiden name if they have one. Then they tell where they went to school. If they went to a residential school or a large day school, they are sure to mention its name, since this is the richest vein of ore when digging for the gold of mutual acquaintances in the Deaf world. If they did not attend residential school, then they simply identify the type of school they attended, such as "mainstream school." The name of such a school is irrelevant because it will not, in all likelihood, lead to any connections. (A possible exception is a local hearing school that everyone who lives in the same community would know, but this would never be told to someone from another state because it would not help to find a Deaf connection.)

After names and schools have been established, the next important piece of background to describe is family status—meaning Deaf or hearing. Since only 10 percent of deaf people have deaf parents, the fact of having them is usually remarked upon. For example, A: MOTHER/FATHER DEAF? B: YES. MOTHER/FATHER DEAF. A: OHHH LUCKY!!! "Lucky," because having Deaf parents signifies immediate acceptance and communication within the family, two elements which are often lacking in households with hearing parents. If it is established that person B in the example above also has deaf children, that fact may be even more envied. If one or both of the people introducing themselves happen to have Deaf family members, their names are shared because they could lead to possible connections.

Consider this brief exchange during an introduction between two Deaf people: C: MOTHER/FATHER HEARING? D: YES. HEARING. C: ME TOO. It immediately establishes a common experience of growing up that does not need to be further described. Each person knows what the other's experience was like. "Hearing parents" generically signifies minimal communication. Perhaps one's physical needs were taken care of, but it may have stopped there. "They fed me. That's all." "They loved me, but they didn't really understand me."

If one's relationship to one's hearing parents had some positive aspects that go against the stereotype, these will be mentioned at this point with a *but*. For example, "I had hearing parents ..." (1) "... but they could sign," (2) "... but I was lucky, they sent me to residential school early," or (3) "... but I had a deaf sister."

The search for a connection during introductions is a dogged one and not easily abandoned. If the exchange of names, family members, and schools does not bear fruit, more obscure associations may be tried. Each person will share the names of a list of friends and acquaintances in the hope that the other person may know one. Possible events that both people may have attended will be enumerated. For example, a woman who was a graduate of Gallaudet University in the 1980s met a man who had never gone to Gallaudet himself but had attended a couple of events in the area around Washington, DC. When the time frame of the early 1980s was established, intense questioning back and forth finally proved successful. They pinpointed a certain New Year's Eve party given by a man named Joe in 1983. He: "Yeah, I was there. . . . I was so drunk I fainted and they had to call an ambulance." She: "Oh sure! I remember you now! So, have you seen Joe lately?"

The search for connections is the search for connectedness. In the small world of the American Deaf community everyone is somehow connected to everyone else, either through their own experiences or through mutual friends. For us, the hearing, it would be like meeting a distant relative whose relationship to you is unclear. You might both run through the names of your grandparents, aunts, and uncles until you finally figure it out. "Ohhh. Your uncle Jack from Boise was my cousin Frieda's first husband."

The "You are who you know" maxim can help establish one's place in Deaf society. If a relative newcomer to a community can enumerate the names of well-respected Deaf people with whom he or she has connections, it serves as an unwritten list of references and can hasten acceptance. This is especially true for hearing people/interpreters who may not have a history of personal connections. There are, however, exceptions to the rule. People change. If asked, John may name all his old pals at Gallaudet, but knowing that this crowd was famous for its drinking and partying, he may feel he has to add, "I was wild then, but I've changed—I grew up."

Mediated Introductions. In the second category of introductions, Jane introduces Fred to George (all are Deaf). Jane will attempt to speed up the connection search between Fred and George. She will introduce them by name, tell where they live, the school they attended, and her own connection with them. The occupations of Fred and George are not usually related because this line of questioning is another dead end (unless one of them works at a residential school, which would likely lead to mutual Deaf acquaintances). If necessary, Jane will tell the names of Fred's and George's current friends, former girlfriends, and so forth, in order to find a link between them. Of course, if no other connection can be found, Jane is herself a de facto mutual acquaintance.

A note about name signs (which will be described in more detail in the next section): name signs are not usually volunteered during the first introduction, unless specifically requested or unless one is introducing a renowned person with a name sign that is widely known. They may be shared at a later meeting or—since their main purpose is to refer to someone who is not physically present—they may come up more naturally in a situation where the person being talked about is not in the room. However, in a group of Deaf people with limited English proficiency, name signs may be employed instead of spelling out names, since they may refer to a small group of possible mutual friends. In fact, it is not unusual to know people by name sign only and not know the spelling of their English names, because names themselves carry less importance than in mainstream culture. This is the source of a particularly thorny cultural dilemma that comes up in legal situations. Suppose a Deaf suspect's alibi is "ME NOT THERE, ME WITH GOOD-FRIEND D-on-the-shoulder." Even if the interpreter delivers a translation such as, "I wasn't there, I was with my very good friend, the one we all call 'D'." The obvious next question is "What is D's full name?" If the Deaf witness replies that he does not know, the incredulous cross-examining lawyer will undoubtedly remark, "Oh, he's your *really* good friend, but you don't even know his name?"

When a Hearing Person Is Introduced. The introduction of a hearing person to a Deaf person, either directly or by another Deaf person, does not share the same emphasis on the search for a mutual connection. Unless the hearing person grew up in the Deaf community (as a CODA), he or she will not have the same history of friends and associations. Two items that are often checked out are the hearing person's "attitude" and why and how he or she has learned sign language. The "how" might involve the name(s) of some Deaf people or well-respected sign language teachers, at which point these individuals serve as a point of connection, and the discussion may lead off in their direction.

Something that hearing people—even interpreters—often misunderstand is that when the Deaf person questions them regarding their Deaf connections, for example, "Who taught you sign language?" the Deaf teacher named in response will generally become the focus of the conversation. The hearing person may feel bewildered, as if he or she has somehow lost a place in the limelight. Hearing people who are involved with the Deaf community should become accustomed to the fact that the names of the Deaf people with whom they have had connections serve as an invisible "set of references" that helps newly introduced Deaf people know how to place hearing people in context. In Deaf culture namedropping serves the important function of validating one's place in the community. One way to accomplish this is to find the appropriate moment to explain a little about your "background" and then mention the names of some well-known Deaf people with whom you have had connections. While in mainstream American culture name-dropping is seen as showing off, for hearing people involved in the Deaf community, it shows that you can be trusted.

In Deaf culture, with its emphasis on insider/outsider distinctions, it is extremely important that hearing people be immediately identified as such. Often the hearing person's nonfluent signing style will give that person away, but if there is any doubt, it is always safer to say right away, "Hi. My name is Anna and I'm hearing" or "I'm an interpreter." One of the strongest taboos in Deaf culture is for a hearing person to try to "pass" as a deaf person.

When a hearing person is introduced to a Deaf person by another Deaf person, the information he or she relates (or subtly conveys) tells the other Deaf person if the hearing person is to be trusted: "An introduction is a gift, not to be given lightly . . . [it provides] entree, a certain stamp of approval" (Smith 1996, 100). If the hearing person is a novice signer, quickly signed comments can be made in front of that person's face that will probably not even be noticed (e.g., "Lousy attitude. Tell you later."). As discussed earlier, hearing status carries a generic set of (negative) assumptions. If Deaf people feel positive about the hearing people they are introducing, they must present information to counter the stereotype, again using a *but*. For example, "This is Mary. She is hearing . . ." (1) ". . . but she has helped me a lot with my community work," (2) ". . . but she is a CODA," or (3) ". . . but she is a very good interpreter."

The Name Sign System in ASL

Name signs represent the identity of individual Deaf people and at the same time symbolize their membership in the Deaf community. In chapter 3 we briefly touched on the subject of name signs in ASL as they exemplify a collective orientation; in chapter 13 we will examine the ramifications of hearing people having name signs. For now we will look at the traditional system of inventing and using name signs in ASL, which has been deftly described by Sam Supalla.

There are two types of name signs in this system, *arbitrary* and *descriptive*. Arbitrary name signs are the type consistently given by Deaf parents to their children and consist of a handshape representing an initial of the person's English name, which is made in a specific location with a certain movement. The location and movement can only come from a limited set of possibilities. Most important, arbitrary name signs contain no meaning.

Alternatively, some Deaf people possess a descriptive name sign that uses a classifier handshape to represent a salient physical feature, for instance, a big nose or a scar. These are most often bestowed on deaf children (from hearing families) when they enter the residential school without a name sign. As these children grow up, they may decide to change to an arbitrary name sign if they feel uncomfortable with their descriptive name sign. Since all their friends are already accustomed to using their original descriptive name sign, however, it may be difficult to effect this change unless they move to a new community. Since one of the functions of name signs is to provide the Deaf community with an efficient method to unambiguously refer to its members, "a name sign is expected to represent the identity of the person for the rest of his or her life" (Supalla 19).

One of the most interesting features of name signs in ASL is the way they exemplify connection to the group.

The smallest group is, of course, the family. Hence the common practice for Deaf parents to express family unity in the name signs for their children. Many parents ... pick one location (e.g., on the back of the passive hand, on the forehead, or in neutral space) for all their children's name signs, changing only the handshape ... [of] ... the child's English name's first initial. If the family picks for the children English names that all start with the same letter, then the handshape is held constant and the location changes. (Mindess 7)

Another way of establishing connections through name signs is by giving one child in the family a name sign that matches the location of the mother's name sign, while the next child is given a name sign that matches the location of the father's name sign. Occasionally, a child is "given the name sign of a deceased relative or old friend of one parent to honor that person's memory" (7).

Possession of a name sign symbolizes membership in the Deaf community. Often Deaf people fondly remember the occasion of being "baptized" or "initiated" into the group by being given their sign. There are exceptions, however, and not every member of the community may need a name sign. Very short English names (e.g., Joe or Ann) can be fingerspelled with relative ease, as can other rare names in which the handshapes flow smoothly (e.g., L-A-R-R-Y).

Name signs are not used the same way that names are used in spoken English.

For example, in a regular conversation, one can use a name to get someone's attention (e.g., "Hey, Mike"); for emphasis (e.g., "Mike, I cannot believe you."); and to refer to someone who is not present (e.g., "Can you tell Mike?"). In comparison to English, ASL name signs are used only for the third example; thus name signs are used only to refer to a third person who is not present. (Supalla 20)

Name signs can also illuminate the power structure of the community. If two people in a local area happen to have the same name sign, the situation must be quickly rectified to eliminate confusion in the group. Regardless of the fact that the two people feel strongly possessive of their name signs, a change will be made to accommodate the group. Whose name sign will change? The newcomer to the group or the younger person are common answers. If one person is Deaf and the other hearing, of course the former keeps the sign and the latter changes. And if both people are Deaf, the one who had the name sign the longest or is better known gets to keep it (Mindess 10–11).

Most Deaf people feel strongly that the Arbitrary Name Sign System, which can be traced back to the early 1800s, is an important part of their culture that should be preserved. To that end, in the second half of *The Book of Name Signs*, Supalla provides drawings of 525 name signs from which parents may choose in order to pass down to future generations the traditional name signs of ASL.

Hugs

Every culture has a greeting ritual: bows in Japan, kisses on cheeks in France, and handshakes in the United States. Deaf culture has hugs. Just like bows, kisses on cheeks, and handshakes, hugs follow an internal system of rules. Children learn the proper way to do it from watching their parents; outsiders who don't know the rules seem awkward. It may be difficult for outsiders to get members of the culture to describe their greeting system explicitly because, like so many other rituals, to the members of the culture "it just feels right."

Even though hearing Americans employ greeting hugs on occasion, the Deaf system appears to differ in certain respects.

+ Deaf people hug *more* than hearing people.
+ Deaf people hug *a wider range* of people than hearing people. The hearing hug seems to be reserved for a smaller set of intimates.
+ The Deaf hug has *more body contact* than the hearing version. (Deaf people often tease their hearing friends about their "hearing hug" in which there is minimal body contact and the bodies of the huggers make an inverted V shape. Hearing people are sometimes also chided for "patting" during the hug.)
+ The Deaf greeting hug is important, but the *parting hug may be more important.*

Other aspects of hugs in Deaf culture:

+ There are individual variations. A particularly physical Deaf person may add a kiss with the hug.

+ One hugs a person with whom one shares a connection. Most often that would be a friend that one has not seen for a while. (One does not hug the same person in greeting more than once a day.)

+ Hugging shows respect, just as in a family gathering, where hearing children are expected to say hello to or kiss all the aunts and uncles (even those who pinch cheeks).

+ Hugs are noticed by others who carry assumptions about who should be hugged by whom. For example, Jill and Gloria are old friends and haven't seen each other for a while. They happen to run into each other at a shopping mall when Jill is there with her mother (who is also Deaf). They do not hug, but greet each other in a cool manner. After Gloria leaves, Jill's mother asks, "What's wrong? Why didn't you hug her?" Jill explains that they have had a recent falling out. In another example, Jim arrives at Laura's party, where a group has already gathered. He goes around hugging everyone hello but misses Charles. Charles acts hurt and quizzes Jim, "Hey, why didn't you hug me?"

+ There is a right moment for the hug—usually immediately after the "Hi." If something distracts one or both greeters at that point, it becomes too late to hug; the moment has passed.

+ Whom one hugs is also a variable, depending on the circumstances. The more foreign the environment, the more one hugs someone who is not that close a friend. (Just as if you were traveling in a foreign country and happened to bump into someone you barely knew at home, you might greet that person very warmly at the sheer relief of seeing a familiar face and finding someone with whom you could converse in English.) At a large, all-Deaf event, one would only hug one's closest friends, but at a mostly hearing event, two Deaf acquaintances would probably hug because their connection would assume greater proportions set against a hearing backdrop.

+ The parting hug seals the moment of farewell. It is an expression of closeness and closure, and it is almost mandatory at social events. If one leaves in a hurry without hugging the appropriate people, it is seen as very rude. At a party, one may make several rounds of hugs. One may say good-bye to everyone, hugging each person in turn and exchanging a few last words. As often happens, however, one of these exchanges turns into a longish conversation. When one is finally ready to walk out the door, one has to again make the rounds with perhaps a quicker set of hugs. This is one reason why leave-taking in Deaf culture takes so long.

+ Interpreters often feel uncomfortable when Deaf clients want to give them a parting hug at the end of an assignment. In our role as "professionals" we are not used to hugging our clients. In American culture, for example, we do not usually hug our accountant (unless he or she just saved us a lot of money). Deaf hugs, on the other hand, convey a different message. They may be the Deaf person's way of saying "Thank you. I felt you really understood me. I feel connected to you now."

The subject of hugs in American Deaf culture deserves more research, and a more enjoyable topic to study would be hard to find.

Attitude

The sign ATTITUDE carries a specific connotation. It is used most often to refer to one's perspective on what the Deaf community cherishes most: ASL and Deaf people. Someone is said to have a "GOOD ATTITUDE" if they respect sign language and the people who use it. Hearing people have a "good attitude" if they support Deaf people's decisions regarding their own lives, rather than taking a pitying or paternalistic stance. Deaf people label other Deaf people as having a "lousy" attitude if they try to act superior.

As a collectivist culture, Deaf culture places importance on identifying with the group. Therefore, even college degrees or an advanced position of employment should not lead one to distance oneself from other Deaf people. "If a Deaf person were to try to lord her abilities over other Deaf people, she would be ostracized immediately" (Rexroat 19–20). "There are a number of ASL signs referring to presumptuousness, arrogance, bragging, or self-centeredness, all of which are deemed an immature putting forward of oneself" (Smith 1996, 95).

A particular type of bad attitude is referred to by a sign that places the sign for "hearing" on the forehead and could be translated as "thinks/behaves like a hearing person." It is used to describe a deaf person who rejects the values of the Deaf community and tries to follow the ways of the hearing majority. "Deaf people who adopt hearing values and look down on other Deaf people are regarded as traitors" (Lane 1992, 17). Following the same principle in reverse, one can praise a hearing person's attitude by describing him or her as "thinks/behaves like a Deaf person." A person so described would be lauded not only for signing well but for supporting and contributing to the goals of the Deaf community, for example, volunteering time for Deaf causes and attending Deaf events.

The Value of ASL and the Preservation of Deaf Culture

> For many members of the Deaf Community, they and ASL are indistinguishable. Their self-concept is based on being Deaf and being Deaf to them means using ASL. Their feelings about ASL comfort them, just as using ASL in communication with other Deaf people is made comfortable by ASL. (Schein 1989, 37)

ASL is loved and cherished by the Deaf community. As their creation, ASL is "rooted biologically and culturally in Deaf people, [and] is a unifying force in the Deaf community" (Tucker 1994, 368). Yet, it is oppressed by those who do not recognize its existence, its validity as a language, or its value in allowing deaf children to access education with a language naturally suited to their needs.

Perhaps it is the very oppression of ASL that engenders such strong positive feelings about it. The experience is similar to other "oppressed language communities" around the world. In France, for example, two regional languages, Breton and Occitan, were not allowed to be taught in school for hundreds of years. Yet they were kept alive in the hearts and mouths of their speakers, who passed them on to their children and wrote poetry and songs in these languages. Often the subject of this art was how much the language meant to them. This intense love for an endangered language is something that we English speakers have probably never experienced.

How Deaf People Feel about ASL

"Deaf adults often tell stories about the first time they saw ASL, remembering in vivid detail their sense of 'connection' or 'liberation' with the new language" (Rexroat 19). "When ASL entered my life, I felt like I was born again . . . It is my language. It is my identity" (Finkle 1992, 7). Learning sign language "was like waking up in heaven . . . I felt almost as if ASL were biologically innate to me. It was developed, refined and kept alive by deaf people, and it *feels* right. It's designed to meet our needs" (Ogden

1996, 143). As former president of the National Association of the Deaf George Veditz so eloquently put it in 1913 in a lecture preserved on film,

> Enemies of the sign language, they are enemies of the true welfare of the Deaf . . . As long as we have Deaf people on earth, we will have signs . . . It is my hope that we will love and guard our beautiful sign language as the noblest gift God has given to Deaf people. (as translated by Padden in Padden and Humphries 1988, 36)

Storytelling Skills

As a rich visual language that employs the narrative mode of expression, ASL is a storyteller's dream. A good storyteller is part actor and part cinematographer, because a good story in ASL involves changing character as well as perspective, including extreme close-ups and long shots from every conceivable angle. Skill in ASL storytelling is admired regardless of educational background. Everyone knows who the best storytellers are. These people are in heavy demand at parties, talent nights, storytelling festivals, and other events, and favorite old stories are requested again and again. One's skill in ASL might even take precedence over other personal characteristics. I have heard of an excellent storyteller who is still invited to share his talents even though people in the community do not approve of how he runs his personal affairs. Stories are not only saved for formal entertainment but are also used in everyday discourse to present, emphasize, warn, instruct, or inspire (Smith 1996, 221–34).

Traditional Folklore

Deaf culture is very rich in folklore. Because ASL is not a written language, stories, games, and humor are shared and passed down through performance, both formal and informal (and nowadays by videotape). Simon Carmel, a Deaf folklorist, has identified several genres: jokes, tales about the old days, stories of personal experience, legends, games, and signplay including ABC and number stories (Carmel 1982). Anthropologist Susan Rutherford has described several additional folk traditions: group narratives, fingerspelling mime, one-handshape stories and skits (Rutherford 1993).

There are a few "old chestnuts" that are often given in response to a request for examples of Deaf humor. One classic joke with many variations involves an interpreter. One version told by noted Deaf educator M. J. Bienvenu in a videotaped collection goes like this: A hearing man happens to acquire $100,000. Worried about its safety, he waits until nightfall, and then he buries the money in his backyard. When he goes to check on his booty in the morning, he finds the money gone and footprints leading to his deaf neighbor's house. Incensed, he grabs his gun and storms over to his neighbor, bringing along an interpreter. After the man threatens to shoot his neighbor if he doesn't reveal what he did with the money, the Deaf man calmly explains in sign language that he put the money in an even safer place, under the elm tree in his own backyard. "So, what did he say?" asks the hearing man. Shrugging, the interpreter replies, "Sorry, he won't talk." This joke clearly reflects Deaf people's fears regarding the unreliability of interpreters and their anger against those who take advantage of the knowledge gained in interpreting situations (Carmel 1981).

Other well-known jokes like "Please BUT," "The Hitchhiker," and "The Motel Joke" express such themes as deaf people's struggles with English, a hearing person trying to pass as deaf and getting in trouble, and a clever deaf person overcoming obstacles. Clearly, Deaf humor relieves the tension of the daily challenges faced by the Deaf minority, just as African American humor and Jewish humor help those groups cope with the difficulties encountered in a white Christian society. Although these jokes have been told thousands of times, Deaf people seem to enjoy their repetition, since the struggles they illuminate are ongoing.

Tales of the old days often focus on ingenious ways deaf people solved practical problems before such modern conveniences as visual alarm clocks or visual doorbells were commonplace. Cannonballs, wooden planks, and pillows were cleverly rigged to fall and wake the Deaf person so he or she could be on time for work. In one well-known story, the sound of a heavy iron crashing down on a wooden plank was so resounding that the entire hearing population of a small town overslept the week the Deaf man went on vacation. Legends include stories of Deaf people in bygone eras such as the Revolutionary and Civil Wars. These two genres give Deaf people connections with their forebears; only in this case a common language and culture are thicker than blood. Other oft-shared stories recount embarrassing situations faced by deaf people in the hearing world, such as an elevator whose doors opened in the back unnoticed by a panicking deaf woman. Like Jewish stories in which a rabbi outwits a priest and a minister, or American Indian jokes in which an American Indian bests a white man, Deaf people also enjoy stories in which they

turn the tables on ignorant or mocking hearing people, who end up looking silly or stupid. Bienvenu has written, "When you analyze minority
cultures . . . [you] realize that they all incorporate fighting back into their
humor. It is a common response to the frustration in our lives, for in
humor, the storyteller determines who will 'win'" (Bienvenu 1989).

Because of lack of communication and differing values, many Deaf
people may not identify strongly with their family of origin. Folktales of
Deaf people's experiences throughout the ages, however, supply a family
of ancestors that one can rely on for inspiration, a feeling of connection,
or a good chuckle.

In recent years a new form of Deaf cultural expression has evolved—
ASL poetry. Such artists as Dorothy Miles, Clayton Valli, and Ella Mae
Lentz have created pieces that paint vivid pictures with ASL's rich capacity for visual expression. Conventions from spoken/written poetry are
easily adapted into a visual vernacular. Rhyme, for instance, is deftly por-
trayed using similar handshapes, rhythm, or movement paths in place of
similar sounds. American Sign Language poetry, by virtue of its visual
mode, can achieve effects impossible in a linear language form, such as
portraying two images simultaneously and exploring their relationship to
each other as they meld and transform. Themes in ASL poetry run the
gamut from the ever-present struggle between the oral and manual
methods of instruction in deaf education to exquisite depictions of the
natural world as seen by Deaf eyes.

Collectivist Values

Loyalty to the Group

Insider/outsider distinctions, as mentioned earlier, are crucial in determining the behavior of Deaf people. Always conscious of their minority
status, Deaf people feel it is incumbent upon them, for the survival of the
group, to take "the Deaf side." A puzzle I have heard posed several times
to assess a Deaf person's attitude goes like this: Suppose you were on an
interviewing panel and had to decide which applicant to pick for a job. If
there were two candidates with equal skills and experience except that
one was deaf and one was hearing, whom would you choose? The easy
answer, obviously, is the deaf candidate, but that is just the setup. Suppose
this time there were two candidates, one deaf and one hearing, except that
the hearing candidate had more skills and more experience. Now, which

would you choose? The correct answer, from many of those with a strong Deaf cultural perspective, is still the Deaf one.

Loyalty can be a feeling of unity, as evidenced in the mass outpouring of support for the students and faculty at Gallaudet University during the "Deaf President Now" revolt in 1988. It can lead Deaf people to defend the actions of a Deaf coworker to their hearing boss, while later, in private, scolding that person for careless actions which might evoke negative judgments about the Deaf as a group. Loyalty is one reason why Deaf people will frequent a Deaf-owned dry-cleaning business even if there were hearing-owned dry cleaners closer to home. It predisposes them to first look for a Deaf worker to paint their house or mow their lawn, whom they might also assume will give them a better price. It also explains the feeling of outrage expressed by the Deaf club members in the play *Tales from a Clubroom*, when one character is found not just to have stolen money, but to have stolen it from *fellow Deaf!*

Reciprocity

One of the strongest collectivist features of Deaf culture is seen in the way members of the community share their time and skills. In mainstream American culture, we practice a balanced type of reciprocity. If Susan gives Rachel a birthday present, Rachel will probably give Susan a present on *her* birthday. Members of the Deaf community also practice this type of back-and-forth giving between one person and another; however, they follow a system of group reciprocity as well. In this system, one donates "favors, energy, information, and work for the community" into the pool, and one knows that in time of need he or she can draw from the common pool of resources as well. Some skills that are commonly shared include fixing a car, giving someone a ride, helping someone write a letter, sewing, woodworking, going to the market for someone who must stay at home, and helping someone move. There is no specific tallying of hours of work donated. As Marie Philip, a noted Deaf educator, put it, "You can't find a specific glass of water in a pool." But somehow there is a collective awareness, and "those who consistently do not contribute are not readily supported" (Smith 1996, 158).

One way the community keeps tabs on who helps out and who doesn't is that credit must be given to whomever it is due. "Oh, you like the new color of my house. Jackie helped me paint it." Collective memory spans generations. One Deaf couple was known for their generosity in helping their Deaf friends and neighbors. When their daughter needed help moving to a new house, her parents' old friends showed up in droves.

In her telecourse, "Cross-Cultural Comparisons," Philip explained that even if someone she didn't know asked her for help, she couldn't refuse. If she did, that person would tell his or her friends, "Marie is so busy she couldn't help me!" If this continued, when Marie needed help herself, she would be turned down.

Philip also described conflicting expectations between interpreters and the Deaf community in regard to reciprocity. Some interpreters see themselves as having learned sign language from one program or a few teachers, a transaction which is now finished. Since they have worked so hard to attain a professional standard of competence in the language, they now expect to be paid for services rendered. On the other hand, Deaf people often view the language skills interpreters acquire as coming from the Deaf community as a group. Since interpreters have gained so much (skill in the language, the means to make a comfortable living), they are now expected to give back proportionally to the community (Philip 1993).

Group Decision Making

In an individualist culture like that of the United States, people pride themselves on making up their own minds. We mark our ballots the way our conscience tells us and are suspicious of anyone who wants to sway our vote. In collectivist cultures, by comparison, the welfare of the group takes precedence over the interests of the individual. Or as it is probably internalized: the good of the group *is* the interest of each individual. In Deaf culture, "consensus, not majority rule, is the managing principle. Decisions are made by a majority vote, but rarely is there a close vote. Most pass unanimously, or with only one or two abstentions. Disagreements are resolved before the vote is taken" (Smith 1996, 261).

This does not mean that there is no discussion. On the contrary, in collectivist cultures there are often lengthy discussions of the merits and disadvantages of a proposed course of action. This may happen, however, before the motion is formally proposed. At many Deaf community meetings "votes are virtually foregone conclusions before they are taken. Each member has had an opportunity to make both opinions and feelings clear. The vote is not taken until everyone feels comfortable or at least resigned to the pending decision" (201).

On a more personal level, Deaf people ask their friends for opinions before they make a major decision, such as what car to buy or which job offer to accept (Philip 1993). At a party, the host might canvass the guests to gauge what most of them would prefer to do next, instead of just announcing an activity. The members of an organization expect to be consulted even on relatively minor matters. It has happened more than once that a president of an organization who was judged to be making too many decisions on his or her own was thrown out of office.

Importance of Getting Together

One aspect of collectivist cultures, which does not seem to be examined as often as the way they vote or their patterns of sharing, is the sheer enjoyment of doing things with other members of the group. The essence of Deaf culture is events: sports tournaments, bowling leagues, plays, panel discussions, parties, and community meetings, to name but a few. "Events are in one sense an excuse to get together. Getting together provides social opportunities for people to celebrate, exchange news or practical information, conduct community business and simply share company" (Smith 1996, 50).

In past generations, each major city had a Deaf club, which may have been the only gathering place for regulars as well as visiting out-of-towners. For a number of reasons these cultural institutions are on the wane, but that does not mean that getting together is any less popular. Recreational organizations are booming. Sports events are a major draw and have the added benefit of enabling people to travel and keep up on old ties. The event itself is not always the main draw. After the game is over many attendees will stay on for hours, socializing. Scores of Deaf people who are themselves "not on the team or officially involved will even travel hundreds of miles to attend such events. These events . . . serve to nurture, preserve and maintain the Deaf Community and its culture" (51).

Conversational Behavior

Lack of Importance of Speech

Many outsiders hold the misconception that speech has a negative value in Deaf culture. It would be more accurate to say that speech carries no weight. Possessing the ability to speak does not elevate a person's status in the Deaf community, nor does it diminish it. One's ability in this area is extraneous. The speech skills of a candidate running for office within a Deaf organization, for example, are never considered. They may even be viewed as the least important qualification of such a candidate. By contrast, the ability to speak is often the first thing a hearing person would notice when meeting a deaf person.

Ironically, however, when it is noted that a Deaf person does have usable speech skills, other Deaf people will not hesitate to ask him or her for assistance when ordering food at a restaurant, requesting information at a store, or engaging in other encounters with hearing people. As this may create unwanted pressure on the speaking Deaf people to function in the role of interpreter/helper, they may refuse to use their speech skills in the presence of other Deaf people. For many others, the painful memories of long hours of childhood spent in speech training, trying to perfect their pronunciation only to find that hearing people still had to struggle to understand them, has left a bad taste in their mouth and they want nothing more to do with speech.

Attention-Getting Behaviors

Hearing people use their voices to attract the attention of others. In the Deaf world the following attention-getting techniques are employed instead: tapping someone on the shoulder, waving in the direction of the intended person, banging on the table or stomping on the floor (using vibrations to catch the person's attention), asking a nearby person to tap the intended person on the shoulder, flashing the room light, or throwing a lightweight object at the target person. Sometimes one uses a sort of chain reaction to get the attention of an entire group. For instance, if a group of Deaf people is seated in a semicircle chatting prior to a meeting or lecture, the lecturer may make a sign with both hands that refers to tapping someone on the shoulder. Made in this context, it asks for those who are presently watching the presenter to alert those seated next to them, and so on around the circle until everyone is looking up and the presentation can begin.

Each of these techniques is more appropriate in certain situations than others. For example, flashing the lights is an effective way to get the attention of a large room or auditorium full of people and is often used to signal the start of a meeting. The use of some techniques varies according to the distance away from the intended target. A large, waving arm movement would be appropriate for getting the attention of someone on the other side of the room. It would be inappropriate, however, to use such a sizable gesture to get the attention of someone standing just a few feet away—comparable to yelling "HELLLOOOOOOO!!!!!!" in the ear of a person standing right beside you.

It has been observed that in the Deaf world people touch one another more than in the hearing world. This may be partly due to the fact that a light touch on the arm is often used to get someone's attention or make one's presence known. If one is approaching a Deaf person from behind, it is polite to avoid startling him or her by subtly signaling one's presence, either by a light touch on the arm or by a small movement that will be noticed in the person's peripheral field of vision. A rough touch is again like shouting a greeting in someone's ear.

Just as techniques for getting the group's attention at the beginning of a meeting differ between the Deaf and hearing worlds, so does the way to show appreciation at the end of a performance. In the mid-1980s a new cultural behavior, "Deaf applause," appeared on the scene, to the dismay of some old-timers. Deaf applause, instead of using the noise of clapped hands, relies on the movement made by arms vertically stretched, hands fluttering quickly back and forth to achieve a visual equivalent of an overwhelming ovation. This distinctive cultural movement, which resembles a forest of excited trees to the performers being saluted, reportedly originated in the French Deaf community and has since spread across the Deaf world through its use at international conferences and events. Previously, simply clapping over one's head was employed and is still preferred in some circles. Another form of Deaf ovation used in the past, primarily at banquets, was a mass waving of napkins, an attractive sight, but one that had the unwanted side effect of scattering bits of food upon the revelers.

When Conversations Are Temporarily Halted

It is considered polite in the United States to temporarily halt a spoken conversation when one's mouth is full to avoid spraying one's conversational partner with half-chewed bits of food. A signed conversation, on the other hand, suffers no such limitations when the mouth is otherwise occupied. The restrictions that apply to signed conversations are mainly concerned with the eyes and hands. Most critically, signing stops when the eyes are needed to avoid danger. When crossing a busy street, for example, where cars may whiz by unexpectedly, a couple's conversation is temporarily halted until they reach the opposite curb. When crossing a relatively small and peaceful street, by contrast, the conversation may be on a short hold while the conversing couple looks both ways and steps off the curb, and it may resume as they walk across the street. While doing so, both know that they are responsible for checking out their partner's path for any obstructions or unexpected danger.

"How Can They Talk and Drive at the Same Time?"

To the surprise of most hearing people, Deaf people are adept at carrying on signed conversations while driving. Although this may seem hazardous to the uninitiated, "statistics show that deaf drivers are just as good as hearing drivers and, on the whole, a better safety risk" (Moore and Levitan 1992, 190). Some adjustments to conversational style are made, however. When both the driver and the passenger are well versed in Deaf culture, a regular signing conversation may be carried on. The passenger may choose to utilize less fingerspelling than normal or else move his or her hand to the left so that the spelling is directly in the driver's sight line. It also helps the driver's sight line to move up the passenger's seat a little. In the case of hearing drivers or deaf drivers who have not had much practice in such situations, on the other hand, it is usually easier if the driver does most of the talking, with the passenger responding at red lights or stop signs. "Most deaf passengers will share the responsibility of keeping watch with the driver and are quick to alert him or her [to any danger]; everybody looks after each other" (191). Increasing darkness may mean that conversations are reduced to essentials or sometimes stopped altogether.

Polite Behaviors

Polite Signs and Facial Expression

In English and other spoken languages, there are a vast number of special phrases which, when added to one's speech, make it seem more courteous: "Would you be so kind as to . . ." "Would you mind terribly if I asked you to . . ." ASL does not employ flowery phrases to indicate politeness. There are, however, a few signs that, when made with the appropriate movement and facial expression, do convey a polite or deferential attitude. One such sign is CURIOUS; when used to precede a direct question, it acts as a little warning that what follows may delve into a personal area. It may be used before asking people how old they are, how much money they paid for something, or other more personal inquiries, Other signs such as DON'T-MIND, WELL, and, SORRY also convey a polite demeanor when asking for a favor or expressing an inability to comply with a request.

In *It's Not What You Say, It's How you Say It* (forthcoming), Jack Hoza builds upon the work of Daniel Roush (1999) in his sociolinguistic examination of two common types of speech acts in ASL, requests and refusals. He identifies certain lexical items (signs) and non-manual modifiers (facial expressions and body movements) in ASL that work to lessen the assumed imposition of a request or soften the negative force of a refusal. From his extensive study, Hoza is able to rank five non-manual modifiers (NMMs) by their potential to mitigate an imposition. From the weakest to the strongest they are: "polite pucker," "tight lips," "polite grimace," "polite grimace-frown" and "body/head teeter." By examining in his study a variety of relationships, such as employee to supervisor and coworker to coworker and a range of tasks such as asking to borrow a pen and asking to borrow $50, Hoza demonstrates that ASL possesses a wide range of strategies to express varying degrees of politeness.

To cite just a few of the significant findings about NMMs in these two important studies: the polite pucker is used to signal cooperation. The tight lips marker "serves as a general 'default' politeness marker for most requests (of medium imposition) and rejections" (Hoza, forthcoming). It is often used in conjunction with the signs DON'T-MIND (in requests) and WELL and SORRY (in rejections). The polite grimace, which is described as a tight symmetrical smile, "seems to add the meaning of 'sorry, can't do it', 'I don't think it can be done' or 'I don't agree'" (Roush, 43). The body/head teeter is described by Roush as a "side to side head movement or shifting of weight between one foot and the other" (43). It is often used in conjunction with other NMMs and serves to intensify them.

These studies refute the oversimplification that Deaf people are always direct. Rather, they demonstrate that ASL users, like speakers of all languages, utilize a variety of strategies, both direct and indirect, depending on the relationship, task, and communicative goal.

Disclosing Personal Information (or Not)

In Deaf culture one is expected to share the details of one's life with others, and it is rude not to do so. There is not the same expectation of a right to privacy that hearing people may claim. Questions that probe into what hearing people would consider private matters serve the important function of educating the community and sharing often hard-won knowledge. It is generally expected, therefore, that one will answer inquiries regarding how much money one earns, what one paid for a car or house, why one is getting a divorce or does not have children. To take one example, buying a car is different from the purchase of any other consumer good in that the price on the sticker is not final. Some Deaf people may not be aware of the negotiation dance one is expected to do with a car dealer. Sharing these details means that one is concerned about one's friends (or those Deaf people who have grown up with more limited access to information).

Even so, Deaf people do not always wish to answer every question posed to them. One good reason may be that they know the answer will set them apart from (or above) others (e.g., earning a much higher salary than most other Deaf people). Some polite ways to avoid answering a question involve responding with a humorous retort (e.g., Q: "How much did you pay for that car?" A: "More than I should have."), indicating that the price one paid was within a certain range, or changing the subject.

One Deaf friend told me of the time she was out with a group of girlfriends and the conversation turned into a comparison of whose ex-boyfriend was the worst. As each woman around the table told her tale of increasingly offensive behavior, my friend decided she did not want to be compelled to do the same. She thought to herself, "How am I going to avoid spilling the beans? Certainly not by saying, 'Sorry, that's private.'" So when her turn came, she subtly changed the direction of the discussion by chiding her friends, "Hey, that's enough negative talk. Let's talk about something positive now."

How to Pass through a Signed Conversation

When two people are having a signed conversation, it sometimes becomes necessary for others to pass between them, thus "interrupting" their dialogue. This happens all the time in the Deaf world, especially at crowded parties, and goes unnoticed. For a hearing person unfamiliar with the ways of the Deaf, however, it seems like a daunting task to walk through a visual conversation. Hearing people, in consciously trying not to be rude, often end up interrupting far more than they would have, had they walked right between the conversing parties without a second thought. The polite way to handle such a situation is for the person walking through the conversation to bring as little attention to him- or herself as possible. One moves quickly between the conversing parties without making eye contact. It is not necessary to sign SORRY, although it is permissible to execute the sign EXCUSE-ME with a very small movement, almost to oneself.

Sometimes it is almost comical to watch well-meaning hearing people hovering uncomfortably on the edge of a signed conversation, wondering how to walk through it. Unfortunately, they usually end up doing the opposite of what would be considered most polite: they wave their arms in a large gesture that captures the attention of the signers and stops their conversation. Then they exaggeratedly mouth "I a-m s-o-o-o-o s-o-r-r-y—p-a-r-d-o-n m-e!" so the signers must reassure them that it is perfectly permissible to walk on through.

Catching Someone Up on a Conversation in Progress

As mentioned in chapter 3, conversations in ASL may be harder to follow if you are not present for the introduction of a new topic and miss the setup of the time frame and names of the people being discussed. Therefore, if someone approaches a conversation in which several people are already involved, to be considerate, one of the people in the conversation may take a moment to catch this friend up on who and what the conversation is about. If, however, someone whom the conversationalists do not care for approaches, they may not bother to catch that person up at all.

Reconfirming Appointment Details

Traditionally, when Deaf people made a date to meet each other or a hearing person, it was common for both parties to repeat the details (i.e., time, date, place) several times to make absolutely sure of mutual understanding. This probably stemmed from the fact that if a miscommunication occurred and one Deaf person arrived at a restaurant at what he or she thought was the right time only to find him- or herself waiting alone for hours, it would have been hard to call the friend to find out what had gone wrong. For those with text pagers, these situations do not pose the same dilemma they once did. It will be interesting to see if this tradition continues or fades away.

Rude Behaviors

Stephanie Hall, in her study of communicative behavior in a Deaf club, observes, "One basic principle of etiquette [is that] . . . one should always act in a way that facilitates communication and access to information. Rudeness inhibits communication. . . ." She enumerates behaviors that are considered rude in such contexts: holding down someone's hands to stop them from signing and turning your back on someone trying to tell you something (S. Hall 1989, 101).

We have already mentioned several behaviors that are considered rude in Deaf culture: withholding information, refusing to watch someone signing to you, pretending to be deaf if you are hearing. Here are a few other taboos.

Asking Inappropriate Questions

Just as one's ability to speak is irrelevant in Deaf society, so are the details of one's audiological status. Questions regarding one's decibel loss or when and how one became deaf are more germane to those who have recently lost their hearing. It is the use of ASL and the identification with similar cultural values that make someone culturally Deaf, not the percentage of hearing loss on his or her audiogram. Those who have grown up in Deaf culture focus more on what they have than on what they are missing. Questions from hearing people about how they feel about "missing out" on music or birdsongs are considered ignorant.

Another type of remark that is considered rude are statements or questions that seem aimed at trying to make Deaf people act more like hearing people. Comments such as "Use your voice," "You should wear your hearing aids," or "Why don't you get a cochlear implant?" demonstrate a lack of understanding and respect for Deaf identity and values.

Hearing People Talking behind the Backs of Deaf People

One of the rudest things a hearing person can do is deliberately talk in front of (or behind) Deaf people in a manner that prevents them from understanding what you are saying. Talking through clenched teeth with a frozen smile like an amateur ventriloquist will only garner more attention. Sometimes a hearing person may be in the middle of a conversation with a Deaf person when the phone rings. The hearing person will probably answer the phone immediately and start gabbing away without a word or a sign to let the Deaf person know what is going on. If this happened with another hearing person, that person could get the gist of the call (business, personal, or family emergency) by subtly eavesdropping on the tone of voice or noting even a few words. Leaving the Deaf person completely in the dark, therefore, is definitely impolite. To show respect, one can give an indication of one's own part of the phone conversation (it is optional to convey what the other party said). One's choices in such a situation are to wait until the call is over and summarize to one's Deaf friend what it was about or do what has come to be known as "sim-com" (simultaneous communication).

Because the structure of the two languages is so different, it is a well-recognized fact that it is impossible to simultaneously speak English and sign ASL. When native English speakers try to do so, they generally sign a poor approximation of their spoken English. Nevertheless, in this situation, some Deaf people prefer sim-com over waiting, without a clue, for the phone call to end, especially if the call is a long one. In this case one's memory may be hard put to reiterate the entire conversation, and one is tempted to use a phrase such as "Oh, it wasn't important," a rebuff that painfully reminds some Deaf people from hearing families of the isolation they felt around the dinner table.

It is a good idea to check with your friends to learn their preferences. Or better yet, consider letting your voice mail pick up the call.

Many hearing people find Deaf culture as fascinating as an exotic flower, because it seems so different from their own experience. Yet, as we have seen, although it does contain several unique features, it also shares numerous attributes with Japanese, French, and Israeli cultures, among others. American Deaf culture takes its place in the panoply of world cultures as the collection of ways this particular group of people has found to meet challenges, perpetuate what they hold dear, and enjoy rich, fulfilling lives.

6

Multicultural Deaf Culture

Hanuman, the monkey god, approached Brahma and found him crying.
"Lord Brahma, why do you cry?"
"I had a perfect jewel that held all wisdom," answered Brahma, "but I
dropped it and it fell to the earth and broke into many pieces that scattered all
around the world."
"Ah," said Hanuman, "Then you are crying because the jewel of wisdom is
broken."
"No," said Lord Brahma. "I am crying because everyone thinks their piece
is the entire jewel."

—*Tale from India as retold by*
RHONDA MARGOLIS

As both interpreters and citizens of the world, we cannot afford the luxury of self-deception: to think that we possess the entire jewel of wisdom. Just as the label "American" does not necessarily refer to a white person of European descent living in the United States, the designation "American Deaf Culture" must also include and reflect the various and diverse backgrounds, traditions, and identities of its members.

How is it possible for us to operate as bicultural mediators in our work as interpreters if we are not familiar with the values, vocabulary, and worldviews of our diverse clients? Our field is fortunate to have the fruits of five years of dedicated labor by scores of multicultural team members in the National Multicultural Interpreter Project (NMIP). Under a grant from the U.S. Department of Education and the able direction of Mary Mooney, of El Paso Community College, they have produced an impressively comprehensive work entitled *A Curriculum for Enhancing Competencies for Working within Culturally and Linguistically Diverse Communities*. At 500 pages, it is not possible to summarize the entire document in this chapter. My aim is to highlight some of the information it contains, focusing on the sections most pertinent to interpreted settings. I appreciate the permission granted me to borrow freely from the document. (The entire curriculum is available free online at *www.epcc.edu/Community/NMIP/Welcome .html*). I hope you will be inspired to read it in full or seek out other sources of material to deepen your understanding of the multicultural society in which you live and work.

Lest we think that learning about the multicultural aspects of the Deaf community is only necessary for interpreters who live in culturally diverse regions of the country, consider the new wrinkle in our profession. As more and more interpreters are working in Video Relay Service (VRS) and Video Remote Interpreting (VRI) environments, we are interpreting for dozens of Deaf and hearing consumers a day from all parts of the country with little or no preparation. It behooves us to learn as much as we can about all the people who might pop up unannounced on our computer screens in order to do a more accurate and effective job.

We will now briefly discuss the four cultural groups included in the NMIP. Each section includes selected cultural features, a discussion of the Deaf members of each group, and a few comments about interpreting issues. Chapter 9 will present interpreting scenarios based on this material.

Asian American Culture

When crossing the bridge into Asian American culture, we are faced with many paths. What complicates our journey is the fact that there is not a single "Asian American culture." The term encompasses more than 30 national and ethnic groups. Asian Americans are a diverse group including people of Chinese, Japanese, Korean, Filipino, Vietnamese, Cambodian, Thai, Laotian, and Hmong descent. Furthermore, each of these countries is culturally diverse as well.

Even though we use the term Asian American, it is important to note that most foreign-born people prefer to be identified with their city or country of origin. If asked, "Where are you from?" typical answers are "I am from Hong Kong" or "My parents were born in Korea." In fact, the very question "Where are you from?" posed by a non-Asian, may be perceived as offensive to people born and raised in the United States. A reply such as, "I'm from Los Angeles," may be indirectly addressing the rudeness of the question. When other Asians pose the question, however, the answer may be more direct. For members of the Deaf community, the preferred term is Asian Deaf, as in the name of the association, the National Asian Deaf Congress. Individuals may have their own preferences for terms, and these should be respected.

Another factor to consider before making any generalizations is the degree of assimilation or acculturation. There may be a great difference in values between a family that has been in the United States for three generations as compared to a family who recently immigrated. Immigration itself is a complex topic, because of the distinction between voluntary relocation (often for educational and/or economic opportunities) and involuntary refugee status. Refugees may be dealing with post-traumatic stress as well as intense culture shock.

Asian Americans practice a wide variety of religions and belief systems. These include Taoism, Buddhism, Confucianism, Shinto, Hinduism, Islam, and Christianity. No attempt will be made here to describe their teachings in depth, but we should be aware that many underlying beliefs such as "life is difficult and full of suffering" or "children must honor and obey their parents" may be deeply rooted in religious systems.

Cultural Features

Even though it is impossible to generalize about members of so many different groups, religions, and generations, most Asian societies can be described as collectivist cultures and share the features described in chapter 3. Loyalty, conformity, and group harmony are highly valued; consideration of other people's feelings is of paramount importance.

Family and Authority

The family is the cornerstone of Asian culture. Within the family, the roles and responsibilities of each member are highly structured. Unquestioned authority is given to the father. The mother is responsible for passing on the lessons of culture to the children. The role of the first-born child is that of duty, while the youngest child may be more indulged. It is not unusual for children to live with their families until they marry, and the household often includes extended family members.

Asian societies tend to favor hierarchical structures, where it is clear who has authority over whom. Proper respect must be paid to one's elders and those of higher status. Interestingly, teachers are considered to have the same high status as doctors (even though they earn lower salaries).

Asian students tend to listen to their teachers without questioning or challenging them. In Asian cultures, it is rude to maintain eye contact with a person of higher status. Students and parents will show respect to teachers by keeping their gaze pointed down. In Western culture, this behavior is often misinterpreted as avoidance (Akamatsu in Christensen and Delgado 1993, 139).

Communication Style

Key features of high-context Eastern cultures are indirect communication (see chapters 3 and 5) and the use of silence (see chapter 2). In a society where maintaining harmony is of utmost importance, speaking directly may cause a loss of face. The height of polite behavior, therefore, may be in leaving the most critical point unsaid. Disagreeing publicly is taboo because it destroys the cohesion of the group. People often limit their discussions to "safe subjects" and employ strategies to suppress conflict, arguments, or debate. One way to avoid the embarrassment of speaking to someone directly is to use an intermediary to deliver an unpleasant message.

Asians use a soft-spoken voice to show deference. The pacing is slower than typical American discourse, with pauses for reflective thinking before speaking. Subtle clues to the intended meaning of a remark are provided nonverbally. Sometimes what is meant is the *opposite* of what is said. For example, *maybe* or *yes* can actually mean *no*. When rejection is conveyed, it may be couched in effusively apologetic language. Many Asians feel that to say "no" directly risks hurting other people's feelings. When communicating a negative response nonverbally, they may smile, scratch their heads, or remain silent to avoid confrontation.

Facial expressions are controlled. One's face is seen as a public mask. Smiling in many Asian cultures expresses embarrassment or it may mask other emotions. Instead of a verbal response, a smile may be used to accept a compliment or an offer without seeming overly eager.

Most Asian cultures are reserved about physical contact, especially between the sexes. In several Asian cultures, touching another person's head is taboo because is believed to be the seat of the soul.

Emotional restraint is highly valued because expressing emotion is viewed as a sign of immaturity. Asians often refuse something the first and second time it is offered, because to accept immediately would seem overly eager and impolite. This may apply to food and beverages or even pain medication. While Americans tend to offer food once, assuming that a "No, thank you" is an honest response, "In traditional Asian society, to extend an invitation only once for dinner would be considered an affront, because it implies that you are not sincere" (Sue and Sue 1990, 58).

While Americans are encouraged to take credit for their talents and accomplishments, this behavior is judged negatively in many Asian cultures. The dictum against boasting is so strong in many Asian cultures that one might apologize for one's lack of knowledge, effort, or expertise even when there is clear evidence to the contrary. For example, after spending hours preparing an elaborate dinner, the host or hostess often apologizes to the guest for not serving anything special.

Asian Deaf Culture

Asian Deaf immigration patterns mirror those of other Asian American communities and lead individuals to congregate in large metropolitan areas. Although some recent Asian Deaf immigrants may struggle to simultaneously learn English and ASL, they may already be fluent in several written languages. Others might not be truly fluent in any language and may communicate in a combination of gestures as well as use oral and written communication methods. This may be because of the lack of special schools in their home country or due to parental protectiveness.

Asian Attitudes toward Deafness

Several strong beliefs in Asian culture color the way a deaf or disabled child is seen. The yin-yang balance is well known in Asia. Perfection is seen as a balance of opposing forces. An imbalance, it is believed, can create a problem such as deafness (Chough 274). A belief in karma often leads Asians to feel that a disability is their own fault. Parents may believe that something they or their ancestors did in a past life caused the disability. The concept of fatalism, however, leads them to accept their burden and the added responsibilities of caretaking. Because of the desire to conform to the group, a disabled child is often seen as a loss of face for the family. Sometimes the shame is so great that the child will be hidden away. Other families move abroad in order to obtain special services and a better education for their deaf children. Because of reliance on the authority of professionals, doctors may be the first persons consulted for a "cure" when a child is discovered to be deaf.

Asian/Pacific Island families may reject sign language due to its highly emotional use of facial expression and body language. Many Asian Deaf signers shift to a more neutral register and style when signing in an Asian context and cultural settings than when communicating with their non-Asian Deaf peers. (NMIP 5b, 25)

➤ Points for Interpreters

Gestures may be misleading. In several Asian cultures, pointing with one's finger is impolite. An open hand is used instead. To refer to oneself in American Deaf culture, one points or gestures to oneself at chest level. In certain Asian cultures, one points to one's nose instead. Our crossed fingers for good luck is an obscene gesture for Southeast Asians.

Conversely, the outstretched middle finger, which Americans consider a rude gesture, is a part of many Asian sign languages. A story related in the NMIP materials describes the shame felt by an Asian student whose interpreter laughed when she used this gesture in class. The student felt so embarrassed that she stopped participating in class out of fear of suffering future humiliation. Unfortunately, she never shared her feelings with the interpreter who caused her to lose face (38–39).

Interpreters need to become familiar with many culture-specific words and signs. As noted in chapter 3, it is now expected that interpreters use the sign that individuals from a foreign country use to refer to themselves. It is a good idea to ask a cultural consultant for the appropriate signs for countries and cities. Other important signs are the names of religions and culturally rich terms such as *saving face*. Some English words can have a culturally specific meaning. For example, *camp*, when used by a person of Japanese descent to refer to internment camps during World War II, would be more accurately signed as PRISON, not the sign glossed CAMP.

It is common for Deaf clients to ask their interpreters about their motivation for learning sign language or becoming an interpreter. "Some Asian Deaf individuals, however, have been perplexed when interpreters stated they entered the field because it was 'fun' or gave other less 'serious' answers. They were expecting a response indicating that a high level of professionalism or skill was required to be a good interpreter" (33). Students of Asian heritage who wish to become interpreters have encountered some initial resistance from their parents about their choice of occupation. In order to conform to parental ideals, they need to emphasize the serious nature of the profession, the academic preparation required, and the important benefit to the community.

African American/Black Culture

Many authors use the terms *African American* and *Black* interchangeably in order to respect the preferences of a broad range of people. These terms refer to individuals whose ancestors came from the continent of Africa, which was and is composed of a multitude of ethnic and cultural groups, languages, and traditions. Also included in this group are individuals from the islands of the West Indies, such as Barbados, Jamaica, Haiti, and Trinidad, as well as people who identify themselves as biracial or multi-racial (NMIP 3b, 2).

In our discussion of diverse cultures in the United States, one of the most striking contrasts between African Americans and other groups whose ancestors settled in the United States is that Africans were *unwilling* immigrants, having been forcibly removed from their homes and brought as slaves to the United States and other countries.

> They became a group robbed of much of their cultural identity: slaves were forced to adopt a new language and religion and were even assigned new names. Being denied access to the culture of their captors while being told they could not preserve their own culture, they attempted to forge a new one. It was a culture that, in order to survive, stressed companionship and group solidarity.... (Samovar, Porter and Stephani 1998, 114)

African American history and identity development as well racism and the economic and social disparities that exist today are complex areas of study. Unfortunately, it is not possible to do these subjects justice in this limited space. We will limit our discussion, therefore, to selected features of Black culture and its impact on language use, after which we will move on to an examination of Black Deaf culture. It is important to reemphasize that there is great diversity within Black culture, just as in the other multi-cultural groups discussed in this chapter.

Cultural Features

Even though African American/Black communities include a wide variety of ethnicities, several features are shared across these diverse groups. Among them are strong collectivist values, such as working for the welfare of the group and showing concern for others, along with individualist values such as the expression of personal style and creativity.

Style is the way individuals within a culture express themselves. Distinctive expressions of Black style pervade every aspect of daily life. Black culture embraces an open expression of one's personality through colorful dress, speech, art, dance, poetry, and behavior patterns.

Family

The extended family has been essential to the survival of African American people in the face of historical oppression. During the era of slavery, caring for one's "family" meant taking responsibility for any person of color. These values still endure. The African American family often relies on a network of relatives and close friends for emotional care and economic support and to share in raising the children.

Elders have strong roles in the family, community, and the religious arena. They pass down the oral traditions and collective stories within the family. Grandparents often take care of the children. They, in turn, are cared for at home, within the family system, when they become frail or elderly.

Discourse Style

Perhaps the one area that carries the most potential for misjudgments is the differences between European-American and African American discourse styles, including contrasts in negotiating styles, male-female interaction, argument forms, presentation styles, and turn-taking.

Anthony Aramburo, a member of the NMIP team, describes African American presentation style as "emotionally intense, dynamic, and demonstrative" (NMIP 3b, 23). There are also frequent references to scriptural passages and an interactive style of discourse termed "call and response" that began in the church and has spread to other settings (29).

"Call and response" refers to a form of back-channeling or active listening behavior. In a religious setting, the preacher supplies the call and members of the congregation provide the response by adding their voices to those of the preacher or the choir. There are unspoken rules for the timing of such responses. In chapter 11 we will compare call and response to back-channel feedback in ASL.

Conversations may seem to have more emotional intensity in Black culture because overlapping and interjections are common. Turn-taking rules are different than in mainstream American culture. "The white classroom rule is to raise your hand, be recognized by the instructor, and take a turn in the order in which you were recognized. . . . The black rule, on the other hand, is to come in when you can," which means, in effect, that the floor may go to the most assertive person (Kochman 1981, 25–26).

Certain nonverbal behaviors are also part of Black discourse style. These range "from simple facial expressions and head gyrations to 'slapping' five and full-body gyration." (Lewis 1998, 232). Eye gaze behavior in Black culture also contrasts with mainstream white expectations. While listening, whites make eye contact with the speaker about 80 percent of the time. When speaking to others, they tend to avoid eye contact about half of the time. Conversely, African American children are taught that it is polite *not* to look at an older person who is speaking to them unless they are instructed to do so. Generally, eyes are averted to show respect; however, eye contact may be more direct while speaking (Sue and Sue 55–56).

"Black English" and Code-switching

What is referred to as Black English or Black Vernacular English, "is a highly complex, rule-governed communication system. It is one of the many varieties of English, albeit one that seems to be the most highly stigmatized" (Lewis 229). Black English reflects the influences of many African languages and has been passed on through the generations, not by formal education, but by socialization. As is the case with other oppressed language varieties, it lives on in songs, stories, and everyday use. Linguists have documented many of its features.

Many Black speakers will switch to a more standard version of English when interacting with whites. Black English reinforces the strong delineation between "ingroup" and "outgroup" members in terms of language use. It may be seen as insulting if outgroup members try to use ingroup communication style without having received permission to do so.

African American/Black Deaf Culture

Signs of Interest

Signs that refer to a group of people are as culturally loaded as words people choose to describe themselves and others. Currently, there are at least two different signs in ASL to refer to "Africa" and, by derivation, "African American." There is no consensus on their use and people have strong feelings on both sides.

An older sign traces a circle around the face with an "A" handshape. According to Emmanuel Azodeh, a Deaf Nigerian, the sign comes from Africa and depicts the shape of the African continent. The newer sign for Africa commonly used in ASL also traces the shape of the African continent, but does so off to the side of the body. According to Mr. Azodeh, Deaf Nigerians in Africa do not like the new sign because it "forces viewers to end eye contact and move their eyes down to the sign, evoking feelings of someone 'looking down upon' or being ashamed of Africa or being African" (Azodeh 1994, 3). Many American Black Deaf people have a strong distaste for the older sign that circles the face and ends on the nose because to them it makes a disparaging reference to physical appearance.

There are older signs in ASL used to refer to African American people that use the "N" handshape on the nose, or circling the face and touching the nose. The NMIP materials caution that "these are very socially restricted signs" that some older signers may use them "in the same sense as the older term 'colored' but [they] are not considered appropriate for non-Black signers and interpreters to use" (NMIP 3b, 2).

Identity

Deaf people often comment on which of their several identities is the strongest. A 1989 study found that 87 percent of the black Deaf people polled identified with their Black culture first. Respondents in this study explained that they were not denying either culture, but placing them in the order of social acceptance. "Black deaf individuals believe that society views them as black first because of the high visibility of skin color. Deafness is an invisible handicap" (Aramburo 1989, 113).

The NMIP describes the African American/Black Deaf community as "a mirror of the greater African American/Black population," grappling

with the same challenges. Yet, as members of both a minority and a disability group, they experience the "double jeopardy of ... double discrimination" (NMIP 3b, 9).

Legacy of Segregated Schools

In researching the history of the African American/Black Deaf community, all roads lead to one striking fact. For more than 100 years, Black
Deaf students in at least 15 Southern states were schooled in inferior facil-
ities completely apart from their white Deaf peers. Some state schools
subdivided their campuses, maintained two sets of dormitories and two
infirmaries, employed different teachers, and even conducted separate
graduation ceremonies. Unfortunately, not many detailed accounts of this
chapter of history still exist. "A combination of shame, fear, neglect, and
ignorance have led to a massive loss of historical records from this period"
(Padden and Humphries 2005, 41, 47).

This legacy of segregated education has had far-reaching effects on the
lives of Black Deaf people. "As in the rest of society at that time, African-
American men and women often could not get the same jobs as white Deaf
men and women" (40). Black Deaf people are gaining ground today. In
addition to attending historically Black Colleges and Universities, more
Black students are attending Gallaudet University and NTID, but their
"enrollment is still considerably behind their White Deaf peers" (NMIP
3b, 16–17).

Black Deaf Clubs and Churches

Schools were not the only institutions that were segregated during the last
century. Deaf clubs, where Deaf people traditionally gathered to socialize
after work and on the weekends, were also divided into Black and white.
There was rarely any crossing over, even though the Black club and the
white club might be located only a few blocks apart. Black Deaf clubs
were important places for young people to connect with role models.
Unfortunately, many of these clubs are now gone.

With the strong religious tradition in the Black community, many min-
istries serve Black Deaf people from various denominations. Some provide special training to develop interpreters. Many skilled interpreters
began their careers in religious settings and have moved out into the
wider interpreting arena (NMIP 3b, 20).

African American/Black Variation of American Sign Language

The language used by the Black Deaf community is ASL. "Yet, variations of ASL occur when members of this community engage in conversations among themselves, as opposed to others who are outsiders" (Aramburo 119). There have been only a few studies of this Black Sign Language variation. Most have focused on different, or regional, signs. Aramburo cites three common ASL signs that have alternate "Black forms," FLIRT, SCHOOL, and BOSS, which may trace their roots to language use in the segregated schools (115–117).

Even when Black signers use the same signs in the same syntactic structures as white signers, something in their signing gives it a distinctive quality (Lewis, 233). Clearly, some of the nonverbal aspects of Black Vernacular English (facial expression, head tilts, and body movement) are carried over into the Black signing style. A larger signing space has been observed, a more dramatic style, and a certain elongated rhythm (236). "Call and response" behavior is also incorporated into Black Deaf settings, such as large meetings. It must be remembered, however, there is not just one Black signing style. Significant differences between generations of signers exist because of the transition from segregated schools to integrated programs (NMIP 3b, 26).

➤ Points for Interpreters

As previously noted, Black signers often code switch between more standard ASL and a distinctive Black variety of ASL. An interpreter voicing for a code-switching speaker should be able to match this shift in their use of Standard English and Black Vernacular English. Without mentoring from an African American interpreter, it would be difficult for a non-African American interpreter to effectively mirror the language switching choices that are purposely used to produce a certain effect on the audience. Hearing Black speakers making a presentation to a largely Black audience will also often employ the same code-switching strategy. An interpreter working from spoken to signed language must also possess the capacity to code-switch between the standard and Black variety of ASL.

Languages are living, breathing entities; they are in a constant state of change. Black Vernacular English is a vibrant example. The new vocabulary of today will soon be old. Not only do interpreters who work with the Black community need to keep up with the latest slang, but they also need to be aware that words that sound like Standard English may carry a completely different connotation in Black Vernacular English. A well-known example is the word *bad*. When pronounced with emphasis it means the opposite—good. Another example is the word *phat*, pronounced "fat," which refers not to physical weight or looks but rather to something that is desirable or someone who is wealthy.

The NMIP materials caution non-Black interpreters to be careful not to exaggerate their emotional/expressive affect when interpreting for Black speakers and signers. By trying to take on a "Black style" that does not come naturally, one may unconsciously paint a caricature of the style and people one means to emulate. The goal is to understand and be sensitive to cultural differences and interpret respectfully (NMIP 29).

Latino/Hispanic American Culture

Our discussion begins with the choice of a name for the fastest-growing minority group in the United States. The terms *Latino* and *Hispanic* are often used interchangeably, but strong feelings prevail about both of them. *Hispanic* is rejected by some because it is a bureaucratic term devised by the U.S. government. "Latino . . . is the term that persons who trace their origins to Latin America use to self-describe" (Chong 3, 2002). Most individuals from Spanish-speaking countries prefer to identify themselves by their country of origin (e.g., "I am Puerto Rican"). Latinos are a diverse group of mixed-race peoples including Mexican Americans, Spaniards, and Native Indians (Mestizos), Puerto Ricans, Central Americans, South Americans, Cubans, Dominican Republicans, and Spaniards. Given those diverse backgrounds, there is no one Hispanic appearance.

The Spanish language is a cultural bond that unites Latinos/Hispanics, although not everyone who identifies as Latino speaks Spanish. Much depends on the level of acculturation. Recent immigrants may be monolingual in Spanish, while the third or fourth generation may speak mostly English with a few words of Spanish.

The term *la raza* translates mostly closely into English as "the people" and is used to "reflect the fact that the people of Latin America are a mixture of many of the world's races, cultures, and religions—Europeans, Africans, Native Americans, Arabs, and Jews" (NMIP 6b, 3). Even though many Latinos/Hispanics have immigrated to the United States, "the majority (60 percent) of individuals of Hispanic descent living in the United States are native-born Americans" (NMIP 6b, 5).

Cultural Features

Since each Spanish-speaking country possesses its own culture, one must be careful about making generalizations. However, the following elements seem to carry strong meaning across the various borders:

"La Familia"

The family forms the central network of life in Latino/Hispanic culture. It includes a large, extended group of relations including godparents, grandparents, uncles, aunts, and cousins. Elders are respected and have important places of honor in the family structure. One is expected to take care of one's elderly parents within the family home. Children may continue to live at home after graduating from school. It is not uncommon to find several generations sharing the same house, possibly sharing bedrooms or even beds (20).

Traditional gender roles are strictly defined. The father is the protector and the provider of the family and makes many decisions as head of the household. The mother also holds a powerful role. Her responsibility is the house and the children. She is the one who negotiates with educational officials and agencies.

Because interdependence is more valued than independence, children are expected to depend on their parents. The first-born is expected to excel. The entire family may contribute in order to put the eldest child through college, with the expectation that he or she will help with the expenses of the siblings' education. When a child is discovered to have a disability, there may be a feeling that one is being punished for a sin or given a special cross to bear, but there is also a dignified acceptance because *la familia* is there for support (21).

Time Orientation

To generalize, Latinos live in the present. Those North Americans who are obsessed with time may criticize Latinos' apparent disregard for punctuality at social events. Yet from the Latino view, it is considered rude to be the first to arrive or the last to leave. In work settings, however, clock time is taken much more seriously. Although a business meeting may commence punctually, small talk about family issues will precede business matters, in order to create a feeling of mutual trust and rapport (23).

Politeness Norms

Latinos are proud of their traditional food and are pleased when an outsider accepts their offer to share a meal. It shows respect. A rejection of an invitation or food is considered extremely insulting.

Politeness is also demonstrated by the way people are addressed, including the use of formal titles (*Señor, Profesor*) and *usted*. When a stranger enters the room, everyone is introduced, beginning with the older persons. When leaving, one is expected to shake hands. Questions about the health and well-being of the family are part of the greeting and demonstrate courteousness.

In terms of body language, lowered head or eyes signify respect, not humiliation. "In general, touching shows affection. Children greet adults with a handshake. Men greet women with a *beso* (kiss) on the cheek. Men greet other men with an *abrazo* (hug) and a couple of pats on the back" (25).

Religion

"The Catholic religion often has a major influence in Hispanic groups and is a source of comfort in times of stress" (Sue and Sue 230). When Catholicism was first introduced in the New World by the Spanish Conquistadors, the indigenous people already had their own spiritual traditions, yet many were forced to convert to the new religion. Sometimes the indigenous beliefs are combined with the practices of the Catholic Church.

Medicine

Traditional medicine is an important part of the Latino culture. It may include herbal cures and trust in *cueranderos* (healers). It can also lead to intercultural conflicts. For example, outsiders may misjudge seemingly dramatic expressions of pain.

Mexican women are notorious for loud behavior during labor and delivery. It is often possible to identify a Mexican woman in labor simply from the "*aye yie yies*" emanating from her room. Although this chant can be annoying to nurses and patients alike, it is actually a form of "folk Lamaze." To repeat "*aye yie yie*" several times in succession requires long, slow, deep breaths. *"Aye yie yie"* is not just an expression of pain. It is a culturally appropriate method of relieving pain. (Galanti 94–95)

Latino/Hispanic Deaf Culture

The Latino/Hispanic Deaf population faces a "double barrier" which can be complicated by the conflicting values of the Deaf and Latino communities. John Lopez, a Deaf activist, writes that despite the "diversities within and among our Hispanic Deaf community, we ... are bonded together by the same reasons: adversity, the language we speak, and cultural values" (Lopez, 1989, 12).

Educational Concerns

Latino Deaf students face extra difficulties in school. "The academic achievement of these students is lower than their Anglo and African American peers, and they are less likely to leave school with a high-school diploma" (Gerner de Garcia in Christensen 2000, 149–150). Educators of Deaf children should be aware that language and culture are inextricably intertwined, yet the cultural needs of the Latino family are often ignored. The school may feel that hiring a Spanish interpreter for one meeting a year fulfills their obligation, yet complain that Latino parents are not sufficiently involved in their child's education.

Another reason for conflict between the family and school professionals is that they may each have different expectations regarding the role of parent and family, and the role of teacher and school (Gerner de Garcia 1993, 72). Anglo teachers of Latino students criticize parents for failing to demand their rights to obtain special services for their child and characterize the parents as "passive." The Latino parents' point of view, however, is that teachers are experts, and it would be disrespectful to challenge the plans that these experts have devised.

From a Mexican cultural perspective, the idea of sending a Deaf child to a residential school is insulting to the family. "Sending a child away is a sign of incompetence, weakness, and not behaving like a proper Mexican parent" (Ramsey in Christensen 2000, 141). It is believed that childrearing should take place in the home. Family elders may not understand the reasons for sending their grandchildren to a residential school and react with anger, feelings of shame, and heavy criticism of the parents (137–138).

Language Needs

The language needs of Latino Deaf people vary considerably. Those who immigrate may come with fluency in another sign language such as Mexican Sign Language (LSM) or Puerto Rican Sign Language (PRSL). They may prefer to communicate in written Spanish or use "home signs" that are only understood by their immediate family members. Even after having lived here for several years, many Latino Deaf people use a mixture of ASL and their first sign language. Or they may use signs from ASL while mouthing the word in Spanish. Others may prefer to communicate by lipreading Spanish, because of the strong tradition of oral education in Latin America. Unfortunately, "the language diversity of Hispanic/Latino students is [often] characterized as a 'problem' . . . rather than seeing different languages as a resource" (Gerner de Garcia 2000, 162).

A recent event epitomizes the vulnerability of this group. In 1997, it was discovered that 57 Mexican Deaf people had been lured to New York City with the promise of a good life, nice jobs, and money. The immigrants were forced to live in cramped quarters, and had to sell trinkets seven days a week on the subway. They were often beaten and molested. At the end of each day they turned over all their earnings to their bosses, who, ironically were also Deaf Hispanic Americans (Deborah Sontag 1997).

When a few of the Mexican Deaf peddlers were brave enough to go to the police station and complain, the ensuing legal process proved to be a logistical and linguistic challenge. Trilingual (English, Spanish, ASL) interpreters were recruited from all over the country. Interpreting teams were comprised of ASL interpreters, Deaf relay interpreters, spoken Spanish interpreters, consultants, and anyone who knew Mexican Sign Language. This dramatic example points up the fact that a team of interpreters with different language strengths is often the best solution.

➤ Points for Interpreters

Latinos maintain a relatively close conversational distance. You may find yourself unconsciously leaning or backing away if you feel your personal space is being crowded.

After interpreting for a Latino family you may be thanked effusively, hugged, even kissed on the cheek. Sometimes you will be given food. Try to accept graciously.

Remember that lowered eyes mean respect. If the Deaf woman you are interpreting for is speaking to someone she considers to be of a higher status and her gaze is at the floor, try to match her nonverbal behavior. Your direct eye contact could send a contradictory message.

If a Latino man is hospitalized, it would not be unusual to have many members of his family "camped out" in his room, helping to feed him (even if he is physically capable of doing so). Family members may even answer questions for him. Love and concern are shown by completely caring for otherwise independent family members who are ill.

American Indian Culture

No simple label is satisfactory for this vast group that encompasses more than 550 nations and tribes. Nations and tribes differ in language, beliefs, family structure, traditions, and organization. Each nation refers to itself by a word in its own language that means "The People" and considers itself a sovereign nation. The preferred English terms are currently "American Indian," "Alaskan Native," or, in Canada, "First Nation." Most Indians, however, refer to themselves with the name of their tribe (i.e., "I am Cherokee," or "We are of the Diné nation" [formerly called Navajo]). The term "Native American" was coined by the Department of the Interior to refer to a generic grouping of all indigenous people. Some urban Indian nations accept it, but others resent its use (a parallel to the supposedly politically correct "hearing impaired") (NMIP 4b, 2–3).

Prior to the arrival of Europeans, an estimated 5 to 30 million individuals were living on the North and South American continents. American Indians welcomed their visitors with hospitality during the "first contact," only to be repaid with betrayal, oppression, and genocide. Their population was decimated by war and disease. Their land was seized and they were forced to relocate to reservations. The federal government assumed control of Indians' schools, land, and affairs. A history of broken treaties left a legacy of mistrust and suspicion of outsiders (NMIP 6, 37; Sue and Sue 175).

No generic term in any Indian spoken or signed language includes all First Nation people. That doesn't mean, however, that the nations feel separate and disconnected from each other. On the contrary, they share many values and cooperate to achieve Pan-Indian goals (NMIP 4b, 2–3).

Shared Cultural Features

Just like the other cultures we have discussed in this chapter, the Indian population is very diverse, including their level of acculturation. "Walking in two worlds" refers to the reality of leading a bicultural life. Assimilation varies, depending on many factors. Some Indians may be monolingual in their native language and have spent their entire lives on a remote reservation. Others may have grown up in an urban setting and only recently rediscovered their native roots.

Although no two tribes display the same cultural characteristics, most Indian groups do share the common values of community, cooperation, generosity, and a deep reverence for nature. "Taking charge" in the dominant culture is synonymous with a strong, healthy personality. Conversely, Indians are taught to stay in the background and avoid attracting attention. They prefer to observe rather than interfere with others' way of being. Listening quietly and saying only the minimum is one way to respect the rights of other people (14).

Time Orientation

Indians are rooted in the present, with a deep respect for the history and traditions of past generations. They do not feel the same urgency to plan for the future as the majority culture does. Indians are not obsessed with gaining or losing time. Time is always there; it is not something that will run out. The "right time" to do something is not necessarily dictated by the clock or the calendar. It may be when the right thoughts are present. "This emphasis on the present can be frustrating to non-Indians who schedule appointments that may be broken by Indian families when events arise at the last minute" (Hammond and Meiners in Christensen and Delgado 152).

Family

Given the many different nations and clans, it is difficult to generalize about the Indian family. For most tribes, though, the extended family is crucial. It can include aunts, uncles, grandparents, and cousins. It is not unusual for children to be raised by several members of their family and reside in a variety of different households.

Elders are deeply respected members of the community because they carry knowledge, wisdom, and tradition. When they speak, they are not to be interrupted; younger members will wait until after all of the elders have spoken before they take a turn to speak, if at all (NMIP 4b, 32).

Many tribes are matriarchal societies with women taking on important roles as clanmother, warrior, farmer, or spiritual leader. However, "women's 'moontime' is considered powerful and taboos may ... [include] possible exclusion from some activities" (21).

Medicine

Most Indian nations share a spiritual view of health. Wellness is conceptualized as harmony in the body, mind, and spirit. Sometimes conflicts arise between the practices of Indian cultures and Western medicine. Dr. Lori Alvord describes her unique perspective as the first Navajo woman to become a surgeon. In her work with Indian patients, she makes what interpreters might recognize as "cultural adjustments." For example, one problem is the Navajo taboo against speaking of death for fear that talking about it will make it happen. When Anglo nurses ask their Navajo patients if their charts should be noted as "put on life-support systems" or "do not resuscitate," they are often met with silence. Well aware of the cultural taboo, Dr. Alvord approaches the question indirectly. She describes a fictitious "other person" who has to make this choice and asks the patient's opinion of what this "other" person should do. Then quietly she inquires, "And would you pick the same thing for yourself?" (Alvord and Van Pelt 1999)

Eye Gaze and Gestures

Many American Indians consider direct eye contact rude, especially between a child and an elder (Sue and Sue 179). In a group of men talking in a circle or standing side by side, the gaze is directed downward. "Deaf Indian people still rely on 'eye contact' for communication and may have taken on the Deaf Culture use of eye contact from their educational experiences and social contacts, while others may use a more indirect or peripheral use of vision to receive the interpretation" (NMIP 4b, 20).

Pointing with the index finger to refer to people is considered rude among some tribes. Indians may indicate reference with the eyes, a nod of the head, or point with the chin, nose, or with pursed lips instead (20).

Discourse Features

One of the most striking features of American Indian discourse is the use of silence. Silence is not empty space. It is time used to think carefully before replying. Turn-taking is accomplished without overlapping the previous speaker. Words have power and must be chosen carefully. There are taboos about certain topics that should not be discussed with outsiders or with members of the opposite sex (32).

American Indian Deaf Culture

The traditional ASL sign glossed as INDIAN is still preferred by the members of The Intertribal Deaf Council to the newer, more "politically correct" sign, in which an "open B" handshape rubs the back of the "S" handshape, which was derived from a few Indian signs meaning *color*, or *dirty*. It specifically refers only to the Utes, although some Deaf individuals may continue to use it. Again, it is better to refer to a specific Indian nation than to lump them all together with a generic term (2).

Indian Sign Language

In the sixteenth century, when Spanish explorers traveled across the southern plains of North America, they came upon Indians who were using signs. This intertribal sign language, known as Plains Sign Language, developed as a lingua franca between the Indian nations of the Great Plains. It is not a universal language and its use has declined. Certain tribes have their own sign languages, which may be used by both hearing and Deaf members for conversing in noisy situations or to accompany speech in storytelling and religious ceremonies (Farnell, 2005).

Current language use and literacy levels vary considerably among American Indian people. Some may use only ASL, or ASL and English; some may use a specific Indian signed or spoken language, some may use an elaborated "home sign system" or some combination of all of the above (Davis and Suppalla in Lucas 1995, 77–106).

American Indian Deaf individuals vary in their identity formation. Those who attend Deaf residential schools apart from their families may experience a lack of cultural knowledge and Deaf Indian role models. To make matters worse, some Deaf Indian children have suffered discriminatory behaviors from their fellow Deaf students and even from the school staff. For example, Donette Reins, a Muskogee Creek Deaf Indian, recounts how the other students tried to "clean off" her dark skin with abrasive cleanser and how the dorm counselor "chopped off" her long hair without asking permission (Life Experiences of Donette Reins, NMIP video 2000).

➤ Points For Interpreters

Try to educate yourself about the culture of American Indian groups in general and those in your local area. Be aware, however, that your well-intentioned questions may not always elicit useful answers, because sacred cultural and spiritual information cannot be shared with non-Indians. The best solution is to find a cultural liaison who can advise you (NMIP 4b, 35).

Adjust the pace of interpreting to allow for a pause between speakers and do not interrupt an elder.

Indians practice less physical touch than other cultures. They may "shake hands" by lightly grasping the fingers. Typical instances of physical contact that interpreters use in other settings, (i.e., hugs, shoulder rubs), may be viewed as inappropriate by traditional tribal members (20).

Female interpreters should dress conservatively, possibly with skirts or covered legs. Ask a cultural informant for specifics. If you are interpreting for traditional events, inquire discreetly if there is a "moon time" taboo.

Be aware of specialized vocabulary. For example, when voicing into English, drums are "sung" (not "played"), special dance clothing is called "regalia" (not "costume"). "Drumming" in an Indian context is signed with one hand. Learn the signs for "Elders," "powwow," "reservation," or "rez" (fingerspelled R-E-Z), and other culturally rich terms.

Traditional Indian families may not feel comfortable inviting non-Indians into their homes right away. Meetings may be held outside the home sitting on benches, on the ground, or even in the flat bed of a family truck (Hammond and Meiners 158).

When attending ceremonies such as a powwow, it is important to observe certain guidelines. Do not enter the blessed area without invitation. Maintain silence during prayers. Do not talk to or touch the dancers or their regalia. Do not pick up fallen feathers (NMIP 4b, 29–30).

.   .   .

We have briefly examined the cultural features of four groups. This is not meant to infer that these are the only four communities whose cultural practices we need to study. The image of the American cultural mix as a "salad bowl" recognizes that there are many ethnic and religious identities that make up our distinctive American mix.

In conclusion, learning about cultural groups is a lifelong endeavor whose aim is to give other people the same respect that we desire for ourselves. It may be an unattainable goal, but if we gather the individual pieces of the "jewel of wisdom" mentioned in the opening to this chapter and bring them together, there is hope and power in our collaborative efforts.

7

Culture, Change, and Technology

Cultures change. If they didn't, they wouldn't survive. The strength of a culture is reflected in the manner it adjusts and adapts to inevitable outside influences, and Deaf culture is no exception.

In this chapter, our aim is to examine the ways American Deaf culture has been affected by recent technological innovations; specifically, changes relating to communication devices. A qualification is necessary at the outset. The moment one finishes describing the current state of technology, it will undoubtedly have already changed. Trying to foresee the next advance in digital devices is like trying to predict next year's teenage slang and fashion trends. There will always be unexpected developments. Understanding that, we can begin.

In order to broaden our perspective, we will start with a brief investigation into ways technologies such as the cell phone and text paging have affected other world cultures.

New Technology and Changes in Cultures

It is known as *le portable* in French, *handy* in German, and *el movil* in Spanish. In America, the cell phone has altered many of our lives by, among other things, filling up the "dead time" spent standing in line, waiting in traffic, and walking from place to place.

Cultural differences color a variety of attitudes toward cell phone usage. In collective cultures where people are used to living close together, few complain about the volume of their neighbors' conversations or the details that are overheard. Americans, who place great value on privacy and personal space, however, would probably have a hard time tolerating the din of voices in competing conversations on street corners in

Rome or the one-sided cell phone dialogues heard throughout movie houses in Bangkok (Plant 2003).

Let us now examine in depth several instances where the use of cell phones and text paging has had dramatic effects on society. Several themes will be explored: (1) how cultures adapt to new gadgets and, in turn, adapt the devices to existing cultural habits; (2) how new technology can empower a group; and (3) how new technology has the potential to both support and erode cultural values. Finally, we will focus on developments within American Deaf culture and examine how the introduction of new technology has posed similar challenges and resulted in various adaptations.

Japanese "Thumb Tribes"

A good place to begin is Japan, where the use of cell phones and text paging, especially by the younger generation, has taken over the country on a scale that is unparalleled in the United States.

Most traditional Japanese homes are so small that there are neither private bedrooms for children nor enough room to entertain friends. The space is crowded and controlled by parents. "Texting" has given teenagers a way to assert their independence and identity, not the traditional values one associates with collectivist Japan.

The younger generation of Japanese texters, called the "thumb tribe" because of their heavy usage of pagers, utilize their new communicative freedom to create a "portable place of intimacy" as they stay in almost continuous contact with their friends (Plant 53). The home phone formerly allowed "parents to monitor and regulate their children's relationships with their peers. Texting has made it possible for young people to conduct conversations that can't be overheard" (Rheingold 2002, 4). Whether the transformation that has placed this new power literally and figuratively in the hands of Japan's younger generation will remodel other features of the Japanese cultural landscape remains to be seen.

Technology Supports Cultural Values

Instead of changing to adapt to mobile phones, many cultures make mobile phones adapt to their unique needs. For example, "In Malaysia you can now get mobiles that come with a built-in directional finder to help Muslims pray in the direction of Mecca" (Hermida 2003). In Israel, the

ultra-Orthodox Jewish community convinced one company to manu-
facture a modified handset in which potentially "corrupting influences"
such as Internet access, text messaging, and voice mail are disabled. These
phones are then given the "kosher" stamp by rabbinical authorities (Mac-
Kinnon 2005).

In Africa, where land-line phones are still unavailable to many citizens,
cell phones have become extremely popular while supporting traditional
values and societal structures. For example, storytelling and oral communication are key features in traditional African culture. "Cell phones allow
average Africans to entertain each other through conversation, which is
what Africans have always done. It's a relatively inexpensive entertainment" (Hall 2003).

African cultures' collectivist tradition of sharing also makes cell phones
accessible to many who would not otherwise be able to afford them. The
system is called SOMU, or "single-owner-multi-user," and the person
who "owns" the cell phone allows his or her friends to give out the number
and takes messages for them (Hall 2003).

Technology Erodes Traditions

Despite gains in communication access, cell phone usage may have some
unwelcome side effects. In Nigeria, for example, the practice of paying by
the minute for phone conversations has corrupted the traditional greeting
ritual into a "soulless, impersonal, and snappy form which only twenty
years ago would have been considered rude by many Nigerians" (Odunfa
2004).

In many African cultures, the polite way to greet someone, either in
person or on the phone, begins with a mandatory exchange of inquiries
after the health of each person's spouse, children, and other family members. This ritual exchange, lasting up to two minutes, was until recently
seen as a necessary courtesy. To omit it and jump right to the matter at
hand was considered quite offensive.

On costly cell phone conversations, however, courtesy is a luxury that
many Nigerians are now doing without. To economize, callers sacrifice
the traditional opening exchange of pleasantries. Like the plunk of a
pebble in a lake, innovations in technology inevitably cause far-reaching
ripples that extend beyond their point of origin. In Nigeria, this terse
greeting has spread beyond the phone. "Unfortunately, the same soulless
attitude is destroying face-to-face conversations. Hardly anyone has the

courtesy anymore to ask after your mother, your wife, your children, your health or your appetite" (Odunfa 2004).

Keeping these themes in mind, let us turn our attention to the series of inventions and adaptations that have transformed Deaf people's lives in the last 40 years.

Technology and Deaf Culture

It is ironic to consider that early in the last century, prior to the invention of the telephone, Deaf and hearing people relied equally on writing letters or the occasional telegram to communicate with friends, family, and businesses. The two groups could also enjoy going to the movies to see subtitled silent films.

The telephone, motion pictures with soundtracks, radio, television, and finally the cell phone, have driven a technological wedge between the two communities' ability to enjoy the same forms of communication and entertainment. Interestingly, those divergent paths may be converging again with the increasing use of closed captioning, fax machines, computers, e-mail, the Internet, and text pagers, which again allow both groups to enjoy popular forms of entertainment and communication.

Life after the Telephone

Life, for Deaf people, in the years after the widespread adoption of the telephone, is described in *A Phone of Our Own* by Harry G. Lang. He explains that without easy access to instant communication, Deaf people could leave nothing to chance; "we had to carefully plan visits, vacations and business transactions." Telephone calls were made thanks to the kindness of hearing neighbors or by enlisting the aid of hearing children. (Lang 2002, 1). A common feature of Deaf life was receiving surprise visits from friends who happened to be in the neighborhood, and who would be made welcome even if they had arrived at an inconvenient time. Conversely, when setting off to visit one's Deaf friends, there was always the distinct possibility that the trip would be for nothing as one would arrive to find no one at home.

Emergency situations presented even larger obstacles. Lang relates the story of a Deaf man in New Jersey who suffered a heart attack in his home in the late 1960s. "His wife frantically sought help. She rushed out of their home, screaming, but her frightened neighbors kept their doors shut. By the time she spotted a squad car on a patrol and asked the officer to make the emergency telephone call, it was too late—her husband had died" (5).

The Birth of the TTY

In 1964, Robert H. Weitbrecht, a Deaf physicist and ham radio operator, developed a device that allowed Deaf people to use the telephone in conjunction with old bulky, floor-model, teletypewriter machines. By typing on these machines, Deaf people could make calls independently.

Interestingly, when TTYs first became available for purchase in the late 1960s, Deaf people did not flock to buy them, because there were not many people to call. Eventually, the network of TTYs grew. The original TTYs were ungainly but beloved monsters whose vibrations could be felt throughout the house. Growing up in an all-Deaf household, Priscilla Moyers remembers that a phone call was a big event. When she and her siblings felt the floor shake, they would run into the room with the TTY and peer over their mother's shoulder to try and read what she was typing.

With the spread of TTYs, the habit of dropping in on friends unannounced began to change. Access to this new mode of communication ushered in a new category of etiquette, with requests such as "Please call before you come over" or "Please don't call after 9 P.M., we will be asleep."

A Need for Text Relay Services

Despite the convenience of the TTY, one problem remained. Deaf people could only call other Deaf people or the few hearing people who also had TTYs. Thus was born the relay center. It started with a few individuals who set up switchboards in their homes. A hearing person with a TTY would act as go-between for a Deaf caller who wanted to contact a hearing person. Eventually, the passage of the ADA in 1990 mandated nationwide access to text relay services (TRS) regulated by the Federal Communications Commission (FCC). Finally, Deaf people could call their doctor, inquire about job opportunities, and order delivery of a pepperoni pizza. "Telephone access made nearly *everything* possible for deaf people" (Lang 122).

Although TRS gave Deaf people the ability to call any hearing person, the process was not exactly smooth. Hearing people, receiving what may sound like a sales pitch, often hang up. If the hearing caller speaks too fast, the Communication Assistant (CA) must keep interrupting in order to slow the speaker down and catch up typing the message. The callers must cooperate and take turns speaking or typing. Conventions from TTY usage include typing or saying GA ("go ahead") every time one is finished with an utterance to let the other person know it is their turn. As Tom Holcomb points out, many Deaf people are unaware of how painfully tedious and frustrating text relay is for hearing people. Additionally, even though it may not be their primary language, Deaf people must conduct their TTY conversations in English. For some people who are not comfortable with English, this can be a real struggle, especially as there is no visual feedback from facial expression or body language. Tom adds that Deaf people may also not realize the impact of their poor English usage on hearing people's perception of them.

Television Becomes Accessible

Even before closed captioning was added to television shows to make them accessible to Deaf viewers, many Deaf families had TV sets in their homes. As CODAs tell it, their Deaf parents were hungry for news and entertainment and often (even nightly) requested their hearing children to interpret these shows for them. For example, one CODA remembers when she was a young teenager and shared the emotional experience of watching the weeklong *Roots* miniseries with her mother by sitting in front of the TV set interpreting for her. Her mother was so involved in the story that she went to her job at the post office an hour late every night, but during her dinner break she regaled her Deaf coworkers by repeating the details of the story she had just seen, thanks to her daughter (Millie Hursin, personal communication).

While TTYs enabled Deaf people to contact hearing individuals, the closed-captioned television programs that began to emerge in the 1970s allowed them a wider connection with the world around them. Two Deaf researchers, in a 1994 article, wrote "Captioning has had profound social, political, educational, and cultural impacts, both positively and negatively" (Schragle and Bateman 1994, 101). On the positive side, they report that Deaf people "have become more aware of current issues" and developed increased political activism (101–102).

On the negative side, however, the authors feel that "captioning has contributed to greater isolation of many within the deaf community." They describe how prior to the availability of captioned TV, "deaf people congregated at centers or clubs to find out the latest news and events and to share their thoughts and opinions. This reliance on each other for information promoted social contacts" (102).

Movies

"During the early silent years of film, deaf persons sat in movie house audiences everywhere in the United States and participated, on a comparatively equal basis, with their hearing peers, as dramas, comedies, and the news unfolded on the theater screen" (Schuchman 1988, 21). This "golden era" came to an abrupt halt at the end of the Roaring Twenties. After the introduction of sound in motion pictures, Deaf people's movie-going options were severely limited until a 1956 law set up Captioned Films for the Deaf. The captioned movies, loaned out and sent around the country for weekly showings, were one of the biggest draws at Deaf clubs for many years. (Van Cleve 1987,v. 2, 248).

Nowadays, most Deaf movie buffs must wait until the latest blockbuster comes out on captioned DVDs for home rental or purchase. Selected movie theaters offer special screenings of current movie releases with open captions. And a growing number of cinemas offer a "rear window captioning system" in which Deaf and hard-of-hearing patrons borrow special reflectors that attach to the armrests of their seats. This device enables them to view the captions that are projected (in reverse) on the back wall of the theater. New technology will probably introduce more ways for Deaf and hard-of-hearing movie patrons to again enjoy a scary thriller or a romantic comedy alongside their hearing friends and family.

Has Technology Led to the Demise of Deaf Clubs?

Popular sentiment blames technology for the dramatic decline in Deaf clubs, once the mainstay of the Deaf community. Matthew Moore and Linda Levitan, authors of the third edition of *For Hearing People Only*, explain that "after closed-captioned TV removed the main barriers to the nation's favorite information and entertainment medium, and after captioned home videos began making their way onto the market, more Deaf people became less inclined to go to the clubs, preferring to stay home and get their news and entertainment there." They conclude that, "... the upsurge in accessible mass media had led to the downfall of the club"

(353). This viewpoint is echoed in a recent newspaper article in Florida, entitled "Deaf Culture Fades." Members of the Orlando Deaf community sadly acknowledge that the few remaining Deaf clubs seem to attract only older community members, while the younger Deaf generation prefers to stay in touch by e-mail, text messaging, and through Internet chat rooms. "There is a big fear that we are going to lose deaf culture because of technology" (Kunerth 2005).

Interestingly, in their new book, *Inside Deaf Culture*, Carol Padden and Tom Humphries refute the widespread assumption that the disappearance of Deaf clubs is due to technological innovations. Even though the timing of the emergence of technology and the decline of the clubs seems to link the two trends, Padden and Humphries find this argument flawed. "The Deaf club was on the wane by the time most of this modern technology became available." Instead, Padden and Humphries offer an alternative explanation, citing "powerful shifts in Deaf people's work lives leading to the growth of a Deaf middle class" and a subsequent move to the suburbs (87).

Whether it is due to the emergence of accessible technology or a Deaf middle class, the image of the traditional Deaf club as a building where a variety of Deaf people gather to play bingo and cards, watch captioned movies, enjoy skits, and exchange news may now exist mostly in nostalgic memories. The majority of Deaf people have not, however, retreated to live isolated lives in front of their TVs and computers. In fact, they are enjoying a new mainstream American luxury—choice. Instead of a one-size-fits-all club, there are now a multitude of venues that cater to individual tastes and interests. Deaf sporting events and athletic organizations still draw many followers. Deaf churches also serve their traditional function as gathering places. Additionally, with the rise of Deaf professionals in many occupations, Deaf ASL teachers, rehabilitation counselors, and computer programmers now all have their own associations and meetings. "The Deaf middle class [has] turned to more professional affiliations, identifying themselves increasingly by job and profession" (95). Newer events are "Deaf chat nights" at local coffeehouses, "Deaf pizza nights," or specialized meeting places, such as a bar that has a Gay Deaf following. With the increase in awareness and interest in sign language from the hearing majority, it could be that Deaf people feel more comfortable holding some of their events out in public, instead of in the old, protected Deaf club.

Text Pagers

What started out as a way for corporate travelers to keep in touch with the office has become a godsend for Deaf people. The size of a deck of cards, pagers take the gamble out of being away from home. The most basic devices send and receive e-mail messages. Some models can receive news and traffic reports, have Internet access, and connect to a relay operator or leave a synthesized voice message. Besides offering instant communication with family and friends, text pagers can get you out of a jam. Before the advent of pagers, without access to public phones or cell phones, Deaf people were stuck incommunicado when a car broke down, a flight was delayed, or a friend did not show up at the expected time. Tom Holcomb recalls that he used to keep in his memory all the locations of his Deaf friends' homes as well as public pay phones equipped with TTYs. In the event that his car broke down or he needed help, he could go to the nearest TTY. Now that he carries a pager, these feats of memory are no longer necessary. Not only has the pager revolutionized communication access for Deaf people, it has also remodeled the rules of politeness in Deaf culture.

New Rules of Politeness

When text pagers arrived on the scene in the late 1990s, they challenged one of the most basic tenets of Deaf culture: the primacy of face-to-face interactions. Deaf people found themselves pulled in opposite directions by competing values operating simultaneously. I remember observing my Deaf friends in conversation with each other. Suddenly, someone would tense up as she felt the pager clipped to her waist vibrate. What to do? Stay focused on the live conversation, or find out what new information was coming in? It seemed an impossible choice. Priscilla describes her impatience with her Deaf mother, who in the early days would read every text message in its entirety as soon as it came in. "We couldn't have a normal conversation; her head kept dipping down to read an incoming message; she couldn't help herself," sighs Priscilla. Daniel Langholtz likens the early heady days of text pagers to being in a new romantic relationship. "We were lovesick, totally consumed with our new companion, it was out of perspective" (personal communication).

For years, Deaf people had been accusing their hearing friends of behaving rudely, always answering their cell phones as soon as they rang, for yakking away and ignoring their Deaf friends standing right in front of them. Soon they were guilty of the same crime. Moving from the impolite to the dangerous, hearing people are not the only ones tempted to converse while driving. Just as blabbing on a cell phone distracts hearing drivers, precariously holding a pager atop the steering wheel and typing out a message with the thumbs while shifting one's eye gaze and attention is formidable, if not foolhardy.

Since text pagers have been around for a few years, the all-consuming infatuation that Dan Langholtz described has begun to mellow out. Perspective and politeness are once again surfacing. In one-on-one conversations, there might be some negotiation at the beginning. Will the pagers be on or off? Will they be laid on the table, left in the purse, or locked in the car? It is more polite to let friends know ahead of time when one is expecting an important or emergency call. If someone's pager vibrates when in a conversation with friends, it is polite to ask permission before answering it. On the other hand, as an example of rudeness, Dan cites a meeting where one of the principal participants repeatedly checked his pager, then belatedly returned his attention to the meeting, asking, "What did I miss?"

Different situations have different protocols. In a large lecture hall, it might be acceptable to surreptitiously glance down at an incoming message. At a workshop or smaller gathering, where the Deaf presenter depends on eye contact and responsive back-channeling to modulate his or her presentation, it is terribly distracting to see participants' heads bobbing up and down as they continually glance at their pagers. At some Deaf events, there may be a short announcement at the outset to remind audience members to refrain from using their pagers until the break. Then, when the break is announced, with the intensity of smokers rushing outside for a cigarette, people hurry to check their messages. Of course, one can always retreat to the bathroom to use a pager without being rude to the presenters.

Web Cameras and Video Relay

Although TTYs, e-mail, and text pagers constituted a big step forward in communication access for Deaf people, there was one drawback; the language used to communicate was always English. Finally, advances in broadband (high-speed) Internet technology made possible a huge revolutionary leap forward: real-time communication in ASL. At the time of this writing, one uses either a special videophone with the TV set or a web camera and PC hookup. If both parties have this capability, conversations are almost like being in the same room. Deaf people describe the joy of making calls using ASL, complete with facial expressions, to show emotions, tone, and meaning. Sitting comfortably in their living rooms, they can have long conversations with friends all over the country. There is no going back now and no way that the expressiveness of ASL can ever be equaled by typed English, even with smiley face icons.

If a Deaf person with a videophone or webcam wants to speak to a hearing person, there is also a new kind of relay. In video relay service (VRS), a sign language interpreter takes the place of the text typing relay operator. Wearing a headset to communicate with the hearing caller, the interpreter and Deaf caller can see each other on a TV or computer screen. Deaf callers delight in the clarity and comfort of using ASL on their relay calls, especially compared to the slow pace and misunderstandings that were common to TRS relay calls. Hearing consumers also appreciate VRS for sounding much more like a natural phone conversation, without the awkward pauses and stiff "go aheads" that characterize TRS.

Recall the earlier description of changing etiquette in Nigerian cell phone calls. There is a similar phenomenon occurring in Deaf culture. Ironically, the new interpreting environment of VRS is now operating under the older conduit model of interpreting. This is partly due to the fact that the FCC views VRS as another form of text relay: in essence, a mechanical process of taking dictation. Sign language interpreters, conversely, tend to view their work as a cognitively discriminating process of interpreting between languages and cultures.

Additionally, the current fee structure for VRS providers only reimburses them for minutes when the caller is connected to the person being called. That means that VRS interpreters are strongly encouraged to connect the Deaf caller to the hearing party immediately, foregoing the traditional "warm-up chat" that occurs in community interpreting situations. Interpreters identify themselves only by number and are prohibited from disclosing any personal information, even the state they are located in. Initially it was difficult for many Deaf callers, as well as interpreters, to accept this new colder, more businesslike way of relating. After only a few months, however, it seems most Deaf callers adapted to the situation and no longer try to initiate the kind of chat that is common when meeting a new interpreter face-to-face.

There is currently one aspect of VRS that some Deaf people do find rude. It involves the use of what is known as "the privacy screen." Certain VRS providers employ a technology that allows interpreters to activate a barrier that covers the screen for long hold times. Tom Holcomb explains that many Deaf people feel it is a visual equivalent of slamming a door in their face, as it cuts off all information access to the Deaf caller. Whether the new impersonal relationship between Deaf callers and VRS interpreters will spread to community interpreting remains to be seen.

Thus far we have looked at video relay from the Deaf consumers' viewpoint. Although it is a welcome new twist in communication access for Deaf people, it has been more like a giant twister in its far-reaching effects on the interpreting field. We will discuss video relay in depth from the interpreter's perspective in chapter 12.

Common Themes in Cultural Change

Delving into the history of technological change in Deaf culture has brought to the surface similar themes to those found in our brief survey of world cultures. Although technological innovation has allowed easier communication and accessibility to entertainment, certain cultural traditions are disappearing. VRS has introduced a quicker, but less personal, way to obtain interpreting services. Without a crystal ball, it is hard to predict the future impact on other cultural traditions. Will the traditional reconfirmation of appointment details disappear with the ease of texting friends when a plan goes awry? Will long "deaf good-byes" fade away as the spread of videophones allows friends to keep in closer contact? How will Deaf culture change as new inventions give birth to new rules of politeness?

There is another by-product of all this new innovation. Deaf people and hearing people have more in common than ever before, as they both make use of the latest technology. Whatever the future holds, Deaf culture, like a supple branch in a high wind, is strong and flexible enough to adapt to innovations.

PART TWO

Practical Applications

8

The Impact of Cultural Differences on Interpreting Situations

If you travel to a new country and stay there long enough, you will probably go through three stages of acculturation. Stage one we may call *confusion*. The language you hear is a jumble of sounds. The behavior of others might seem arbitrary. Sometimes people bow to you; at other times they don't. A policeman shoos you off the grassy lawn in a park, while dogs are welcomed in restaurants. You think you are being polite by bringing your hostess flowers, yet when she sees they are yellow, she can barely hide her dismay. It all makes little sense.

Stage two we may call *delayed understanding*. If you watch what goes on around you carefully, begin to converse in the language, and have a few friends of whom you can ask questions, things start to become a little clearer. Yet it may only be after an embarrassing moment or two that you belatedly figure out what went wrong. You arrived too early or too late. You brought a gift when you should not have or failed to bring one when you should have. You used the polite form of address when the familiar was appropriate or vice versa. Most of the time no one informs you directly of your mistake, but you grow sensitive to a raised eyebrow, a sharp intake of breath, a muffled giggle. Slowly, slowly, the pieces begin to fit together.

By stage three, you have seen the same transactions repeated so many times that you have now become capable of *prediction!* You know what behavior is expected in a range of situations and can act accordingly. These small successes mean a lot. You feel a thrill of accomplishment when you go to the bakery and actually leave with the precise item you had planned to buy. Your feeling of pride is increased when the baker's facial expression informs you that you used the appropriate greeting to the people in the store. Now you are even able to anticipate when your ingrained values are likely to clash with those of the locals, so you can prepare yourself mentally beforehand.

As sign language interpreters, we face a similar challenge. Since the majority of us learned ASL as adults, we went through the same three stages as the foreign traveler described above when we entered the Deaf community. Our job now, however, is to be bicultural mediators, so we had better operate as often as possible on a stage three—prediction—basis, foreseeing the inevitable cross-cultural clashes that lie in wait. If we are still in stage two—delayed understanding—we won't be able to do anything except commiserate with our Deaf or hearing consumers over the rudeness of the other.

With the goal of prediction in mind, let me offer the following scenarios. The following are examples of culturally influenced miscommunications. In order to focus on the points of cultural difference, I will not attempt to represent the exact signs used by the Deaf consumers either by gloss or by any written version of ASL. For the sake of flow, I am assuming that an interpreter was present and translated the statements back and forth in a literal manner without making any cultural adjustments. They take place in settings familiar to most interpreters: a doctor's office, a college, and a workplace. I will describe a few common exchanges we are likely to encounter. I am sure that you will be able to add your own experiences to the list. So much the better! The more thoroughly we anticipate the cultural misunderstandings that are likely to come our way, the more successfully we can plan our strategies for dealing with them.

THE MEDICAL APPOINTMENT

Scenario 1

Hearing Doctor: Hi. How are you?

The doctor is probably expecting a general introductory statement grounded in the present. Perhaps something like, "Not too well. The last few mornings, I've been feeling quite dizzy." Then it's up to the doctor to further question the patient about what led up to the current state of affairs.

Deaf Patient: Well, that first pill you gave me last year was awful, made me itch all over, then the blue one made my headache worse, and this one made me feel dizzy in the morning. . . .

Deaf patients often begin their discussion with the doctor by relating their relevant medical history starting at whatever point they consider to be the beginning, probably to give the doctor enough context with which to view the present situation. In ASL discourse the present moment does not hang isolated in space but exists on a timeline connecting past, present, and future. Depending on how far back the narrative is started, the doctor may become impatient waiting for the patient to get to the point.

Scenario 2

Hearing Pediatrician: I'm sorry, I have some bad news. Our test results show that your baby is deaf.

Deaf Mother: Hurray!!!

This scenario is just one example of the numerous misconceptions that hearing people hold about deafness and Deaf people. Many hearing people see deafness as an affliction. A significant number of Deaf people, on the other hand, are proud to be Deaf and would not change it even if they had the choice. So while the doctor in this example may pity the Deaf woman for having a child "with the same condition," the Deaf mother feels happy at the thought that her child will be a continuation of her family and culture.

Scenario 3

Hearing Doctor: How many hours of exercise do you get a week?

The doctor is expecting the answer to come in the form of a number and assumes the patient will do the necessary mental calculations and come up with an average estimate.

Deaf Patient: Well, Monday I went bowling, Tuesday I was sick, Wednesday I was supposed to play softball, but I had to help my friend John with his car, Thursday . . .

Again the answer takes the form of a chronological narrative and includes more specific details than the doctor wants to hear. The Deaf patient might very well calculate the hours for this particular week after having finished his recitation, but the doctor will probably interrupt him out of frustration first.

Hearing Doctor: Wait a minute, didn't you understand my question?

Deaf Patient: (thinks) Why doesn't he let me explain?

Scenario 4

Deaf Patient: My friend told me she has glaucoma too and she used a blue bottle of drops that made her vision blurry, but then she got a red bottle of drops that made her eyes feel better. . . .

As noted in chapter 3, the peer group often acts as the primary source of information as well as the authority to be trusted.

Hearing Doctor: Never mind about your friend.

The doctor tends to view each patient as an individual and he or she may be concerned about the danger of a patient's using someone else's medication, even if his or her medical condition had the same diagnosis. Discounting the patient's concerns, however, conveys an attitude of disrespect.

EDUCATIONAL SETTINGS

The following scenarios take place in a college professor's office.

Scenario 1

Hearing College Professor: Tell me, which high school did you attend?

Deaf Student: I attended the State Residential School for the Deaf in Pleasantville.

To many Deaf people, the state residential school is a focus for fond memories and positive feelings. It is the place where they may have first acquired sign language, developed a sense of Deaf culture, found a community of Deaf people who held similar values and who could act as role models, experienced a feeling of identity and belonging, and made lasting friends and contacts.

Hearing Professor: Ohhhhh, I see . . .

To most hearing people, the idea of a state residential school conjures up a whole different set of images, more like being in a mental institution—remote, cold, harsh, impersonal, a depressing place where children are forced to live away from their parents.

Scenario 2

Hearing College Professor: If you did not understand this key concept when we first discussed it in class weeks ago, why did you wait so long to tell me about it?

To overgeneralize: Americans are impatient. If we don't understand something, we want clarification *now*! We feel we have a right to understand and the assertiveness to ask for an explanation immediately. We may even blame the teacher or professor for not being clear in the first place. As opposed to many other cultures, we feel no shame in admitting we don't know something. In fact we respect people, even those in positions of authority, who honestly admit their ignorance of a certain word or concept. The professor assumes that the Deaf student holds the same set of values as the majority of American students and therefore should, from the professor's perspective, have been more aggressive in seeking clarification earlier on.

Deaf Student: Well . . .

There are many possible reasons why the student did not promptly bring his or her confusion to the teacher's attention, including feeling uncertain or embarrassed about admitting that he or she did not understand something, having a different time frame for needing or desiring to obtain clarity, feeling less uncomfortable with ambiguity, or pursuing other avenues to resolve confusion. Perhaps Deaf people are more accustomed to not understanding everything because of the many linguistically inaccessible situations in which they find themselves. They also may have different ways of clearing up confusion: waiting to see if the information becomes clear over time, getting notes from another student, checking with a tutor, learning on their own through printed materials, checking the Internet, or asking a friend for clarification.

Scenario 3

Hearing Professor: I am glad you came in to discuss your paper. Hmmm . . . your choice of topic is fine, you have a few good examples . . . but I do have some concerns about your thesis. . . . I'm not sure it is strong enough to support a paper of this length.

The professor will organize his or her comments in this feedback session using the common American "sandwich approach." In this technique, one introduces and concludes one's critical remarks with positive statements that are supposed to make the negative comments sandwiched between them easier for the recipient to swallow. In this first comment, the professor, after making a couple of positive comments, pinpoints a major fault of the paper: if the thesis is not strong enough to support the rest of the paper, the entire essay will fail. The professor assumes that the student will easily detect the "meat" of his crucial criticism underneath the faint praise in his opening "slice."

Deaf Student: You mean, make the thesis statement longer?

The student is unsure of where he or she stands. Deaf culture is more direct and one may very well start off a discussion with a precise description of what needs to be changed. Also, the value of starting a discussion with a broad introductory statement is not always shared in the structure of Deaf discourse.

Hearing Professor: Well . . . that certainly is one option, but I would really like to see some restructuring. So play around with the thesis statement and let it inform the rest of your paper. Oh, and you need to clean up your punctuation.

The first statement is an extremely subtle way of saying that it takes more to improve a thesis than just making it longer. "Play around with the thesis" is a vague but ominous statement that only hints at the possibility that the entire paper may have to be redone.

Deaf Student: Oh, the punctuation, yes, I know I have trouble with commas and semicolons. Sure, I will work on that. So you think the rest of the paper is okay?

The student finds it helpful to hear a concrete example at last (this one regarding punctuation) but is still unsure if the professor's basic take on the paper is positive or negative.

Hearing Professor: Uh . . . let's just say it's on the right track. Tackle these things I've mentioned and I'm sure your paper will be fine.

The second positive "slice" of the feedback sandwich.

Deaf Student: (to interpreter after professor has left) Whew! I'm relieved! He thinks my paper will be fine.

The student seems to be leaving with a very different feeling about the paper than the professor thinks he or she has communicated.

THE JOB INTERVIEW

Scenario 1

Hearing Interviewer: Why do you want this job?

Although this seems like a simple, straightforward question, it is all part of the game we play when we participate in a job interview. Employers are not necessarily looking for honest answers, but they do expect applicants to try to present themselves in the best possible light. Ideally, applicants are expected to compliment the employer while describing their own abilities and virtues. For example, "I believe that this company, with its deep commitment to saving endangered animals, would give me the opportunity to use my secretarial skills to benefit our natural world."

Deaf Applicant: I need the money and you have dental insurance. I have to get a couple of crowns.

Deaf applicants may not be aware of the rules of the game. Of course we all want a job for the salary and benefits we would receive, but in a typical job interview, no one would admit that up front. The interviewer's seemingly direct question elicits this honest, direct answer, which is not at all what he or she is expecting.

Scenario 2

Hearing Interviewer: Why do you feel you are the best-qualified candidate for this position?

The interviewer is expecting the answer to be in "outline form" (i.e., introduction, supporting examples, summary). Also, the interviewer is not only interested in a recitation of the facts but is also waiting for the interviewee to present a compelling argument about why he or she would be the best choice to fill the vacancy.

Deaf Applicant: Well, my first job was as a secretary, my second job was as a claims adjuster, and my third job was as a supervisor.

The Deaf person answers in time-sequential narrative form, assuming that the sum of the details is sufficient and does not need to be elaborated upon. Even though the job history demonstrates advancement and increasing responsibilities, the applicant fails to highlight these important features, thus missing an opportunity to "sell" him- or herself to the prospective employer.

Scenario 3

Hearing Interviewer: Do you have any experience with the XYZ software?

Deaf Applicant: No. None at all.

A direct, honest, negative response will not win many points in a job interview. Applicants are expected to try to turn any question into a chance to laud themselves. The interviewer will be surprised if the applicant does not attempt to dress up a negative answer, as in the following response: "Not with the XYZ software specifically, but I do have five years' experience with the ABC software, which, I believe, is quite similar. And I am sure I could pick it up very easily. I'm a fast learner."

Scenario 4

Hearing Interviewer: Since I just asked you about your strengths, I need to ask also about your weaknesses. What are some of them as they relate to this job?

The classic trick question. The employer does not expect a full disclosure of the applicant's shortcomings, foibles, and bad habits. Instead, he or she wants to see how the applicant can turn this tough question into another positive statement.

Deaf Applicant: Well, I guess I haven't used that accounting software before, and my last accounting class was ten years ago in college, and sometimes it takes me a little while to catch on to a new program. . . . Is that what you mean?

Advice commonly given to job seekers encountering this question is to cite a positive trait in disguise. Two examples of traditional answers to the classic trick question are these: (1) I get so wrapped up in my work that sometimes I forget to take a break or (2) I tend to expect everyone to work as hard as I do. If the Deaf applicants are not aware that they are participating in the "job interview game" with all the rules this implies, it is not surprising that they answer the question literally.

In chapter 10 we will examine our role as interpreters/bicultural mediators and the scope of our responsibility in relation to cultural differences such as those above. In chapter 11 we will consider some techniques to help us deal with these cultural contradictions. This would be a good place, however, to analyze a distinction exemplified in some of the previous scenarios. Let us call it a cultural set of assumptions.

Cultural Sets of Assumptions

Cultural differences that manifest themselves in interpreting situations can be broadly divided into two categories, form and content. In interpreting with a focus on form, we adjust for differences such as active versus passive voice, amount of detail, and general versus specific statements. These challenges certainly warrant much discussion and preparation. At this point, however, I would like to focus on the second category, content, which involves the much more complex factor of cultural sets of assumptions.

This content factor comes in two varieties. The first relates to unspoken, yet pervasive, cultural values or presuppositions (i.e., the importance of the group or the preciousness of time); the second involves assumed cultural knowledge of sets of rules that govern certain types of transactions.

An example of a conflict regarding cultural presuppositions was illustrated in Medical Scenario 2, when the Deaf mother expressed her joy at the thought of having a Deaf child. The doctor's reaction would probably have been surprise or disbelief, because he saw the situation through a different set of assumptions regarding what it means to be deaf. In order for the doctor to truly understand her "Hurray," he would have to be willing to give up his unenlightened view of deafness and learn to understand this woman's set of feelings, assumptions, and beliefs. The only way for this to happen would be if the doctor entered the conversation with a curious and open mind. We hope for this to happen, although we know from experience that all too often it does not.

Similarly, in the first educational scenario, the teacher did not understand the feelings of loyalty, love, and cultural connection that the Deaf student associated with the mention of residential school.

The job interview, as a whole, is an excellent example of the second content factor, in the implicit "rules of the game" that all American job seekers are expected to know.

The Cultural Set of Assumptions in Job Interviews

In contrast with most medical, educational, and other business situations, which vary with each encounter (although they contain certain repetitive elements and routines), almost all job interviews in mainstream American culture follow the same basic pattern and have definite underlying cultural precepts. Usually these conventions are not formally taught in high school or college. If we grew up in the United States, we generally absorbed them through books, TV, movies, or in discussion with others. There are many books and workshops available, however, on how to interview, for people who may not have had much formal education or who wish to practice these techniques so they can hone their job-seeking skills and present themselves to their best advantage.

So what are the rules of the job interview game? In poker, we learn that our advantage is not in the strength of the cards we actually hold in our hand, but in what we can make our opponent think we have through bluffing. Similarly, in a job interview, the point is not to recount our previous positions, education, or skills but to present ourselves in a positive way so as to convince the employer to hire us. (This may or may not necessitate bluffing.) "Positive" seems to be the key word in interviewing well, according to the authors of *Interview for Success*, who use the word in almost every piece of advice they offer (e.g., "Turn what appears to be a negative into a positive." "Use positive form. This means avoiding negatives by presenting yourself in as positive a light as possible." "Present your strengths, skills and accomplishments in a positive way." "Always phrase your answers to questions in a positive manner") (Krannich and Krannich 1982, 87, 119, 121, 123).

While playing Scrabble, good players do not volunteer information about their position that would disclose their weaknesses (e.g., "Darn! I've got all vowels"). Similarly, in job interviewing a cardinal rule is not to disclose any negative information that has not been specifically asked for. Or in the words of the author of *Job Interviews for Dummies*, "Never should the unnecessary be volunteered by the unwary for the unforgetting" (Kennedy 1996, 68).

The job interview is like a game of chess; it begins and ends almost formally with moves chosen from very limited sets of possibilities. The question with which it often begins, "Did you have any trouble finding our office?" is offered as an icebreaker and assumes a short neutral or positive response. It is *not* an invitation to expound on the terrible traffic or lack of available parking. Similarly, the last query the interviewer often poses, "Do you have any questions?" is not an open-ended request to satisfy one's curiosity about the company's quirks or inquire about irrelevant topics, but one last opportunity to sell oneself.

That job interviews are routinely conducted according to a set of procedures not unlike those that govern football, checkers, or Monopoly can be inferred from this quote from *Interview for Success:*

> Like it or not, employers play by these rules. Once you know the rules, you at least can make a conscious choice whether or not you want to play. If you decide to play, you will stand a better chance of winning by using the often-unwritten rules to your advantage. (Krannich and Krannich 95)

The Game Has Different Rules in Other Cultures

Naturally, the rules of job interviews vary in other cultures. In Japan, for example, interviewees are not supposed to brag about themselves. When asked why they are applying for the position, the appropriate response, after complimenting what the company has given to society, is to state, "I hope I can humbly make my contribution to this company." As the saying goes in Japan, "An able eagle hides its claws."

Similarly, Yao Wei in his essay "The Importance of Being KEQI [modest, humble]" describes Chinese immigrants' difficulties with the assertiveness required in American job interviews. When asked to show his woodworking abilities at a job interview, an accomplished Chinese carpenter may downplay his talents by saying, "How dare I be so indiscreet as to demonstrate my crude skills in front of a master of the trade like you?" If the employer persists in his request, the carpenter would probably respond: "If you really insist, I'll try to make a table. Please don't laugh at my crude work." Finally the carpenter may put the final touches on a "beautiful piece of art in the shape of a table" (Wei 1983, 72–74).

In the essay "Performance and Ethnic Style in Job Interviews," the authors, F. Niyi Akinnaso and Cheryl Seabrook Ajirotutu (1982), describe the job interview "as an interrogative encounter between someone who has the right or privilege to know and another in a less powerful position who is obliged to respond . . ." (119–20). The interviewer uses his or her power to start the interaction, introduce new topics, change the topic, and terminate the conversation. However, "miscommunication and negative evaluation often arise when participants do not share the same cultural and linguistic background. . . ." (124). The authors stress the importance of discovering underlying patterns of expected responses. One of the most important challenges for the interviewee is that the interview questions

> are mostly indirect, relying upon the interviewee's ability to infer the type of answer wanted . . . The interviewee's ability to go beyond the surface, pick the relevant cues, infer the intended meaning, and effectively negotiate an acceptable relationship between questions and responses is an important measure of his/her success. (127)

In the job interview scenarios described earlier in this chapter, we saw that Deaf applicants, not versed in the unwritten rules of the American job interview game, repeatedly violated the interviewer's cultural expectations, thereby not presenting themselves to their best advantage, though they may have been eminently qualified for the position. I do not mean to imply, however, that Deaf people never interview well. Of course they do, and they also get hired for many jobs in the hearing world regardless of the fact that they may follow a different set of cultural rules. It is true, however, that Deaf people as a group are underemployed (Schein and Delk 1974; Crammate 1987; Jacobs 1989). I would posit that this results not only from discrimination, fear, and hearing people's lack of information but also from a lack of knowledge on the part of some Deaf people about the cultural set of the job interview. One place to alleviate this lack of information would be in school, where ideally after studying their own Deaf culture in depth, a class in hearing culture, as a contrast culture, should be offered, including a unit on "Cultural Assumptions in a Hearing American Job Interview." I am pleased to report that this idea seems to be catching on in several schools. Let us hope that this enlightened trend will continue.

Dealing with Cultural Sets of Assumptions

While interpreting job interviews or other situations rich in cultural sets of assumptions, can we as interpreters make up for our clients' lack of knowledge of the cultural rules of the game? Even if we believe it is our responsibility to do so, it poses quite a challenge, especially when the underlying meaning of a comment is diametrically opposed to its surface form, or if the point of the whole exchange is so connected to the cultural value system that one cannot separate an utterance from the beliefs that have necessitated it. We could argue that American job interviews simply exemplify many features of American culture: one sells oneself like our advertisements sell soap and soda pop, by hyperbole. The incessant positivity endemic to these interviews is also akin to our national optimism, but is it our responsibility to explain the whole culture while interpreting?

An example of a cultural assumption from another country may help to clarify this idea. When I asked a Japanese/English interpreter what he felt was his responsibility in the face of major cultural differences, he gave me this example. He had interpreted for an American businessman who presented an offer to a Japanese businessman in Japan. At the end of the discussion, the Japanese businessman's closing statement was, "We will consider your proposal with a positive attitude." "Of course that meant no," the interpreter confided to me. I asked the interpreter if he had conveyed that underlying meaning to the American businessman in his translation. "Oh no," he replied. "If an American comes to do business in Japan, he had better learn certain basic things about Japanese culture first, such as the fact that we say no indirectly."

Speaking on the Telephone Has Its Own Cultural Set of Assumptions

With the spread of Video Relay Services (VRS), we are becoming increasingly sensitized to the fact that telephone conversations are governed by a wide range of unspoken cultural rules. These deal with appropriate greetings, lengths of silences permitted, amount of detail expected, turn-taking mechanisms, avoiding gaps and overlap, and polite ways to end calls. We will examine these conventions in greater depth in chapter 12.

How have we hearing people learned all the rules, procedures, and etiquette for conversing on the telephone? We have never taken a class in it, so we probably pick it up as part of the culture. Telephone protocol varies, of course, in different countries, sometimes to the amusement or consternation of unsuspecting callers. In Germany, for example, one answers the phone by identifying oneself, usually by last name only: "Schmidt here." The caller then invariably identifies him- or herself before asking to speak to someone. I know several Germans who have lived in the United States for many years but still find it extremely rude that in this country callers do not feel obligated to identify themselves, but immediately ask, "Hi, is

Jane there?" In French (and in ASL), the appropriate way to give out a phone number is with double digits (e.g., "Twenty-five, fourteen, seventy-nine" not "two five one four seven nine.")

Certain cultural rules are relatively easy to pick up. If we lived in Germany, for example, we could quickly learn to identify ourselves by name when answering the phone, instead of saying "hello." Learning from repeated encounters with automated menu systems, many Deaf users of VRS now give the interpreter a preview of their account number so as to expedite calls to financial institutions. On the other hand, many of the complex conventions of telephone conversation are based totally on sound. Could we even explain that in such and such a situation, it will take three seconds of silence to try the caller's patience, while in another situation one second is the polite limit?

Cultural Sets of Assumptions in Deaf Culture

We began our discussion of cultural sets of assumptions with a distinction between two common types: assumptions about cultural values and the rules of the game that apply to specific situations such as job interviews and speaking on the telephone. Deaf culture has developed its own set of rules for conversing on the TTY, such as the use of "GA" at the end of an utterance that lets the other person know they can "Go Ahead" with their turn.

Another convention has also developed to make up for the lack of emotional affect in reading typed text. Since it is hard to tell if the words moving across the screen are serious or sarcastic without the help of facial expression, clues such as SMILE, SIGH, WINK, or HAHA are added to help the reader correctly interpret the typed message.

In ASL classes, Deaf teachers impart more than signs. Usually the classroom is expected to follow Deaf cultural norms, as well. For example, if a student arrives late to class, the teacher may expect a brief explanation of the reason for the tardiness.

There are many situations such as parties, Deaf club gatherings, school plays, sports events, and international conferences where sets of unwritten rules dictate the norms of appropriate behavior. An uninitiated hearing person attending such an event would undoubtedly violate many of these cultural rules. Given the fact that the hearing are in the majority, the Deaf in the minority, however, most often it is the Deaf person who must venture into the hearing world to work, obtain medical services, or otherwise transact business. If we were more frequently called upon to interpret for hearing people as they came for a job interview at an all-Deaf business or school, we would examine these situations from the opposite perspective.

Different Frames for Understanding the Interpreting Event

So far in this chapter we have focused on the different sets of cultural expectations held by our two consumers, Deaf and hearing. At this point we need to add ourselves to the equation. Let us examine how we view the very act of interpreting, by virtue of our hearing American cultural upbringing. Then we will see to what extent our perspective is shared by our Deaf consumers.

First and foremost, to professional interpreters the interpreting event is our work. And what does "work" mean in mainstream American culture? As we saw in chapter 4, it defines our identity. Not only the way we earn our money, it gives us a sense of value through accomplishment. Many interpreters' self-esteem is tied to visible, measurable indicators such as college degrees, interpreting certificates, or amount of money earned.

The term *professional* seems to be a key to understanding how we see ourselves in the interpreting role. Often we use this word with pride. At other times, however, we use it in a slightly defensive manner when hearing consumers assume that (a) we are related to the Deaf consumer, (b) we are volunteering our time, or (c) we have no training in areas such as confidentiality or ethics. Professionalism connotes neutrality. As section 2.5 of the NAD-RID Code of Professional Conduct states, "Interpreters shall refrain from providing counsel, advice, or personal opinions." As models of interpreting have changed, so has our collective self-image. We do not see ourselves as helpers or machines anymore. We pride ourselves on our professionalism and believe that it entitles us to the same respect accorded other professionals such as doctors and lawyers.

The concept and sign PROFESSIONAL carries a very different connotation in the Deaf world. "While it is sometimes a neutral designation, it is never a compliment . . . to be identified by others as *professional* is sometimes negative, connoting a cool, standoffish, or elitist attitude, someone who attains to principles rather than people" (Smith 1996, 111).

Do Deaf people see the interpreting event in the same way that we do? There are several avenues we can pursue to gather some data on this question. First, let us take a historical perspective and look back before there were "professional interpreters." The Registry of Interpreters for the Deaf was established in 1964. Prior to that time (and doubtless continuing to the present day in many situations), when Deaf people needed to communicate with hearing people, they either did the best they could with lipreading and writing notes, or they enlisted the aid of a neighbor or family member who could hear and speak. Often these were the hearing children of Deaf parents who had learned ASL in the home. There was no formal code of ethics followed by these family "volunteers." They were part of the reciprocal pool of skills in the Deaf community. Were they "professional interpreters" in the sense of the term today?

In the book *Mother Father Deaf*, author Paul Preston, himself a child of Deaf parents, examines the past and present impact that having Deaf parents had on the 150 informants he interviewed. Almost all of these now grown children remember interpreting for their parents in encounters with the hearing world. Asked about which behaviors and skills constituted these childhood interpreting tasks, his informants mentioned the following: "helping," "connecting," "mediating," "bridging," and "caretaking" (Preston 1994).

Is this what Deaf consumers want and expect from "professional" interpreters today? Many Deaf people desire to be in control of their own lives and do not want interpreters to make decisions for them. On the other hand, the complete rejection of the helper model may not take cultural habits and preferences into account.

In her telecourse entitled "The Socio-Political Context of Interpreting as Mediation," esteemed interpreter and educator Anna Witter-Merithew interviews several Deaf consumers of interpreting services regarding the qualities they most value in an interpreter. They confirm the conviction that "a good attitude" is of number-one importance. One of the Deaf consumers, Larry Smolik, says that he has seen many Deaf people express a preference for interpreters who have only adequate signing skills but possess a good attitude over those who have exemplary signing skills but an inappropriate attitude. Elements that constitute an interpreter's good attitude include sensitivity to cultural norms, such as making sure there is enough time to talk with the consumer before and after the assignment, clear communication, honesty regarding one's skills and limitations, adherence to the RID Code of Ethics, and a friendly, personable rapport with the Deaf consumer (Witter-Merithew 1996).

In another example that supports the same point, the head of the special services division of a leading university recently surveyed the Deaf students a few weeks after the beginning of the semester to assess if they were satisfied with the interpreting services they had received thus far. Not one student mentioned anything about the skills of their interpreters. Instead they focused on how "friendly" and "helpful" they had been.

Articles and letters to the editor written by Deaf consumers often reveal their feelings, complaints, and preferences when it comes to interpreters. One article, which appeared in the March 1997 volume of the RID monthly newsletter entitled "Free Enterprise: A Euphemism for Greed?" was written by a Deaf regional RID representative who also works as a relay interpreter. In it the author criticizes the view of interpreting services as a "commodity subject to the rules of economics." He cautions interpreters to stay in touch with the humanistic roots of the profession and states that there are two important elements necessary for quality service: "linguistic/translating skills and personal relationship (or 'attitude' as some deaf consumers call it)" (Teuber 1997, 31).

In a GLAD (Greater Los Angeles Council on Deafness) newsletter article, its outspoken executive director, Marcella Meyer, expressed her belief "that many of the interpreters twenty years ago were much better than the present ones. They seemed so much more flexible and sensitive to what WE had to say and were our friends." In contrast, Meyer sees most interpreters today as "overeducated, overtrained and overpolished and misguided professional robots. . . ." Several of her criticisms regard "interpreters who pull a 'Houdini Act' after an assignment" by leaving at their scheduled time, before an event is actually over, interpreters who "price their services through the roof," and those who are "taking control of our communication away from us." She laments the fact that "interpreters rarely befriend deaf persons" nowadays (Meyer 1994, 5).

In an article that appeared in the *Silent News*, a Deaf publication, the author reports that some members of the Deaf community have been expressing anger against interpreters. The issue appears to be that these Deaf people feel it is unfair that interpreters should be privy to so many details regarding their lives without sharing intimate information from their own lives in return (Schwartz 1996).

Taking a different tone, a newsletter article written by the executive director of the NorCal Center on Deafness in Sacramento, California, is entitled "Sign Language Interpreters: Something Positive." The author reports, "When you ask deaf people what it is they cherish or admire in an interpreter, the response generally points to the willingness of some interpreters to stay and help out in times of crisis without worrying who is going to pay them." She also expresses gratitude "to interpreters for encouraging and respecting the need for deaf and hard-of-hearing persons to be in control in deafness-related situations . . . " (Mutti 1996, 13–15).

Taken together, these comments from Deaf consumers seem to paint a different picture of the ideal interpreter, one in which the "humanness" of the interpreter is most valued. Clearly, there can be great differences between the way hearing interpreters tend to view our job and what Deaf people perceive as our role in their lives.

Assuming Alternative Cultural Roles

A useful parallel may be seen in the field of cross-cultural counseling, which seeks to train counselors to be sensitive to differing worldviews of clients from other cultures and to modify their therapeutic interventions accordingly. For example, in traditional forms of Western therapy, clients are encouraged to make their own decisions, because individuation is a hallmark of maturity. As mentioned previously, in the majority of the world's collectivist cultures, by contrast, to make decisions on one's own (without the input and guidance of the family) is a sign of selfishness and immaturity.

So too, the role of the therapist shifts when seen through different eyes. In traditional Western psychological practice, therapists are cautioned to remain neutral and refrain from giving advice or relating their personal experiences to their clients. Clients who are members of certain non-Western cultures may be used to getting direct help with their problems from other members of the community. They may expect, therefore, to establish a personal bond with the person they turn to for assistance. To them, the very act of the help giver relating his or her own experiences engenders a sense of trust and connectedness.

The quandary of cross-cultural counselors bears a striking similarity to the situation between professional interpreters and Deaf people. What do we do about these seemingly opposing views and expectations? Can we be all things to all people? Is it possible to act in a more neutral manner with our hearing consumers and in a more personal manner with our Deaf consumers?

Why not? While it may stretch our repertoire of ways of relating to other people, it is not an uncommon shift. We do it when we relate to our own families in contrast with how we may act out in the world, so why can't we make a similar shift in performing our work?

By accepting the designation of bicultural mediator, we acknowledge the need to switch cultural modes of interacting when necessary, adopting the appropriate set of behaviors depending on whom we are dealing with. It seems we do this more easily in social situations. At a Deaf social gathering, for example, we readily follow Deaf norms of behavior such as telling someone where we are going when we leave the room. We probably notice that the way we describe our recent vacation in ASL differs from the way we might have told the same story in English, in terms of level of detail, presentation of time, and point(s) of view. Depending on our level of awareness of cultural differences, we may even notice that when socializing with Deaf people, we make direct comments about someone else's personal appearance and check with others before making a decision that affects the group.

Something happens, however, when we assume the role of professional interpreter. Our formerly flexible, culture-switching style becomes stiff, and we get locked into the hearing American definition of that role. The result, I believe, is that we function less effectively for all the parties involved.

One way to visualize the constant shifting of perspectives that is required of us is to liken it to using different pairs of glasses. Some of us have one pair of glasses for reading or close work and another for looking at things in the distance. Each helps us function properly in the environment for which it was designed. It would be clearly inappropriate to wear our distance glasses to do embroidery or to use our reading glasses to watch a football game from seats high in the stands.

As interpreters, our first task is to see each world clearly. Once we can see from our Deaf consumer's and hearing consumer's perspectives, our actions should follow naturally, because we already know what is expected and what is appropriate behavior in each worldview.

Since we have to switch perspectives so rapidly and repeatedly in the course of our daily work, the best guiding image to keep in mind might be an excellent pair of bifocals.

9

Multicultural Interpreting Challenges

What is the most basic precept that sign language interpreters are taught to always follow? The answer, of course, is confidentiality. It is listed as number one in both the old RID Code of Ethics and the new NAD-RID Code of Professional Conduct. But is confidentiality truly universally applicable? Suppose you interpret a medical appointment for a Deaf client from a non-mainstream cultural background. After the assignment, a leader of that cultural community approaches you and asks you what happened. Confidentiality means that you must refuse to reveal any information, right? What do you do if you know that the expectation in this Deaf person's culture is that information is shared with the community so it can provide support to its members?

In a multicultural environment, even our most basic assumptions need to be reexamined. When we think of maintaining confidentiality, we are probably visualizing our clients as individuals. However, "many cultural communities may function at a more 'collective' level including family, extended family, or other significant community persons into the umbrella of confidentiality" (NMIP 8b, 5).

To be effective in multicultural situations, we need to take a step back and examine some of the basic principles that underlie our range of interpreting models. In this chapter, we will look at some of our fundamental assumptions about the role of the interpreter seen from a multicultural perspective. Specific considerations for the four groups in chapter 6 will be discussed. Then we will present some interpreting scenarios and options for dealing with them. Finally, we will offer some suggestions for more effective interpreting in multicultural contexts. As in chapter 6, much of the material in this chapter is adapted from the *National Multicultural Interpreting Project* curriculum. Special thanks go to the many people who contributed their time and wisdom, and Mary Mooney as project director.

In addition to the issue of confidentiality, we need to revisit some of the other principles contained in the old RID Code of Ethics. (After several years of dedicated collaboration, members of NAD and RID developed a new "Code of Professional Conduct" that was ratified in 2005. A great effort was made to update the tenets to reflect a more inclusive perspective. Interpreters who have been trained in the last 30 years, however, have undoubtedly internalized many of the tenets of the original RID Code of Ethics.) We will examine three additional principles.

Interpreters shall not counsel, advise, or interject personal opinions. In some cultures, the interpreter is not seen as a neutral professional but as a "trusted friend" who has received the approval of the community. This may create a potential conflict if there is a community expectation that advice and personal opinion will be injected into the interpretation. The interpreter must maintain a delicate balance of input into the situation, favoring an expansion of the cultural implications over a directive of the appropriate course of action (5).

The interpreter is an outside professional. It is easy to forget that in many countries, there is no such thing as a professional sign language interpreter. The role of language intermediary is filled by the second or third generation of immigrant children. Family members who speak English are expected to perform these services for other family or community members. Although using an untrained family member in the role of interpreter goes against our principle of unbiased professionalism, there must be an acknowledgement of cultural preferences and a balancing of needs. How can the traditional role of these family members be respected, integrated, or transitioned into the communication and interpreting process? (5)

The empowerment of the individual is to be encouraged. From the mainstream American perspective, each Deaf person is an independent consumer of interpreting services. Mainstream culture also regards men and women as equal in legal status. We assume a woman will decide for herself if or when to enter into or leave a personal relationship, an educational program, or a position of employment. In many cultures, however, a woman generally defers such decisions to her male family members. It may be expected that information will be furnished to the Deaf woman's family members so that they can make a decision in her best interest.

Let's examine some issues about the role of the interpreter specific to the four cultural groups discussed in chapter 6.

Asian Americans

Asian Deaf students often have their first experience with an interpreter in the United States in an educational setting. They may be struggling with learning both ASL and English but embarrassed to admit that they do not understand the interpreter. In order not to lose face, they will not ask for clarification during a group interpretation. In a one-to-one or small-group setting, they may want the interpreter to expand on the cultural meanings behind words and signs without focusing on their lack of knowledge (NMIP 8b, 9).

Sometimes Asian students ask their educational interpreters for help in understanding a concept, finding a location on campus, filling out a form, or handling a situation in the United States. In interviews conducted by the NMIP, some Asian students explained that when their requests for help were answered by the signs DO-SELF or THINK-SELF, they felt extremely offended. The Asian expectation of "help" includes the feeling of caring and personal involvement. What we may consider to be "traditional boundaries of the role of interpreter," they found "abrupt and very impersonal" (9).

In situations with religious or cultural content (e.g., a wedding, a funeral, a New Year's celebration), an interpreter of Asian heritage is often preferred. Conversely, when discussing personal or business matters, Deaf Asian families may prefer an interpreter from outside the culture to avoid a "loss of face" within the community. In other situations, the skill of the interpreter is the primary concern (9–10).

Latino Americans

In the Latino community, the interpreter is often seen in the role of "all-knowing" supporter, or advocate. The interpreter is expected to function as a helper and to give advice. The Deaf person may anticipate that the interpreter will relate not only what has been said but also what needs to be done in a situation.

While mainstream American culture encourages the individual's right to self-determination, traditional Latino families make decisions as a group. In a decision-making process, the white American interpreter may feel that his or her job is only to relate to the Deaf consumer. In the Latino family, however, the decision-making process must include not only family members but also other significant individuals as well. Communication and information sharing is of paramount importance. In a crisis situation, disturbing or removing this network of support could be the worst possible thing for the Deaf consumer (NMIP 8b, 10).

Deaf people and their families who have emigrated from Spanish-speaking countries may have had experience with two types of interpreters: (1) family members who help for free and are seen as allies and (2) government workers whose jobs may have been to report information to the authorities. "Depending on the country that the individual comes from, they may have a tremendous fear and distrust of someone who is getting paid by the government." By wrongly assuming that the interpreter is a government worker, the family may feel it would be dangerous "for them to open up and give needed information to the interpreter" (11).

When it comes to establishing our qualifications, European Americans tend to emphasize schools attended, skills learned, and credentials earned. From the Latino perspective, the ability to make a human connection is more convincing than the number of certificates one holds. Most Latinos strongly prefer interpreters from the same background, ideally the same country as themselves. The interpreter will know the country the Deaf person is from, will be able to recognize and pronounce the names of towns and family members, and will be supportive, because this is expected behavior in his or her home country (11). With sensitivity, however, non-Latino interpreters can build trusted relationships with the Latino Deaf community.

American Indians

When working with American Indians, interpreters need to be aware that they may initially be met with feelings of mistrust if they are nonnative because of a long history of troubled relations with the Europeans who invaded their land. Throughout decades of turbulent negotiations, interpreters have been blamed for some of the devastating results. Interpreters were accused by both sides as being "dishonest," "incompetent," and "the root of all troubles" and miscommunication between whites and Indians (14).

Understanding the importance of nonverbal behaviors is crucial to establishing a feeling of trust. As described in chapter 6, these include eye gaze, turn-taking, use of questions, touch, and pointing behaviors. Becoming familiar with Indian communication style presents a challenge for nonnative interpreters who have not lived in native communities.

Intertribal Deaf Council conferences have become a model of multicultural team interpreting, relay interpreting, and mutual mentoring. Several organizations have collaborated to recruit and train interpreters directly from Indian communities. There is currently a small but growing number of Indian interpreters who are RID-certified. Most nonnative sign language interpreters do not possess an in-depth knowledge of the cultures or community languages of the Indian children and adults they work with. It is often essential, therefore, to ask parents, siblings, or other community workers to assist by providing communication using ASL and/or indigenous Indian signs and gestures. Interpreting for religious ceremonies where cultural rules are of great importance is a particularly sensitive area.

African Americans/Blacks

The interpreting field is not immune from discriminatory attitudes. During the 1985 RID conference, whose theme was "Interpreting: The Art of Cross-Cultural Mediation," many issues of sensitivity were addressed publicly for the first time. Phillip Jones presented a paper entitled "Issues Involving Black Interpreters and Black Deaf People." Jones stated that the lack of contact between Black and white Deaf people and Black and white interpreting communities leads to strong feelings and judgments on both sides. Because white Deaf people often do not have much exposure to Black interpreters, "White Deaf consumers will typically assume that the Black interpreter is less skilled. They also tend to express or exhibit more surprise if that interpreter *is* skilled" (Jones 1985, 63).

Black interpreters report that they are often told by white interpreters and interpreter trainers that they are "too expressive" and that they should "tone it down" (e.g., decrease their signing space and lessen their affect). Black interpreters resent these comments because they contend the foregoing is a key component of the signing style used by Black Deaf people. They know when and how to match an appropriate signing/interpreting style with a particular audience and presenter.

At the same time, Black Deaf people often lack exposure to white interpreters outside of educational settings. According to the NMIP, in social, religious, and cultural settings, many Black Deaf people prefer an interpreter who is also Black, probably because of the familiarity and comfort with "what may be termed the black style of discourse and signing" (16).

Myisha Blackman, a respected African American interpreter and presenter, explains that a common, unfortunate, and unfair assumption made by African Americans regarding non-African American interpreters is that they are incapable of following an African American speaker. When non-African American interpreters interpret for an African American speaker or event, they need to be able to produce an equivalent message in the target language and do so without offending their audience (personal communication).

There are some subtle, yet dangerous, assumptions that must be avoided. One is that just because an interpreter is Black, he or she can speak Black Vernacular English. It is a mistake to assume that all African American interpreters have had the same experiences or upbringing and can automatically use the Black Vernacular English communication style. Another dangerous stereotype is that all interpreting situations presented for a Black audience will be full of colorful, emotionally intense slang. They can, of course, be non–code-switched presentations, similar to those of any other cultural group.

Another example of discrimination is the assumption that African American/Black interpreters are only capable of interpreting performing arts, sports, and religious events primarily for Black Deaf people. Myisha states that some interpreters who are members of NAOBI (The National Association of Black Interpreters) have made a strong statement that they do not want to be pigeonholed. They assert their ability and right to present and consult on issues of technology, medicine, law, and business, and interpret for all members of the Deaf community (Myisha Blackman, personal communication).

Scenarios —Group 1

The following scenarios show problems that can occur when interpreters have a less than adequate awareness of the cultural implications of their work.

It's Not What You Say . . .

A group of Asian employees are meeting to plan a program recognizing Asian/Pacific Islander Month. There are eight hearing participants, all of whom seem foreign-born, and one American-born Deaf participant. One interpreter is an American-born Asian woman; the other is a non-Asian male of large stature. The participants speak softly and in measured tones. The male interpreter, when he has trouble hearing, glares at the speakers and commands in a loud voice, "Speak up! You are not talking loud enough!" His command is always met by silence. When discussion resumes, the participants speak even more hesitantly and quietly and with less interaction. The Asian interpreter tries to replace the non-Asian but he will not relinquish his position. Finally, the non-Asian interpreter stands up and mutters, "I give up!" The Asian interpreter takes over. She quickly explains to the Deaf employee that people were speaking very softly and it was hard to hear. At an appropriate moment, she turns to the group leader and says in a very calm and respectful tone, "Excuse me, Dr. Lee, I am having trouble hearing. Could you please repeat that last comment?" Dr. Lee responds and the group begins to interact more (adapted from NMIP case study no. 5 8b, 10–11).

Discussion: Speaking softly is common in Asian cultural situations and direct criticism is seen as impolite. The interpreter's requests should be negotiated in a culturally appropriate manner.

A Matter of Respect

A team of interpreters is scheduled for a young Latina's lengthy medical appointment. The non-Latino interpreter arrives first. Entering the waiting room, she sees the patient, a young Latina Deaf woman, who is accompanied by her hearing parents. The interpreter is a little worried about communicating effectively with the Deaf patient, so she makes a beeline to the Deaf woman and engages her in small talk to establish her language needs. After a while, the parents rise from their seats angrily, motion to their daughter to follow them, and abruptly leave the room. The interpreter is at a loss to explain what happened. On the family's way out, they bump into the Latino interpreter, who, seeing them so upset, asks the father in Spanish what happened. He explains that the other interpreter was very rude by completely ignoring them (the parents). The Latino interpreter apologizes to the parents and explains that the other interpreter doesn't speak Spanish and didn't mean to be so inconsiderate. He calms the parents down and they all go back into the waiting room.

Discussion: Family unity, especially in a time of crisis, is a core value in Latino culture. The role of the elder family members needs to be acknowledged. Even if the interpreter does not speak Spanish, she can still convey an attitude of respect in many ways (e.g., through a handshake or use of titles *Señor, Señora*).

When in Doubt, Play it Safe

During a college lecture entitled "The Effects of Rap Lyrics on the African American Youth" by a Black studies professor at a Black university, there are repeated references to the "N" word. The interpreter, who is not African American, signs the "N" handshape on the nose. There is a noticeable discomfort among the African American/Black Deaf students in the audience. The interpreter is unaware of the tension exhibited by the audience members (adapted from NMIP case study no. 9, 8d, 4).

Discussion: Myisha Blackman advises that it would be safest for the non-African American interpreter to fingerspell the word. The African American Deaf person may then supply their preferred sign. She also cautions that one should spell the word as N-I-G-G-A-H or N-I-G-G-U-H, as that is the spelling in rap lyrics. (These carry a very different connotation than the word that ends in "-ER.")

Going Native?

A non–American Indian interpreter is assigned to interpret an American Indian event. In order to try and "fit in" with this assignment, the interpreter goes through her jewelry box and takes out every piece of turquoise and silver jewelry she has. She even decides to buy more "Indian jewelry pieces" and wears several turquoise rings, a necklace, and a pair of dream-catcher earrings to the assignment. Her attempt to "fit in" has the opposite effect. And some of her sign choices make her audience even more uncomfortable. She refers to *drums* with a two-handed, open palm style of drumming and to *pipe* with a sign for the citation form of the common smoking pipe (adapted from NMIP case studies no. 6 and no. 9, 8d, 8–9).

Discussion: For an outsider to "dress up" in what she thinks is culturally appropriate clothing can be seen as offensive by members of that culture. It would be better for the interpreter to use the time to learn the most culturally appropriate signs.

Rush to Judgment

A Japanese Deaf man has a job interview for a professional position. An interpreter has been arranged. During the interview, many questions posed by the prospective employer are met with long silences before the Deaf man answers. The interpreter assumes the pause means that the Deaf man does not understand the question as phrased. So every time a question is followed by silence, the interpreter repeats and rephrases the question, making it simpler and simpler. The Deaf Japanese man becomes flustered because he had no problem understanding the questions the first time around.

Discussion: The interpreter was unaware of an important feature of Japanese discourse style. The job applicant's silences meant he was composing his thoughts before answering. It would be better for the interpreter to check out her assumption before acting on it.

Make Yourself at Home

A Latino Deaf couple are interested in becoming foster parents. The social worker has arranged to come to their house to interview them. The appointment is set for 1:30 P.M. An interpreter meets the social worker outside (they are both non-Latino) and they approach the door together. After the husband greets them, he brings them inside and motions for them to sit at the dining room table. The wife proceeds to bring out many dishes of food that she has spent the morning preparing. The interpreter explains that she just had a big lunch and is still full, and the social worker brings out her papers, as she wants to get right down to business.

Discussion: Making and serving food to guests is an important gesture. Even if she has already eaten, the interpreter needs to accept the offer of food—at least taste it, pronounce it delicious, and thank the couple. Latinos also prefer to establish rapport and trust with strangers by chatting a while before getting down to business.

The next group of scenarios will portray more positive examples, where the interpreters used their sensitivity and knowledge of multicultural communities effectively.

Scenarios—Group 2

Got the Message?

A Deaf employee asks his Asian-born supervisor if he can borrow the company car to pick up a special order of supplies. The supervisor answers, "The roads have not been fully plowed. I understand it may snow again this afternoon." After signing the supervisor's response, the interpreter signs BORROW CAR? BETTER NOT (adapted from NMIP case study no. 1, 8d, 10).

Discussion: The interpreter is aware that indirectness is a key feature of Asian discourse style. He is able to discern the point behind the supervisor's statements. Because the non-Asian Deaf employee may not be familiar with this type of indirectness, the interpreter decides to make sure that the underlying point of the message comes across.

Homework Pays Off

When a Caucasian female interpreter learns she will be interpreting a presentation by His Holiness, the Dalai Lama, she seeks counsel from a friend she knows who is knowledgeable about Tibetan Buddhism. She goes to the assignment wearing an ankle-length, long-sleeved dress. She seeks out one of the monks in the entourage, introduces herself, explains her interpreting needs, and asks for help. She is led to the highest monk in authority; he gives her permission to stand while interpreting, even though it may place her above the head of the Dalai Lama. While she is talking to the monks, she is careful to not look any of them in the eye (adapted from NMIP case study no. 3, 8d, 10).

Discussion: The interpreter realizes that she is going to be present at an event where cultural sensitivity is important. She realizes she needs more information and identifies someone to advise her. She then follows the advice to be respectful of the members of the other culture.

Maybe Looks Do Count

There are two interpreters at a large event celebrating Martin Luther King Day. One is a Caucasian male and the other is a Puerto Rican female who is often mistaken for African American because of her dark complexion. The culmination of the celebration is the singing of "The Black National Anthem." The white male interpreter happens to be familiar with this song and, in fact, knows all the words; the Puerto Rican female is not. The male interpreter insists that it would not be culturally appropriate for him to stand in front of the largely African American audience and sign the anthem. He offers to "feed" the signs to the female interpreter.

Discussion: Both interpreters know that the manner in which they chose to sign the anthem was more respectful of the audience than a technically perfect but culturally insensitive interpretation (from a story told by Angela Roth on *Multicultural Interpreter Issues: From the Multicultural Interpreter Perspective*, NMIP video 2000).

Teamwork Works

A team of many interpreters has been hired to interpret at a large, integrated American Indian gathering. The Anglo interpreters and one of the Indian interpreters are certified; the other Indian interpreters are not. Before the event begins, the Anglo interpreters discuss how to work out the timing for each interpreter's turn. The Indian interpreters remark that there are things other than time to consider, such as matching the gender of the interpreter with the speaker or giving deference to age. One of the non-certified Indian interpreters explains that if a medicine person offers a prayer in Indian sign language it should not be interpreted at all because it would lose the power it possesses in the original language. Another adds that it is essential to get permission before interpreting certain blessings. The Anglo interpreters share their knowledge of local geographical signs (from a story told by Tupper Dunbar on *Multicultural Interpreter Issues: From the Multicultural Interpreter Perspective*, NMIP video, 2000).

Discussion: In this situation, the multicultural team of interpreters cooperated, respected, and learned from each other. Even though certification is important, at times other skills and knowledge take precedence.

Points to Remember for Multicultural Interpreting

1. Study your own culture(s). The more you know about your own values, attitudes, and politeness norms, the clearer you can see other cultures.

2. Learn about other cultures through reading fiction and non-fiction, watching films, attending cultural events, and talking with people from other cultures. Remember, however, that just because people are from another culture, it doesn't mean they can articulate the subtle nuances of their culture. They might also be tired of outsiders' curious questions or feel that answering certain questions would compromise some sacred knowledge.

3. Visit cultural gathering places and observe what is going on.

4. Become familiar with the manner in which cultural groups establish rapport and resolve conflicts. Other essential areas of knowledge include a cultural group's level of directness, style of humor, taboo topics, and amount of self-disclosure.

5. You may need to adjust your natural behavior or interpreting style. For instance, in collectivist cultural groups, you may need to pay more attention to introductions and formalities and demonstrate more humility and less "ego."

6. Before an interpreting assignment, try to find out any essential cultural information so that you can dress and behave appropriately.

7. Try to find out specific names that will be used and how to spell and pronounce them: people, countries (and where they are located), acronyms, and organizations.

8. If you begin an interpreting assignment and you realize that you are in over your head and not doing a good job, stop and inform the consumers. Maybe an interpreter/relay/consultant with the necessary skills can be found. Better to be honest than to leave the consumers thinking that communication happened when you know it didn't.

9. Don't feel responsible for doing it all. Recognize your strengths and weaknesses and realize that teaming maximizes each person's abilities.

10. Realize that cultural situations are often multilayered and multifaceted. There may be people of several different cultures in the same interpreting situation plus different ages, educational backgrounds, and genders. Often a team approach is best.

11. The keys to multicultural interpreting assignments are knowledge, sensitivity, flexibility, and respect.

12. Realize that as interpreters, we have a common goal: to produce the best work and get the message across in a culturally appropriate manner.

10

The Interpreter's Role and Responsibilities

Suppose you have been invited to a masquerade ball and you are standing in front of a rack of costumes wondering which one to pick. Your behavior will be limited in certain ways depending on your choice of outfit. If you assume the role of the Tin Man, your tight metallic suit will restrict your movements and speaking. If you pick a belly dancer's costume, on the other hand, you will be able to move about freely, but you will have to accept the fact that you will expose more of yourself and that people may expect you to dance. Even though as sign language interpreters we do not don a costume when we do our work, we do assume a certain role that, in part, dictates our behavior. So what is the appropriate role for us to play? Since a look at comparable occupations and the similarities and differences between their work and ours may illuminate this issue, let us begin by briefly examining the roles of mediator and spoken language interpreter.

The Role of Mediator

It is interesting that our profession, for at least the past fifteen years, has been using the term *bicultural mediator* to describe what we do without much inquiry into the *mediator* half of the term. By examining the duties of professional mediators, we may see if the title is truly appropriate.

Mediators can be lawyers hired by the court to expedite conflict resolution, therapists who work with divorcing couples to resolve custody or visitation battles, or volunteers who work on a panel to solve disputes within their community. The one thing that all mediators have in common, however, is that they are called in to help resolve some type of disagreement that the parties involved are unable to solve on their own.

Mediations typically follow a set of steps. They begin with a statement by the mediator laying out the ground rules, goals, and expectations for the session. Then each party gets to tell his or her side of the story without being interrupted. This is followed by discussions, where the mediator, through active listening, validates each person's position and clarifies what is needed to reach a resolution (Lovenheim 1996, 7.3–7.50). While the mediator wields no power to directly influence the decision reached, he or she is in constant control of the mediation session to ensure that it stays focused.

The role of mediator does share a few characteristics with our traditional view of interpreters' roles: neutrality and confidentiality. Also presumed is the fact that the interpreter and the mediator find themselves between two parties who do not understand each other. Their role is to try to facilitate communication to create understanding. But at this point the two professions diverge. Interpreters are not allowed their own voice. Whatever we interpreters do to facilitate understanding must be done inconspicuously and usually simultaneously. Also, although mediation, by definition, is utilized for conflict, we usually interpret situations with no inherent dispute (e.g., a classroom lecture, a medical appointment, a conference).

Furthermore, although power imbalances are common in both interpreted and mediated situations, we, as interpreters, are cautioned to add nothing to the situation. We are severely limited in exercising influence upon this imbalance, while mediators frequently "do their best to ensure that any agreement they oversee is not blatantly unfair to one of the parties" (2.19).

It seems, then, that the bicultural mediator model of sign language interpreting is more wishful thinking than a description of reality. It would be wonderful if we could help each side appreciate the other's reality and, in the words of Peter Lovenheim, "unfreeze the parties from their fixed positions, open them to the possibilities of creative solutions and finally guide them to a mutually agreed-upon result" (1.16). Unfortunately, it would be next to impossible to achieve these goals while interpreting everything being said and signed from one language to another. It might make more sense to conceive of interpreter and mediator as two different roles that share a common goal: when we do our job well, *each participant is enabled to see things from the other's perspective.*

Many interpreters may argue that they identify as a mediator only in regard to their position of being in the middle. However, some Deaf people's complaint about interpreters who see themselves in the role of mediator is that they take over the situation, thereby taking control out of the hands of the Deaf participants and sometimes unknowingly thwarting their carefully conceived game plans. Eileen Forestal, a well-known Deaf educator and relay interpreter, relates several examples in her telecourse, "Understanding the Dynamics of Deaf Consumer-Interpreter Relations." One instance involved a Deaf supervisor who was meeting with a recently hired hearing employee who seemed to be having trouble working under a Deaf boss. The Deaf supervisor decided that what was called for was a firm stance in this meeting with his new employee, yet he noticed that at the end of the exchange the interpreter added a lot of "thank you" and "nice to meet with you" polite phrases as if they had come from the Deaf boss, which seemed to undermine his entire strategy. When questioned, the interpreter, who was apparently unaware of the Deaf client's intended toughness, responded that in hearing culture one must always be polite and say thank you (Forestal 1994).

The Role of Spoken Language Interpreters

The next role we need to consider is that of spoken language interpreter. Since both sign language and spoken language interpreters interpret between English and another language, it would seem at first glance that their jobs are more or less identical. There are a number of important differences, however. One is visibility. In certain circumstances (e.g., medical appointments or legal depositions) spoken language interpreters, like sign language interpreters, have a visible presence right there with the participants and can interrupt, if necessary, to ask for repetition. In simultaneous conference interpreting, however, spoken language interpreters are strikingly removed from the participants in a soundproof booth above the back of the meeting hall and cannot ask a speaker for clarification.

In the courtroom or a small-group meeting, when there is only one foreign speaker, the spoken language interpreter may be placed in an inconspicuous position—seated next to the foreign speaker, for example, where he or she whispers in the person's ear the proceedings of the event, although if the foreign speaker testifies on the witness stand in court, the spoken language interpreter will be up front and visible, too.

Sign language interpreters, by contrast, need to be clearly visible to the Deaf participants (and vice versa). Consequently, we often place ourselves next to the hearing person who will be speaking the most, so that we end up on stage next to the podium, at the front of the classroom, or in the middle of the courtroom. At a small discussion table, we and our Deaf clients sit across from each other instead of side by side (as most people who are used to working with spoken language interpreters expect). This constant visibility, along with the fact that sign language is often a novelty, sometimes makes us, instead of the Deaf (or hearing) speaker, the focus of attention.

A more significant difference between sign and spoken language interpreters is the perceived identity and allegiance of the interpreter. Although it is not necessary for foreign language interpreters to be native speakers of the language(s) they interpret, it is common that a Japanese/English interpreter, for example, is either Japanese or Japanese American. Therefore, the Japanese-speaking client can more readily identify with the interpreter and trust that the interpreter will either share some common values or at least understand where the client is coming from. Although we hearing sign language interpreters may sometimes share an identity factor with our Deaf client (e.g., by being Black, gay, Jewish), we are never deaf. Consequently, there is not necessarily an automatic feeling of trust in the interpreter. As members of the majority culture, we may be seen as being "on the same side" as the hearing judge, boss, or doctor, despite our language skills. An excellent way to alleviate this problem is to use a relay interpreter: a qualified Deaf individual who works as a team with the hearing interpreter. Unfortunately, we don't always have the luxury of this option.

A third distinction involves the majority culture's assumptions regarding foreigners as compared with Deaf people. Americans who are truly ethnocentric assume that the normalcy of everyone they meet should be judged by how much the person conforms to or deviates from the norms of American culture. Other, more open-minded people may expect someone from a foreign country to have cultural and language differences, but they don't assume that a Deaf American has any cultural characteristics that in any way diverge from hearing American culture. Most people naively believe that sign language is just English words and word order on the hands. So when a Chinese person and a Chinese/English interpreter are involved in a meeting with an American, for example, the American may be a little more flexible and forgiving than when dealing with a Deaf person whose sign language interpreter, they assume, is just a device that allows the Deaf person to get the audio input of English through a visual channel—as if they were watching a television show and had turned on the captioning.

With these distinctions—visibility, perceived allegiance, and cultural assumptions in mind—let us look at the manner in which spoken language interpreters view their own job. I recently interviewed several professors at the Monterey Institute of International Studies, one of the few institutions for training interpreters and translators, and perhaps the most respected. We compared the scope of our work, what we see as the limits of our responsibility, and the models under which our practitioners work. Graduates from the Monterey Institute can hope to interpret for the United Nations, the State Department, international trade negotiations, and conferences. In these high-level situations, interpreters may be provided with written documents beforehand for which they can prepare translations. Their clients are often of similar status, so power differences are not so critical.

As sign language interpreters, most of us do not have the opportunity to work at the level of international conferences. The bulk of our work is referred to by spoken language interpreters as *community interpreting,* a designation that includes court, medical, educational, and social service settings. Community interpreting is still a relatively young branch of the spoken language interpreting profession. Even though training programs for spoken language interpreters have not focused on community interpreting in the past, the situation seems to be changing. The Monterey Institute has added some classes in recent years with the aim of producing interpreters who are flexible enough to work in several different types of settings. (We will examine the community interpreter training program at the University of Minnesota after this discussion.) The necessity of using trained spoken language professionals is becoming more accepted, since interpretation in medical, legal, and social services settings can have such a direct and significant impact on people's lives. One of the problems has been the widespread yet erroneous belief that relatives or other untrained native speakers could adequately fill the needs that arise in hospitals, courts, and businesses.

Perhaps this new attention to community interpreting will affect the model under which conference-level spoken language interpreters see themselves operating. When I questioned the professors at the Monterey Institute, there was consensus that they have been using the conduit model, which is primarily concerned with delivering a linguistic equivalent of the communication. They are aware of the cultural implications, however, and may seek to account for these when they feel it is appropriate to do so.

These highly trained spoken language interpreters feel that their responsibility and creativity are generally limited to the linguistic level.
This perception may be due in part to the high level of discourse at international negotiations and because diplomats are presumed to have done
their homework on the culture of the representatives with whom they will
be negotiating. It may also be in reaction to, or to differentiate themselves
from, the untrained, drafted-at-the-last-minute relatives and friends who
end up "helping out" at the doctor's or lawyer's office and may inappropri-
ately interject themselves into the situation. Also, trained spoken language
interpreters may feel that their ability to expand on the cultural significance of a term is more constrained, since their words and those of the
participants might be recorded or transcribed to be analyzed at a later
time. For example, in legal settings they are instructed not to explain but
are directed to use the equivalent legal term in their target language
(which can usually be referenced in a bilingual dictionary), whether or not
their foreign speaker can be presumed to have the sophistication and
experience to understand it.

Since sign language interpreters also work in legal settings, this makes
for a striking comparison. There is no word-to-sign equivalent legal dictionary because ASL, having not been used extensively by its speakers in
certain specialized settings, has not yet evolved signs that refer to all legal
terms. With the small but growing number of Deaf lawyers starting to
practice in what was heretofore a basically hearing profession, signs are
being developed and expanded through usage. A similar phenomenon is
taking place in the computer industry, where, as more and more Deaf
people gain employment as computer programmers, signs for computer
terms are being developed by the Deaf workers who best understand these
concepts. Deaf people outside this field will then be exposed to these
signs, which may ultimately trickle down into more common usage.

In the absence of sign-for-word dictionaries, sign language interpreters
are in a different position from spoken language interpreters in legal situations when admonished to "just interpret, do not explain." In order to
interpret a legal concept or term for which there is no single equivalent sign, we must either resort to fingerspelling the English word (which
would more accurately be considered "transliterating" or shifting from
one mode to another while remaining in the English language) or un-
avoidably expanding on the concept, if it takes two or more signs to adequately convey the meaning of a single word. For example, one way to
express the term *conservator* could be PERSON COURT PICK HELP-

YOU MANAGE-MONEY, DECIDE LIVE WHERE, ETC. Sometimes, although we may be able to translate a word with one compound sign, we end up illuminating the concept in our choice of selected terms. For example, in ASL many terms for collective nouns consist of joining together two or three representative members of the set. Therefore to interpret the word *weapon*, one may sign GUN-KNIFE-CLASSIFIER BIG STICK . . . with appropriate affect to show that this is not a choice but representative of a category. (This compound sign is usually successful in getting the concept of "weapon" across, but may not always be accurate. Recently, a Deaf juror was assigned to a case where the "weapon" turned out to be a bowl of hot soup.)

Sometimes lawyers are purposefully vague in their choice of terms. A sign language interpreter cannot accurately interpret a word such as *battery* without knowing if the aggression consisted of a punch to the jaw, a fist in the stomach, or a knee to the groin, since there is no lexical item to show all the physical possibilities that could be characterized as "battery." This is one of the reasons why legal interpreting can be so difficult and should be undertaken only by experienced interpreters who have had specialized training that has prepared them to deal with these challenging legal nuances.

This disproportionality between the number of signs required to convey the meaning of one word naturally operates in the other direction (just as there is not always a word-for-word equivalence between two spoken languages). When describing a car accident, for instance, an ASL user can show in just one movement the physical relationship between the two cars involved before, during, and after the impact (using one hand to represent each vehicle simultaneously). This is impossible to interpret into English in less than a sentence, since we cannot speak simultaneously about two distinct objects doing different things. For example, the following complex English sentence would be needed to translate a description of an event that could be expressed in basically one signed movement: "I was in the process of making a left turn when the other vehicle, which had been following very closely behind me, attempted to move around my car to the left, but then struck my car forcefully on the driver's side, which resulted in my car careening out of control."

This point about the difficulty in interpreting "just the linguistic elements" between any two languages brings us back to spoken language interpreters. Spoken language interpreters, like those trained by the Monterey Institute, are keenly aware that, unlike oil and water, language cannot be easily separated from culture. In translating almost any sentence or interpreting any remark, they are daily reminded of the subtle cultural differences that color a choice of terms or a line of reasoning. Among the clients for whom they interpret, however, there is a widely held misconception that an interpreter's job merely consists of picking the proper equivalent word in another language (like those new little computers for foreign travelers). So spoken language interpreters are not always afforded the latitude to make the necessary adjustments for cultural differences that we sign language interpreters seem to have accepted as an essential part of our job.

Perhaps surprisingly, the professors at the Monterey Institute told me that they consider sign language interpreters very advanced in our discussions about the cultural aspects of interpreting and in the idea of interpreters as bicultural mediators. In certain ways we are role models for them. Spoken language interpreters are cognizant that, as Condon and Yousef state, "sometimes a faithful rendering of the original into the second language but without adjustment to culture differences can lead to new misunderstandings" (Condon and Yousef 202–203). Even though spoken language interpreters are constrained by tradition and expectations, sometimes they too feel compelled to make adjustments for cultural differences, although perhaps with a figurative furtive glance over their shoulder.

In my visit to the Monterey Institute, it was enlightening to compare jobs with spoken language interpreters. There may be many more differences between us than would appear at first glance. One thing we could all agree upon, however, was the near impossibility of successfully interpreting a joke into another language, especially if the joke serves a purpose in one culture that it would never serve in another culture. For example, an American may tell an off-color story as an icebreaker to open a speech, while the appropriate way for a Chinese speaker to begin a presentation is to humble him- or herself.

Spoken Language Community Interpreters

As previously mentioned, community spoken language interpreting is a very young field. The Program in Translation and Interpreting at the University of Minnesota, which was established in 1991, may well be the first of its kind to train bilingual members of a community to work as interpreters. It offers a series of introductory and intermediate courses that focus on medical and human services settings. The interpreters have a variety of language backgrounds, from French, Spanish, and Russian to Somali and Hmong.

Laurie Swabey, a sign language interpreter trainer, took an eight-year sabbatical from training sign language interpreters and transferred the skills and knowledge gained in our field to that of spoken language community interpretation where she worked as an instructor in this exciting program. She reports that the community interpreters do not restrict themselves to any one interpreting model but rather employ the gamut of models from machine to mediator, depending on the situation. When interpreting for an elderly, monolingual, monocultural member of a rural society who has recently immigrated to the United States, a strict adherence to the machine/conduit model will likely prove ineffective. For example, Hmong people are often shocked and resistant when asked to have a routine blood test. (This may be the first time they have ever set foot in a Western medical clinic.) The type of interpreting/mediating required for the Hmong patient, however, would probably be inappropriate if the patient at the medical appointment is a Russian physician who has recently moved here and already speaks a little English.

One of the differences between training sign language and community interpreters, Swabey points out, is that the spoken language community interpreters are themselves members of their linguistic community. This can lead to certain ethical dilemmas. For example, although interpreters are supposed to observe confidentiality while working, a cultural assumption may be that the leader of a community has a right to know what is going on with any of its members. That leader may therefore expect the interpreter to explain the reason why some member of his or her community is in the hospital. The interpreter, in this situation, may feel torn between duty to the community leader and the boundaries of the professional role.

Other cultural differences tax the interpreter's ingenuity: A hearing American doctor gives a Russian patient four options for the treatment of his condition. The patient, not used to being given such a choice, questions the physician's expertise, "Why should I tell you what to do? You are supposed to know what is best for me!" In another example, the interpreter's identification with the Hispanic culture of a male patient caused her to halt the discussion. In certain Spanish-speaking cultures, one never tells a person that he is dying. When the doctor began to inform this patient of his terminal condition, the interpreter, sharing the culture of the patient, did not feel she could relay the doctor's news. She suggested, therefore, that the doctor discuss the matter with the patient's family in another room.

Swabey finds that this kind of community interpreting works best if all the parties are educated about the process. The interpreters themselves, who may have been "helping out" their friends for years, must learn the professional boundaries of their new role. The patients need education about the American health care system and the role of the interpreter, and the physicians need to be sensitized to the needs and possible cultural conflicts that may arise when treating this special population (Swabey, personal communication).

In 1998, the National Council on Interpreting in Health Care (NCIHC) was established. It maintains an excellent website at www.ncihc.org and promotes training and professionalization for community interpreters in health care settings. One of NCIHC's position papers describes the four role conceptualizations they currently observe in their field: (1) conduit, (2) manager of cross-cultural/cross-language mediated clinical encounters, (3) incremental intervention, and (4) interpreter as embedded in her cultural-linguistic community. There is not yet consensus about the appropriate model for community interpreters. It is exciting and inspiring to see how this emerging field is grappling with some of the same issues as our own field. The ongoing exploration into their role may shed some light on our own process as well.

It seems, then, that, in many respects, neither the mediator nor spoken language interpreter role can serve as a perfect blueprint for sign language interpreters. Though there are some commonalities, our job is so unique that we must determine its scope and fashion its limits for ourselves.

A Closet Full of Models

If we cannot model ourselves on another profession, then we must negotiate with our fellow sign language interpreters (and the Deaf people we serve) to come up with a consensus of what our role entails so that our behavior can be guided by that image. As I noted earlier, our profession has eagerly adopted and then discarded several models for interpreting, as if they had become outdated skirts or trousers. I propose that we see this collection of models (helper, machine/conduit, communication facilitator, bicultural mediator) as different styles of clothing and that we keep all of them in our "closet" to "wear" for an appropriate occasion. In reality, when a new style of dress appears, most of us don't throw out all our older apparel and fill our wardrobes with only the latest fashions. We might just push the older styles to the back of the closet while we enthusiastically garb ourselves with the latest innovation. There comes a time, however, when something more traditional is called for and we reach in, pull out an old classic, and put it on again. Actually, it might be better to think of these models as mix-and-match separates. It is entirely possible that what may be most appropriate for a certain interpreting assignment is an old standby with just a touch of the trendy (i.e., basic conduit with a little bicultural mediator).

One reason we seem to gravitate to new models to use as a guide for every situation is that it is much easier to have a panacea than to adopt the eclectic approach. How do we analyze each interpreting assignment to determine where our responsibility begins and ends and what is called for in that particular case? I hope to shed some light on this question in the rest of this chapter.

What Is *Not* the Interpreter's Responsibility

Our discussion of roles and responsibilities must involve a focus on how we decide which aspects of the interpreting situation are in our charge. It is clear that differences in linguistic structure must be dealt with by the interpreter. This book focuses on the cultural influences that are present in transactions between members of any two cultures. Exactly where to draw the line around culture may be ambiguous, however. During an interpreting assignment, we may notice that things don't seem to be going well between the participants. Neither party seems to be understanding the point the other is trying to make. Is a cultural difference to blame? Or is it something about the individual personalities involved? At other times it feels as if there is a larger issue at the core of the rift, which has something to do with differences inherent in our societal structure itself. Should the smoothing out of *all* these rough spots be part of the interpreter's task? No. Let us begin by examining three areas that are *not* included in our obligation to deal with the linguistic or cultural elements of the interaction.

Individual Factors

Every individual we interpret for, both hearing and deaf, has a right to express the quirks of his or her personality. When communication difficulties stem from our client's shyness or stubbornness, we do not need to feel responsible for "fixing" anything. For example, if a physician becomes annoyed with a Deaf patient who happens to be a hypochondriac, this problem falls outside the boundaries of our responsibility, since it goes beyond the linguistic and cultural aspects of the interaction.

Also, on any given day, our clients may be experiencing a variety of states that will adversely affect communication. Physical states such as feeling ill, tired, or drunk and emotional states such as being upset, nervous, or depressed may all result in miscommunication. Yet we need not take responsibility for eliminating the consequences of these conditions.

Although we should be on the lookout for instances when cultural differences result in an unintended perception of rudeness, individuals whom we interpret for do have the right to express hostility, be intentionally insulting, and use foul language. I remember interpreting in court when the judge announced a decision that greatly upset a Deaf client, who proceeded to swear at the judge and almost pushed over the table before he was restrained by the bailiff. In voicing the Deaf man's comments, it seemed necessary to pick equally strong terms in English in order to accurately convey his intention. Although I was nervous using the "F-word" in a remark to the judge, I concluded that a "nice" translation such as "Your honor, I am very upset with your verdict" would not have been equivalent to the intensity that everyone in the courtroom could see. Perhaps to alleviate my own fears of inappropriate behavior, the judge thanked me for my work when the proceeding was concluded.

One of Deaf people's complaints about the helper model has been that interpreters, in an effort to protect them, often denied Deaf people access to the reality of hearing people's negative comments. If hearing people display their prejudice, they may be shaken out of their ignorance by a pointed retort from a Deaf person. This will not take place, however, if the Deaf person never knows about the insulting remark.

In conclusion, as long as we feel confident that these uncomfortable encounters are *not* the result of cultural differences, then we need to allow our clients to express themselves whenever they are feeling ill, upset, or ornery in any interpreted situation.

Situational Factors

Now I would like to describe six other factors that may alleviate the need for making cultural adjustments in interpreting situations. The first is *parallelism,* which means that the transaction is essentially the same in both cultures. Such simple actions as ordering a meal, buying a toy, or asking the time of day may not be determined by vastly different systems of behavioral norms in the two cultures involved, so the task of interpreting these exchanges can be relatively straightforward.

In recent months, I happened to have interpreted in quite a few situations involving divorce proceedings. Because of my interest in things cultural, I am always on the lookout for some element of an interpreting situation that seems to carry a different meaning in the two cultures (and which in this case might necessitate some cultural adjustment between the divorcing Deaf couple and the hearing family mediator, for example). Perhaps surprisingly, I have not found these to be in evidence in the divorce proceedings in which I have been involved. Although I can imagine instances where cultural issues might come into play, so far it seems that the human emotions of anger and pain, which take center stage in a bitter divorce, are sadly universal.

Second, some *deaf clients may not identify with Deaf culture,* even though sign language is their preferred mode of communication. Depending on the age when they became deaf, whether or not they attended a mainstream school, and other factors, your deaf clients may be functioning in the mainstream culture. Therefore, cultural adjustment may not be necessary.

Third, we must take into account the *degree of biculturalism of the participants* in the interpreted event. Many Deaf people have mastered the art of cultural code-switching and may choose to follow hearing norms in certain situations, thereby alleviating our responsibility for making cultural adjustments. There are a variety of factors that incline certain Deaf people to be more bicultural than others. Some of these influences come from their family's attitude toward and degree of exposure to hearing culture—if they have chosen, for instance, to associate with both Deaf and hearing people at work and in community activities or have attended hearing high schools and universities. Another influencing factor in biculturalism is personality. It seems there are specific personality traits that predispose some people to be more adaptive in intercultural encounters than others. These include patience, not taking oneself too seriously, and the ability to accept the fact that two different worldviews are not necessarily mutually exclusive (Althen 150).

Conversely, there are occasions when we work with hearing people who may have some signing skills and an academic knowledge of or an interest in Deaf culture. I am thinking here of a researcher or a therapist who would be familiar with and want the exposure to elements of Deaf culture. Again, in this case, we can just focus on interpreting the content of the message, trusting that cultural differences will not impede communication and may actually become the basis of an enlightening discussion between the participants.

Fourth, we need to consider the nature of the involvement between the participants. Is it a *one-time meeting or an ongoing relationship?* In an ongoing relationship there will be many opportunities for the Deaf and hearing participants to associate with each other and figure out ways of communicating without the presence of an interpreter. This is a common situation at a work site. An interpreter may be hired only for a specific weekly or monthly staff meeting, where there are many people present, or for a matter of extreme importance such as an annual performance review or safety demonstration. During most workdays, however, the Deaf and hearing employees and supervisors manage to communicate the necessary information through a variety of methods, which may include lipreading, writing notes, typing back and forth on a computer screen, e-mail, or limited use of basic signs and fingerspelling. This means that they have created their own in-house communication style. If the interpreter at that monthly meeting makes so many unnecessary cultural adjustments that the Deaf person seems to have a whole new personality, the hearing workers may be quite puzzled. Whatever cultural adjustments seem necessary to get the meaning across are still justified.

Another example of an ongoing relationship would be a family event. We are sometimes asked to interpret at a family gathering such as a wedding rehearsal dinner, a family reunion, or a Passover seder. Obviously, many of the participants have known each other for a period of years. They want to see dear Aunt Sally or funny Cousin Bert just the way they remember them, except with the greater ease of communicating through an interpreter.

Much of our work, however, involves situations between people who may not see each other after this one meeting, such as an interview at the Social Security office or an urgent doctor's appointment, or between people who may see each other several times but always with an interpreter present, such as regular checkups with one's family physician or a week of work-related training. In these types of situations, when a cultural issue comes up the participants may have no outside information with which to enlarge their perspective and may be more focused on achieving the goal of the meeting at hand than on really getting to know each other.

The interpreter, therefore, should be on the lookout for misunderstandings that may stem from differing cultural behaviors.

The fifth factor would be *special circumstances,* where the literal words or signs used by one or both participants carry special significance and must be preserved. One instance where it is important to convey the literal words used is in an educational situation where a student will be tested on specific vocabulary. A more complex one would be a mental health session, where it is imperative that the hearing therapist know exactly what the Deaf patient signed in order to assess the severity of a mental disorder, so the interpreter must convey the Deaf patient's message literally, even if it appears to make little sense or lacks closure. It is also important to note that in mental health interpreting the interpreter and the client should not engage in the "waiting room chat" that would be expected in other circumstances. The reason for this is that rapport needs to be established between the therapist and the client so they can effectively work together. If the interpreter and client establish their own connection through sharing a common language, it may deter the client from developing a clinical relationship with the therapist.

The sixth and last factor (although you will probably be able to add other factors to this list) is the *presence of a Deaf relay interpreter.* In certain circumstances a team of interpreters made up of a hearing interpreter and a Deaf interpreter can most fully optimize understanding by all the parties involved. Situations where Deaf relay interpreters can enhance communication include working with a Deaf client from another country who may have limited fluency in ASL and/or fluent or limited use of a foreign sign language; a Deaf client with minimal or limited communication skills (this may include some kind of "idiosyncratic, nonstandard signs or gestures" or "home signs"); working with Deaf children or other Deaf people who have had little or no previous experience in an "interpreted setting"; working with clients from a specific region or ethnic group, working in an emotionally charged situation where there may be issues of trust, or in any situation where the hearing interpreter and the Deaf client do not completely understand each other. The benefits of using trained Deaf interpreters are still not widely recognized, and unfortunately they are often used only as a last resort in situations (e.g., legal) where their use at the outset might have avoided many misunderstandings.

The dynamics of the situation and the relationship of the participants are altered when a Deaf relay interpreter is used. In most cases, the hearing interpreter's main responsibility will be to pass on the spoken information to his or her Deaf cointerpreter, who will then make any necessary cultural adjustments in communication with the Deaf client. Then the hearing interpreter vocalizes what the relay interpreter has gleaned from the Deaf client. In practice, the Deaf interpreter can relate to the Deaf client as a peer, and because of the trust derived from shared group membership, he or she can say certain things in a direct way that would be inappropriate, if not insulting, coming from the hearing interpreter. For example, if a Deaf person in a legal situation answers a yes/no question with a long narrative, the relay interpreter, who is aware of the hearing cultural norms of the situation, can inform the Deaf person quite bluntly of the need to keep his or her answers short and to the point.

Societal Factors

Moving on from the levels of individual and situational considerations, there exist imbalances and discrimination endemic to our society that contribute to unfair outcomes in certain interpreting situations. We need to examine these areas carefully in order to determine for what elements, if any, the interpreter can be deemed responsible.

Power. First we will address the power differences inherent in roles. If we look at the most common interpreting situations, we find the following roles: doctor/patient, teacher/student, supervisor/employee, social service worker/applicant, lawyer/client. In most cases the former role is occupied by a hearing person and the latter by a Deaf person. This means that there is an inherent imbalance in the power structure. Describing intergroup communication in general, John J. Gumperz and Jenny Cook-Gumperz point out certain elements of such asymmetrical relations:

> In interviews the interviewer chooses the questions, initiates topics of discussions, and evaluates responses. The interviewees respond, i.e., they answer. Often they are expected to volunteer information but what it is they can say is strictly constrained by expectations which are rarely made explicit . . . tacitly understood rules of preference, unspoken conventions as to what counts as valid and what information may or may not be introduced prevail. (9)

When the participants hail from different cultural backgrounds, the one in the position of lesser power is at a decided disadvantage. However, if the interviewer erroneously assumes that the interviewee shares the same cultural viewpoint, as often happens when hearing Americans encounter Deaf Americans, the resulting miscommunication may be even more subtle and destructive.

> The participant structure of such events thus reflects a real power asymmetry underneath the surface equality, a serious problem when the lesser communicator does not know the rules. The issue is compounded by the fact that what is evaluated appears to be neutral. Evaluators tend to concentrate on presentation of facts and information, or problem solving and reasoning abilities, so that underlying sources of ambiguity are not ordinarily discovered. (9)

Although it is not within the interpreter's role to even out the power imbalance, we need to be aware of its presence. In such situations, the Deaf person may benefit from the presence of an *advocate*, who would work to achieve a greater balance of power between the participants. As more and more Deaf people attain higher positions, however, these power dyads may be reversed, with a hearing person answering the questions of a Deaf principal, Deaf lawyer, or Deaf college professor.

Even though the imbalance of power between our Deaf and hearing consumers is not within our control, there is a crucial power relationship in which we are intimately involved and over which we may exercise some control. I am referring to *the relationship between interpreter and Deaf consumer*. In "Who's in Charge Here? Perceptions of Empowerment and Role in the Interpreting Setting," authors Marina McIntire and Gary Sanderson (1995) examine how the distribution of power has shifted with the interpreting field's shifting models.

In the days of the helper model, interpreters took over the situation, thereby withholding power from their Deaf consumers, who were seen as incompetent, powerless, and in need of their help. The machine or conduit model was an attempt to swing the pendulum strongly in the opposite direction, so the interpreter essentially gave up the responsibility for getting the message across. With the advent of the communication facilitator model, interpreters began to take back some responsibility by empowering themselves to request things (such as adequate lighting) to make their job easier. In the current bicultural mediator model, consumers are seen as equals "who have both the rights to and responsibilities for their own destinies" and "interpreters bear the responsibility for successfully managing and negotiating the communication event" (100).

One result of interpreters' ever-shifting views of their role is that Deaf consumers have no way of knowing what to expect from us. Will we take no control or total control? Forestal observes that this confusion and the resulting lack of trust in interpreters has left many Deaf consumers angry. By deciding what role we will assume, it still seems as if we have all the power. To remedy this situation, Forestal suggests that we take our cue from our Deaf clients and follow their lead regarding our role in the interpreted setting. Even though we may wholeheartedly support the bicultural mediator model, if a certain client prefers a straightforward conduit interpreting style, that is exactly what we should deliver.

Oppression. A deeper issue than the power residing in the interpreters' and Deaf consumers' roles—and one more resistant to change—is the power wielded by the hearing majority over the Deaf. Deaf culture, although similar in many ways to Japanese, French, and other national cultures, differs in one striking feature: *deaf people as a group are an oppressed minority.*

Charlotte Baker-Shenk (1986) introduced this important concept to our profession more than twenty years ago at the 1985 RID convention. It is still true, even though in the ensuing years many advances have been made. Gallaudet has a Deaf president, and Deaf people still feel pride in their united efforts that accomplished that goal. The ADA has given Deaf people more options by expanding their access to communication, education, and employment opportunities as well as increasing the hearing majority's awareness of the Deaf community. The interpreting profession has matured through education, professional forums for sharing our thoughts, and introspection. Yet, inequities and old attitudes still exist in many quarters. If we believe in the basic equality of Deaf people and want to see them achieve even more self-determination over their lives, it might be helpful to revisit some of Baker-Shenk's ideas.

In her presentation, Baker-Shenk cited specific instances, which, taken together, characterize Deaf people as an oppressed minority. ASL is not recognized as a language, and its use in schools is prohibited. Teachers and counselors refute the existence of Deaf culture. Deaf students are blamed for their poor academic performance regardless of the fact that many of their teachers have inadequate signing skills. The hearing majority views deaf people as less intelligent, emotionally and behaviorally deviant, and incapable of self-determination. After receiving a less-than-adequate education, deaf people are subject to a scarcity of jobs, including fewer opportunities for advancement and a lower average income. Deaf people are rarely accorded decision-making power in the very institutions that are supposed to serve them (61). Although recognition of ASL as a language has significantly increased (e.g., it is taught in many high schools, colleges, and universities and may be used to satisfy the foreign language requirement), most of Baker-Shenk's other points still contain some truth.

Baker-Shenk goes on to explain that the effects of oppression on any group, including the Deaf, are numerous and pervasive, including ambivalence regarding the feature that makes them different, horizontal or displaced violence against those who are more accessible than the actual oppressors, a passive acceptance of the status quo, a magical belief in the powers of the oppressor (e.g., they are smarter, they never make mistakes, they easily get jobs and accumulate money), and an emotional dependence on them (what Forestal aptly terms the "hostile dependency" that some Deaf people feel for interpreters). Baker-Shenk is quick to point out that the preceding analysis is not an accurate characterization of all Deaf people. She suggests, however, "that the apparent parallels do warrant our serious attention" (65).

She then describes the characteristics of oppressors as a group. They believe their way is the best way, the right way, and they regard all differences as inappropriate or inferior. From their feeling of superiority comes the belief that the oppressed group wants to be like them. Their paternalistic attitude reveals itself through sentiments such as "I know what's best for you" or "You people need me." They resist the idea of empowerment of the oppressed, in part because that would lead to a reduction in their own power. One curious characteristic of oppressors listed by Baker-Shenk is their desire for approval and gratitude from the group they oppress.

Baker-Shenk cautions interpreters to keep in mind that by virtue of their hearing status, they may be seen as members of the powerful dominant group, as the oppressors. And when interpreters interact with Deaf people, they may unconsciously be "influenced by the way oppressors think and feel about oppressed people" (67).

In the end, our understanding of and sensitivity to these issues are invaluable, even though as interpreters we cannot change the societal roles in which Deaf people are cast. It is up to us as members of the hearing community committed to developing skills and earning a living as sign language interpreters to understand the impact of oppression on Deaf people, to make sure that we do not engage in oppressive behavior, and, when doing so does not conflict with our role as interpreters, to act to alleviate it.

One way to check our attitudes and behavior is to scrutinize ourselves individually and collectively to see if we are guilty of *audism*. This term (originally coined by Tom Humphries in 1977) is used by Harlan Lane in *The Mask of Benevolence* to refer to "the paternalistic, hearing-centered endeavor that professes to serve deaf people" (Lane 43). Although Lane includes interpreters in the list of professions that make up the "corporate institution for dealing with Deaf people" along with administrators of schools for the deaf, experts in counseling the deaf, deafness rehabilitation workers, and teachers of the deaf, he goes into no details about our profession.

Do We Behave as Audists While Interpreting?

The biggest point of contention between the Deaf community and the administrators and educators mentioned above centers on the hearing experts' refusal to accept ASL as the natural language of the Deaf and therefore the most efficient mode of instruction for deaf children. Presumably, if we consider ourselves to be ASL/English interpreters, we recognize and support ASL. However, we may be guilty of more subtle acts and attitudes, perhaps out of our conscious awareness, which effectively take the power of self-determination out of the hands of the Deaf people we work for. It may be the *way* we handle something, which can be perceived as taking over—even something as simple as deciding where to sit.

Setting Up the Room. When we arrive at a job, one of our first responsibilities is to make sure that the room is set up in such a way that we can hear the speaker(s) and that everyone can see whomever they need to see. Although it may be faster and easier for us to make all these decisions, it may be better to involve the Deaf consumer(s), in part for practicality (they have to be sure that they can see comfortably) and partly out of politeness (group consensus is preferable to one person's taking control). If there seems to be some resistance from the hearing person in charge about having us up at the front of the room, it is better to introduce him or her to the Deaf person(s) present and then go back into our role of interpreter and allow them to handle their own negotiations.

"I've Always Wanted to Know..." Since sign language is so visual, we attract a lot of attention. The first time hearing people see a sign language interpreter at work, they are often intrigued enough to come over and interrogate us: "What's the sign for...?" "How long did it take you to learn to do that?" "Where can I learn sign language?" "Are you his daughter?" (Or now that the years have gone by, "Are you his mother?")

Although it may be faster and easier for us to give curious hearing people the answers to their questions, we must keep in mind who the real expert is in this situation. How much better to defer to the Deaf person by interpreting the question to him or her, even though it was addressed to us. It is simple enough to spell the word for which the onlooker would like to know the sign, so that they can see it made by the Deaf person's hands. If the question is specifically about interpreting and the Deaf person is not offering an opinion, by signing the entire exchange at least they are included in the conversation and may be able to add something later on. Recently, a nurse at a medical appointment began questioning me about where she could learn sign language, leaving the Deaf person to wait for her to finish the physical exam. In the interest of getting her question out of the way, I replied hurriedly, "Vista College in Berkeley," while signing both the question and the answer. The Deaf person then jumped in and expressed her opinion: "Sure, Vista is good, but the real way to learn ASL is to associate with Deaf people." The Deaf woman went on to describe her church, where there are both Deaf and hearing members, and it soon became obvious that the nurse had a strong religious background as well. The two of them became involved in a great discussion that never would have occurred if I had only whispered "Vista College in Berkeley," without signing.

"Off the Point" Questions. How many of us can honestly say that we have *never* done the following: The lecturer finishes his or her presentation and inquires of the audience, "Any questions?" We sign the previous invitation while appearing to cast our glance around the room, making sure, however, to avoid eye contact with a certain Deaf person whom we know to be notorious for asking seemingly irrelevant questions. Why do we do that? If we are honest with ourselves, I think, we may admit that we feel embarrassed at being the deliverer of an unrelated question or remark that may provoke a snort or a sigh from the hearing members of the audience. This topic deserves careful research, but I offer a hypothesis that there is a cultural difference at the bottom of it.

To generalize, I suggest that in mainstream American culture, there is a very limited set of comment types that are expected from audience members after a presentation: (1) a question relating to a point that the speaker brought up, (2) an agreement or disagreement about a point the speaker brought up, and (3) seemingly unrelated remarks which *must* be introduced with an explanatory link to the presentation. An example of such a linking remark would be: "Your lecture made me think of something similar that happened to me . . ." or "I know this may seem off the point, but . . ." or "I would like to bring up another topic related to what you just said . . ."

I gained some valuable insight into cultural differences regarding audience comments in a Deaf context at the 1999 Deaf Studies Conference that I mentioned in chapter 2. This forum for Deaf professionals had an overwhelming majority of Deaf speakers and attendees. I noticed a pattern emerge from the question-and-answer sessions that followed each presentation. Comments of the type (1) and (2) listed above were certainly brought up, but other types of remarks were also made without the inclusion of the linking introduction in number (3). For example, (4) a story from the speaker's experience that re-emphasizes points made by the speaker, (5) a memory sparked off by the presentation that the audience member has never had the opportunity to share with other Deaf people before. I have since observed the same type of comments at other similar Deaf venues.

It seems that a question from a Deaf participant may *sound* off the point in a hearing context because it lacks the short introductory phrase that would either connect it to the previous comment or explain that the questioner would like to address a new topic. Since these discourse features would fall into the category of cultural rhetoric, the interpreter can make the necessary adjustments.

Has There Been Audism in RID?

So far we have examined some subtle behaviors by which we, as individual interpreters, may take the power of self-determination out of the hands of the Deaf. We may find ourselves embarrassed to admit that we have consciously or unconsciously acted in ways that could be judged audist. But, what about our national organization, RID? Let us take a brief look at its beginnings. In *Silver Threads*, Lou Fant states that the Deaf and hearing people (most of whom were from Deaf families) who founded the organization in 1964 "were of like mind in [their] attitude toward deaf people and shared a common vision about the role of interpreter" (Fant 34). The charter members were divided into two categories: interpreters and "sustaining members," which was the designation for the Deaf people present. It is ironic that the word *sustaining* has several meanings. We cannot guess which of the definitions listed in *Webster's New World Dictionary of the American Language* the Deaf members were expected to fulfill: "maintaining or keeping in existence," "carrying the weight or burden of," "enduring," "suffering as in an injury," "strengthening the spirit of," and "encouraging." As it turned out, probably a little of each.

Carl Kirchner, president of RID from 1972 to 1978, explains (in a personal communication) that there were several events that gradually created a rift between the Deaf and hearing members of RID. The real rift, however, came in relation to issues involving testing and certification.

In RID's original format for testing interpreters, candidates were interviewed and evaluated by teams made up of three Deaf and two hearing evaluators. The organization felt the need to retain its Deaf members to help with these evaluations. The Deaf members, however, began to resent the fact that, other than for these testing purposes, they were not asked to work much as interpreters. In effect, they were helping the hearing interpreters make money while they themselves were not enabled to do so.

Meanwhile, as the seventies progressed, so did interpreter-training programs. A new generation of interpreters, who had not grown up in Deaf families, was becoming involved in RID, bringing with them values that were different from those of the original group that had founded it. Kirchner explains that these new interpreters focused more on "professionalism," whereas the older generation had focused more on "service." The new group questioned the value of having Deaf people on the evaluation teams, sometimes going so far as to state that they were "only consumers." The balance of the evaluation teams was then reversed to three hearing and two Deaf. Some of the Deaf people who had been involved in the founding of RID began to feel unwelcome and left. Some of the hearing interpreters from Deaf families felt they were being attacked because they hadn't gone through a training program. They were also accused of not being professional enough, and it was said that their volunteering would undermine the professionalism of the organization. Mud was slung back and forth. At the height of the debate, according to Kirchner, a patronizing analogy aimed at the Deaf was "Patients don't certify their doctors, other doctors do"—implying that the issue of certification was better left to the interpreters.

The testing system was revamped in the 1980s in an effort to increase its objectivity, reliability, and validity. During a two-year period in the mid-1980s when RID had placed a hold on testing so they could develop their improved instrument, some Deaf-run agencies experienced a lack of certified interpreters and developed their own interpreter evaluations to fill the gap. This may have also been in some measure a reaction to their perceived exclusion from the RID testing process. Members of RID criticized some of these tests for not being adequately rigorous. Hard feelings remained, with each side claiming that the other had refused to understand its point of view.

In recent years, there have been several positive developments in relations between the interpreting community and the Deaf community. In 1993, after many years of strained feelings between members of RID and NAD, their respective presidents, Janet Bailey and Ben Soukup, were unexpectedly stuck together for hours in a traffic jam. They took advantage of the opportunity and agreed to work collaboratively. In 1994, the NAD-RID Task Force was formed, which has since changed its name to the National Council on Interpreting (NCI). The many dedicated members, both Deaf and hearing, working in partnership over several years, have developed a new joint test, the National Interpreter Certification (NIC), which was unveiled in 2005. Both organizations have given their full support and financial backing to these efforts. (VIEWS vol. 11 March 1994, 1)

In addition, as more Deaf interpreters are getting certified, RID now has a "Deaf Members in Leadership Committee" whose goal is to encourage Deaf members to assume leadership roles within the organization. These hopeful signs point to improving relations between the Deaf and interpreting communities.

As Harlan Lane has eloquently put it,

> The truest friends of deaf people . . . will work together with deaf individuals and organizations to forge a hearing and deaf partnership. . . . For that partnership to be forged, both parties must bring their cultural frames into consciousness, construct a mutual understanding of those frames and make an empathetic leap, trying to position themselves at each other's "center." (1992, 200)

Taking Responsibility for Cultural Adjustment

Thus far in this chapter we have established that rather than modeling ourselves on another profession, we must decide the parameters of our responsibility ourselves. If we agree that the interpreting function concerns language and culture, we can exclude several items (personality differences, situational factors, and the inequalities inherent in society) that would not fall under that domain. Yet, we have noted that as interpreters we must be aware of and take responsibility for our own acts of audism. Before we zero in on the necessity of accommodating cultural differences in certain interpreting situations, we will deal with two arguments that are often presented in opposition to the concept of cultural adjustment.

It Depends on How We See Our Role

Recently, I had an informal discussion with several working interpreters about the differences between Deaf and hearing cultures. When the question of what to do when the literal translation of the speaker's statement would be perceived as impolite in the other culture was raised, one interpreter said, "If we keep putting on Band-Aids to fix their mistakes, how will Deaf people ever learn that their behavior is rude?" Since this point of view may be shared by others in the interpreting community, I think it deserves some analysis. The interpreter who made the statement seemed to assume that it is the Deaf people whose behavior is wrong; that it is part of our job to get them to "fix their wrong behavior"; and that the way for Deaf people to learn what is appropriate behavior in the hearing world is to have their ASL translated literally. Then by observing the negative reactions of the hearing people in the situation, they will become enlightened about the rules of hearing culture.

In response to these assumptions I suggest that we examine our convictions. If we believe that every culture is equally deserving of respect, then no culture is "wrong." It just happens that sometimes there is a mismatch between cultures as to what is seen as polite or appropriate in a certain situation. By focusing on the surface form of an utterance, we lose sight of the speaker's intent. If we see our job as interpreting between two languages and cultures, then it may be our duty to discard the surface form of a statement in order to preserve the speaker's underlying intent

In addition, it is misguided to assume that by interpreting the Deaf person's comment literally he or she will gain an understanding of hearing culture. As anyone who has spent time in other countries knows, it is extremely difficult to figure out the rules of another culture based on what we perceive as people's response to our behavior. To ourselves, our own behavior always feels right. Even if we suspect that we have made a faux pas, how do we guess if it was the words we used, our excessive eye contact (or lack of it), or the clothes we were wearing that provoked a negative reaction?

If we feel that part of our job is to educate Deaf and hearing people about each other's cultures, we can certainly make the attempt, but not while interpreting. We may choose to educate our clients through culturally sensitive suggestions. We might, for instance, say to the hearing consumer, "You don't need to say 'Tell him'; just speak directly to him." "The term *deaf and dumb* is out-of-date. You can just say *deaf*." Or "The interpreter has a suggestion. It might be clearer if you could give some examples." In the same way, we may offer the Deaf consumers some suggestions before or after the actual interpreting takes place, especially if they ask us. I am thinking of one Deaf man who was nervous about appearing in traffic court for the first time and asked me what was the proper way to address the judge. I was pleased to be able to tell him that the accepted term of address is "Your Honor." As an interpreter, however, it is not my job to penalize a Deaf consumer who does not know that we are expected to call the judge by that title or even that there may be a special title at all, because in his or her culture titles are not used. My job is to recognize the facial expression/body posture in ASL that demonstrates a submissive or respectful attitude to authority and translate that into "Your Honor."

Why Should We Do Cultural Adjustments At All?

There is another well-intentioned but misinformed resistance to the concept of cultural adjustment, which I have heard expressed by some hearing and deaf consumers as well as by a few interpreters. Their basic argument is that if the interpreter takes it upon him- or herself to adjust for cultural differences between Deaf and hearing people, members of the two cultures will never be exposed to or acknowledge their different ways of doing things and consequently will miss the opportunity to discover the fascinating richness of each other's cultures and to develop their own strategies for working things out. The problem with this line of reasoning is that *exposure to another culture does not automatically lead to mutual understanding*. In fact there is strong evidence to suggest that it leads to a continuation or even a strengthening of preexisting stereotypes.

An excellent example of this point may be found in relations between whites and Blacks in our own country. The two groups have certainly been exposed to each other over many years. Has that unmediated exposure led to an appreciation of cultural differences and a tolerance of contrasting styles of communication? The answer, in general, is no.

In *Counseling the Culturally Different,* psychologists and authors Derald Wing Sue and David Sue cite an example of cultural misunderstanding that took place at a faculty meeting of a counseling department during a discussion that followed a proposal to add more multiculturally related courses to the curriculum and hire more minority faculty members. When several white professors raised objections to this proposal, a Black male professor, Dr. S., addressed the faculty. During his remarks Dr. S. raised his voice, pounded the table, and "rose from his seat, leaned forward, and made eye contact with the most vocal objector." In the ensuing exchange the white professors urged Dr. S. to calm down and "address these issues in a rational manner." Dr. S. continued to strongly express his views and challenged the other faculty members to justify their reluctance to state their own opinions. Finally, one white male professor requested that the discussion be tabled "until we can control our feelings" (Sue and Sue 1990, 49–50).

In the discussion following this example, the authors identify some features of Black and white communication styles that often lead to such cross-cultural misunderstandings. In the type of meeting described above, the white "mode of acceptable communication is low-keyed, dispassionate, impersonal, and issue oriented." In contrast, "Black styles tend to be high-keyed, animated, confrontational, and interpersonal." These types of differences manifest themselves in many communication arenas. The danger here, as Sue and Sue point out, is that *"differences in communication style may trigger off certain preconceived notions, stereotypes, or beliefs we may have about various minority groups"* (italics added). For example, a common white stereotype about Black males is that they are full of anger, which often leads them to violence (49–51).

In the foregoing incident, it is interesting to note that despite their high level of education and (one would assume) greater than average sensitivity to issues of expressive style, these psychology professors fell victim to stereotypical thinking. In this light it becomes clear that *academic education and interpersonal skills alone do not immunize one against personalizing cross-cultural encounters.* Since we all look at the world from our own cultural perspective, anything that does not fit our expectations seems inappropriate, out of place, and wrong. Our natural tendency when encountering difference is not understanding and acceptance but labeling and stereotyping.

Communicating the Spirit and Intent

How does the foregoing illustration of the possible consequences of cultural difference in communicative style relate to encounters between hearing and Deaf individuals? In a transaction in a doctor's office or a government office, will the Deaf and hearing people involved be able to discover the richness of their respective cultures and come to appreciate their distinctive ways of expressing themselves? What should be the interpreter's role in managing the variations inherent in these situations?

One of the tenets of the old RID Code of Ethics stated that "the interpreter shall render the message faithfully, always conveying the content and spirit of the speaker. . . ." This principle is echoed by section 2.3 in the new NAD-RID Code of Professional Conduct. *Webster's New World Dictionary of the American Language* cites several definitions for *spirit,* one of which describes the term as "the real meaning" or "true intention." So my contention is that *our responsibility as interpreters is to impart each speaker's true intention, making adjustments for differences in communicative style in situations when our failure to do so would result in a misunderstanding of the real meaning of the statement.*

Let us say that a Deaf person goes to a medical appointment with the intention of getting a prescription for his or her ailment from the doctor. The doctor's intent, meanwhile, may be to prescribe the appropriate medication, if any, for this patient's problem and be on to the next patient in fifteen minutes. Then that is exactly what we as interpreters should facilitate happening. If the two consumers' modes of communicating happen to be different enough and if we as interpreters do nothing but literally transmit the words and signs used, the real meaning and true intent will be lost in a sea of misunderstandings and judgments (e.g., "Deaf people go on and on and never get to the point," "Doctors are so rude they never let me finish my explanation").

Naturally it is a different story if a hearing person whom we are interpreting for is interested in Deaf culture and is eager to know more about it. In our normal workday, however, this is a rare event. Mostly we work with doctors, Social Security Administration case workers, and job supervisors, all of whom just want to get this meeting over with as quickly as possible and get on with the rest of their work. When communication breaks down because of differences in cultural styles, everyone involved becomes annoyed. And what happens? The participants do not achieve their original intentions or an understanding of the real meaning behind their communication.

As we have established, the appropriate way to converse varies considerably in different cultures. A Japanese/English interpreter who is interpreting between an American and a Japanese businessman will make the appropriate adjustments for politeness so that no one will feel insulted. There is a complex system of honorifics in the Japanese language that expresses the correct level of politeness and respect between different ages, sexes, and social positions. An American is not expected to know about the use of honorifics in Japanese, let alone the suitable term to use to address his Japanese counterpart. It is the interpreter's job to make the necessary addition or adjustment to ensure that the American does not provoke his host, when absolutely no insult was intended. In the opposite direction, the interpreter in her English translation may leave out a certain term of respect used by the Japanese businessman because to literally translate the term would "sound funny" in American English, where we are used to a more informal conversational style. The interpreter who is aware of such cultural differences between English and Japanese will do her job so that the communication seems as natural as possible between her two consumers, so that each speaker's true intentions are imparted. Shouldn't we do the same? Isn't the point of our job as bicultural mediators to ensure that consumers can convey the intent and real meaning of their utterances without cultural differences getting in the way?

In this chapter we have examined the role and responsibilities of sign language interpreters from many angles. It is clear that our task is too complex to be summed up by a simple model. Not only do we have to concern ourselves with two different languages, but we also need to analyze the situation so as to determine whether cultural adjustments are necessary. Suppose we decide that without a cultural adjustment, erroneous judgments will arise in the minds of our consumers. What then are our options? The next chapter will discuss specific techniques we can employ to prevent cultural differences from obscuring the true meaning of our consumers' messages.

11

Techniques for Cultural Adjustments

So far, we have (1) established that cultural differences greatly affect communication, (2) become familiar with contrasts between American mainstream culture and American Deaf culture, (3) identified specific cultural misunderstandings that occur in common interpreting situations, (4) explored the roles and responsibilities of sign language interpreters and (5) examined features of African American/Black, Asian, Latino/ Hispanic, and American Indian cultures. In chapter 9, we considered specific interpreting challenges in multicultural environments and some effective approaches. In this chapter we will look at a few more successful cultural interventions and examine what the interpreters did well in these situations. I will then offer a set of questions interpreters can employ to assess whether cultural adjustment is needed in any interpreting situation. Next, I will suggest a few useful techniques for cultural adjustment, and finally, I will return to some of the scenarios from chapter 8 and offer some options (based on these techniques) for handling them more effectively. This approach will give us a framework that we can apply to future interpreting challenges.

Every profession has a vocabulary with which to discuss the techniques used by its practitioners. Chefs learn how to scald, sauté, and simmer. Football players can compare the advantages of a double reverse, a shovel pass, and a quarterback sneak. Ballet dancers can work to perfect their jetés, pirouettes, and arabesques. Because the profession of sign language interpreting is so young and the concept of cultural adjustment is itself relatively new, we have not yet developed a set of terms with which we can easily discuss what we do. On several occasions, I have tried to talk about cultural adjustments with other interpreters, only to be reduced to such explanations as "Well, I did this sort of thing..." It is hard to be precise without a special vocabulary that more clearly delineates our options. As a result, I have come up with nine terms for things that we may have been doing for years without having any labels for them (see pages 222–31). I do not pretend that this is the last word on the subject. It is only a starting point; others may add to or modify my terms or throw them out altogether. But it will give us a start in talking and thinking about these subtle yet vital aspects of interpreting.*

Successful Cultural Adjustment Scenarios

1. "Surprise!"

Before an administrative hearing, the interpreter and the Deaf client are seated in the waiting room. The Deaf client briefs the interpreter on the issues he is planning to bring up at the interview, giving him the context and some of the major events relevant to this case. When the administrative official takes them into the conference room, she prefaces the hearing with a list of three topics to which discussion will be limited. The interpreter, on being informed of these topics, is surprised that none of them includes the issues the Deaf client had mentioned in the waiting room. In interpreting the statement about the three topics, the interpreter emphasizes the point that these and *only* these topics will be discussed, adding several phrases that stress that discussion of other topics will not be allowed. The Deaf client responds, "Wait, do you mean that I cannot bring up any other issues? I want to talk about X, Y, and Z." The administrative officer kindly asks to hear the client's concerns and then the two of them work out a way to satisfy the client's needs without ever "formally" beginning the hearing.

2. "My, how you've changed"

At a meeting between a Deaf client and her social security worker, the Deaf client's opening remark to her worker is, "WOW YOU FAT NOW!" The relay interpreter, in this case, asks the Deaf client, "Do you mean that she looks different from the last time you saw her?" The client nods emphatically. The relay interpreter puts the woman's comment as, "I've

---

*I want to thank several superb interpreters who shared their insight and experience with me for this chapter: Aaron Brace, Patricia Lessard, Nikki Norton Rexroat, and Daniel Veltri.

noticed that there's a change in your appearance," intending to convey the caring attitude that was under the surface of the client's first comment. It also leaves it up to the hearing worker to elaborate on the comment or let it go.

3. "It all started when . . ."

At a doctor's appointment, the interpreter is aware of a familiar pattern: the doctor asks the opening question expecting to get a short introduction to the patient's current concerns and is thrown off when the Deaf patient launches into a detailed chronological narration. So when the doctor says, "And what brings you here today?" the interpreter conveys a request for the patient to specifically relate what's wrong now. Nevertheless, the patient begins his comments, "Five years ago . . ." The interpreter realizes that the need to supply the context must be very important to the patient and begins voicing, "Doctor, I need to explain a few things first to give you some background. Five years ago . . ."

4. "Hint, hint"

During a discussion between an official of the Department of Motor Vehicles and a Deaf man about how he could win back a suspended license, it seems to the interpreter that the official is hinting that of two possible courses of action, it might be more advantageous for the Deaf man not to follow the officially sanctioned procedure but to follow another course of action instead. As a DMV employee, however, the woman might not feel comfortable overtly advocating such an alternative. The interpreter realizes that in order to convey the underlying message to the client she will have to be more explicit. So she checks out her hunch with the DMV official by asking, "Are you saying that . . . ?" Getting an affirmative murmur in response, the interpreter describes the two options to the client and states explicitly why the alternate course of action would be faster and cheaper. Then the Deaf man asks the DMV official, "Do you mean that it would be better for me to . . . ?" The DMV official nods, smiling.

Let us look back at these four scenarios and analyze what took place. I believe that in each case the participants' intentions were accurately conveyed. Not only did the interpreters not take over, but also by their skillful handling of the situations and elimination of cultural red herrings, they allowed the participants themselves to control their transactions. Without getting derailed by culturally different ways of communicating, each discussion came to a satisfactory conclusion. (This is not to say that successful cultural adjustment means that all participants must leave every meeting totally satisfied. Sometimes if we do our job well, the participants come to see just how different their opinions and goals really are.)

Awareness and anticipation seem to be key ingredients in recipes for successful interpretation. In each scenario the interpreter demonstrated an awareness of the cultural factors and anticipated what might have happened had he or she not made a cultural adjustment.

1. "Surprise!": the interpreter realized that if he had matched the offhand, flat affect of the administrator in delivering the line, "The discussion will be limited to three topics," it might have slipped by unnoticed, only to become the crux of confusion later on.
2. "My, how you've changed": the relay interpreter foresaw that the Deaf woman's comment would sound extremely insulting to her social security worker.
3. "It all started when...": the interpreter, correctly anticipating a common cultural mismatch, tried to take preventive action. When that did not bring about the desired response, he was flexible enough to try another technique.
4. "Hint, hint": the interpreter realized that the DMV worker was subtly suggesting a beneficial course of action to the man. Knowing the limitations of her skills as a nonnative signer, the interpreter decided that she might not be able to achieve the same subtle hinting quality in ASL and so decided to opt for explicitness. She was careful, however, to check out her understanding of what was hinted at before proceeding.

I want to reemphasize that the choices made by the interpreters above were not the only possible solutions. There are many options that could have produced similar results. Also, the same situations with different clients would probably have led these interpreters to make alternate choices. The point is that the interpreters saw as their paramount responsibility that communication and understanding take place unimpeded by cultural differences.

One of my goals in this book has been to install a "cultural early-warning system" in your brain that will light up to signal a possible cultural misunderstanding. The next time you are in an interpreting assignment and notice that something does not seem to be going right, stop for a moment and assess the situation. Perhaps there is a feeling of tension in the room, a restless shifting of a body in a chair, or a fleeting expression of puzzlement that tips you off. One way to ascertain if there is indeed a need for cultural adjustment is to go through a mental checklist, asking yourself if any of the following elements are present. (Feel free to add your own questions to this list.)

1. Does there seem to be an intention of *rudeness*? If not, and I interpret the comment literally (without a cultural adjustment), will there be a perception of rudeness from the other party?
2. If the surface form of the comment seems to be troublesome, can I look for the *function* of the statement and convey that?
3. Are the points being presented in an *order* that the other person may find unclear?
4. Can I use my *own reactions* as a barometer in this situation? (Am I confused? Am I surprised or offended at something?)
5. Is there a *hidden implication* that I should make explicit? (Do I need to check it out first?)
6. Does this comment assume *prior knowledge* or *shared assumptions* that the other party may not possess?
7. Are participants leaving with basically *the same conclusion* that I came to?

After we have asked ourselves questions like those listed above and concluded that there does indeed seem to be a cultural difference that might get in the way of clear communication, the next question is surely, "What can I as the interpreter do about it?" I will now offer nine techniques for cultural adjustment in face-to-face interpreted situations, labeled so that we can discuss their relative merits for a given situation.

The Waiting Room Chat

Chatting with the Deaf client for a few minutes before the appointment gives us an opportunity to get a picture of the context, timeline of events, and main point from the Deaf client's perspective. It is also gives us a moment to examine his or her use of language and to establish rapport. Give the Deaf client an opening line which invites his or her story without demanding it, for example, "Is this your first time here?" or "Can you tell me a little bit about what this meeting is for?" Contrary to some opinions, it is not "cheating" to get background information. Without some kind of briefing by the patient, when the doctor refers to "that procedure we tried last year" or "those tests I told you about" or "my concern about your condition," you will probably have to stop the conversation to ask for a more specific explanation (so you can convey the "procedure" as a D and C or a triple bypass, the "test" as a blood test or an eye test, and the "condition" as high blood pressure or diabetes). The more information we can obtain in an overview of the situation, the better we will be able to structure the Deaf client's comments in a way that is clear to the hearing client and vice versa.

A few notes of caution are needed, however. First, take the information gleaned from the waiting room chat and hold on to it *lightly*. Once in the actual meeting, the Deaf client, just like anyone else, has a right to change his or her mind, forget, or even lie about what he or she told us previously. Second, sometimes we are so good at establishing rapport with Deaf clients that they develop too great an expectation of our support for them. It might be necessary, if this seems to be happening, to remind the client that we are there to serve both parties and that once we go into the office, the client will need to explain everything he or she just told us to the doctor or lawyer or social worker. Third, remember that the waiting room chat is a nice but optional bonus. For a variety of reasons, the Deaf client may decline to give you a preview of the upcoming appointment.

Targeted Translation

Cultural misunderstandings in interpreted settings can be broadly divided into two categories: those that stem from variations in *form* and those that come from surprises in *content*. Quite often in a question-and-answer session, for example, if we pay attention to the expected form of the answer and structure our translations so they elicit the anticipated form, things will flow smoothly. A question might require a numerical response (How many times? How often?), a narration (What did you do after the accident?), or a description (What did it look like? What kind of pain did you feel?).

Also, the questioner expects an answer based on a certain time frame: the present (What is your current position?), the past (When did these headaches first start?), or the future (How will you pay for your college tuition?). The more we hone our ASL skills to be able to target a specific kind of response to a question, the more we can eliminate misunderstandings based on form.

Inoculated Questions

Medical inoculations often inject a person with a mild form of the unwanted disease in order to achieve immunity. Similarly, when the cultural tendencies are very strong, it can sometimes be effective to specifically state what kind of response you wish the respondent to avoid in his or her answer. For example, one challenging task is to interpret a question from English that asks for a simple yes or no response. Knowing that in ASL it is common to supply background or context in answering questions, it can be helpful to acknowledge that fact instead of just hoping it won't happen. Strict expectations of adherence to a yes/no format are of critical importance in legal settings, but this type of question comes up in many other situations as well.

In the following example, "Have you informed your supervisor of these problems with Joe, your coworker?" you can predict the types of elaborative details the Deaf client may be tempted to add but which may be more appropriate for a later time. Instead of ruling out any mention of these details, your inoculated question could specify that those will be asked about in a moment. Here is one option: FINISH INFORM SUPERVISOR PROBLEM WITH J-O-E? (HAPPEN++ JOE BAWL-YOU-OUT, YOU MAD CLASH, HOLD EXPLAIN LATER) WANT KNOW SUPERVISOR YOU INFORM FINISH. YES NO WHICH?

Signposting and Road Mapping

Just as signs on the highway such as "Detour" and "Construction Zone" alert us that the road ahead is not what we anticipated, we can add phrases or sentences to our interpretations that clue in consumers that the statements to follow may not be in the form they expect. For hearing consumers, prefacing your interpretation with phrases such as "Let me give you some background . . ." or "I would like to go back to the beginning and explain how this all started . . ." may help them wait patiently for the point or allow them to see why the Deaf consumer began his or her comments with details instead of an introductory statement.

What form would signposting take for Deaf consumers? A more visual analogy might be called "road mapping." Instead of adding an explanatory phrase, road mapping lays out a picture of the conversational journey ahead. Suppose that a hearing boss calls a Deaf worker and his hearing coworker into her office to resolve a conflict between them in the work environment. If the interpreter gets a sense of the sequence of events to follow, either explicitly or implicitly from the boss, she can lay out a road map for the Deaf client; for example, "First Fred will tell his side of the story, then the boss will ask him some questions, then you will get your turn and she will ask you some questions. Then you and Fred can ask each other any questions you have and try to come up with a mutually satisfactory solution."

Very often in the types of meetings we are called upon to interpret, the Deaf person is not the one in power and does not have control over the order in which things are presented. The way a Deaf boss would structure the same meeting might very well differ from the hearing boss above. A road map does not grant you the ability to change the road ahead, but at least it tells you what to expect.

Identifying the Function

This is a critical skill that is not easily taught. What does it take to figure out what a person is *really* expressing? It calls for the intuition of a therapist, the clue-gathering skills of a detective, and a chess master's ability to see things from different points of view. One way to prepare for this task is to become familiar with basic functions of language acts, such as requests for information, connection-building comments, criticisms, explanations, and so forth. Just as an actor working on a role looks for the intention behind each line, we, too, can analyze what is behind the lines we deliver.

To help us anticipate what the function of some of our Deaf clients' comments may be, we can refer to the most central values of Deaf culture. In the scenario "My, how you've changed," the interpreter saw the intention of the client's opening remark as connection building and interpreted it to retain that function, instead of insulting the intended target. Some other themes in Deaf culture we might want to keep in mind are the value of clear communication and sharing information about oneself and others, loyalty to the group, and the insider/outsider distinction.

On the other side, one of the most common confusions occurs when the hearing client expresses a veiled criticism or a negative remark that is covered in a positive coating in order to make it more palatable. If we conclude that the underlying intent of a comment is critical, we should try to bring that out.

A note of caution: since divining the intent underlying a statement involves an intuitive guess, it is often a good idea to check out your hunch before proceeding. Note that the relay interpreter in "My, how you've changed" did so. In another circumstance a more bicultural client could have conceivably answered, "Just interpret what I signed, it's this joke we have—every month we tease each other about being fat."

Highlighting the Point

We probably all have some kind of "third eye" that monitors our interpretations to see if we are communicating effectively. It may help us to identify the major point each of our clients is trying to make and mentally check that the point is getting across. The point may get lost due to a less direct style or different order of presenting arguments than the participants are used to. Two questions we can ask ourselves are "Do I need to add an introduction, a conclusion, or a summary in order to bring out the point?" and "Do I need to stress the important points through emphasis in the appropriate channel: vocal inflection, facial expression, sign choice, or repetition?"

Sometimes you, as the interpreter, may have difficulty identifying the point. You may therefore choose just to relay the muddy thought and then translate the Deaf person's puzzled expression or the hearing person's "Huh?" Or you may subtly insert a query for clarification of the point. One interpreter told me that when the doctor says "Your blood pressure is 150/80," she feels she cannot deliver that line without knowing if it's good or bad news. So she might ask "Is that good?" in order to be able to convey the point of the statement.

Context Balancing

Shelley Lawrence, Anna Witter-Merithew, Theresa Smith, and other interpreter educators have noted that one of the major differences in discourse style between English and ASL is the latter's use of expansion, amplification, and elaboration. As discussed in chapter 3, these include adding layers of detail, reiteration, faceting, and describing things by indicating what they are not. More recently, Lynn Finton and Richard Smith of NTID have further examined the effect of these discourse features (Finton and Smith in Maroney 2004). When interpreting from English to ASL, therefore, a common strategy is to increase the amount of context, making use of these features.

English discourse structure, in comparison, is more linear. Where the point in ASL may be implicitly understood from the accumulation of details, in English the point of a lecture or a large chunk of discourse is usually stated explicitly at the outset. In ASL one clarifies a concept by demonstrating it, acting it out, or showing how it works. In English, a label (word, phrase, or technical term) is often sufficient. In other words, when interpreting from ASL to English, we may often need to reduce the amount of context in order to make it sound appropriate in English (Finton and Smith refer to this technique as "compression").

Another type of context balancing occurs when there is a reference to cultural information that one party erroneously assumes the other party shares. For example, hearing Americans make reference to many aural aspects of their culture without thinking twice. Theme songs from television shows and famous lines from TV commercials or popular songs are woven into everyday conversations. Interpreters cannot usually explain the entire reference, but a parenthetical "G-I-L-L-I-G-A-N'S ISLAND (an old TV show from the 1960s)" helps clarify a little. By the same token, references to artifacts of Deaf culture such as "TTY," "residential school," "relay service," or "NAD" may need a parenthetical short explanation to bring hearing consumers up to speed.

A cautionary note: sometimes the other party's ignorance of the cultural reference becomes the whole point of the rest of the conversation. In her teleconference, Forestal mentions a job interview where the Deaf applicant was asked if he had any last questions for the employer. The applicant asked, "YOU HAVE TTY HERE?" to which the interpreter, with all good intentions, added, "a telecommunications device that deaf people use to talk on the phone." That added clarification essentially ruined the Deaf person's strategy, which was to check out the level of awareness of this prospective employer.

Back-Channel Feedback

One feature of ASL that is easily observable is that it is a language of conversational interaction. The receiver of the communication is involved in active listening (often called back-channel feedback), which includes head nods and signs such as UH-HUH (nodding Y hand shape), REALLY, KNOW, and nose wrinkle (YES). Many languages require some form of back-channel feedback to demonstrate attentive listening, including spoken English and Japanese. Typical expressions used for back-channel feedback in English are *uh-huh, okay, mmm,* and *right.* In Japanese, one uses lexical items such as *un, ee, aa* and *hai.* Other vocalizations, including laughter, coughs, and sniffs, can also serve the same purpose.

In a study of back-channel feedback in English and Japanese, authors Ward and Tsukara describe the way it works.

> One person is explaining something or telling a story, the other person is paying attention and understanding, and produces a typical word or sound to indicate this, and also to indicate that he wishes the story-teller to continue. The story teller, without showing any awareness of this response, continues with his story, perhaps slightly encouraged to know that his listener is still interested. (1999, 1178)

Ward and Tsukara list some of the most common uses of back-channel feedback as expressing "attention, understanding or agreement" as well as judgment, sympathy, and approval (1183). They state that these collaborative conversations demonstrate that being a "good listener requires ... being responsive" (1201).

As we mentioned in chapter 6, the African American discourse style known as "call and response" is also a form of back-channeling. "This rhetorical style does not permit passive listening on the part of the audience. Listeners in both formal and informal settings are expected to actively give the speaker verbal feedback" (Lewis 1998, 232).

Even though white Americans practice a form of back-channel feedback when speaking English, they may not be sensitive to its usage in other language contexts.

> Call-response can be disconcerting to both parties in Black-white communication, presenting a real case of cross-cultural communication interference. When the Black person is speaking, the white person, because call-response is not in his cultural heritage, obviously does not engage in the response process, remaining relatively passive, perhaps voicing an occasional, subdued "mmmmhhm."

Judging from the white individual's seeming lack of involvement in the communication, the Black communicator gets the feeling that the white isn't listening to him, and may repeatedly punctuate his "calls" with questions, such as "Are you listening to me?" "Did you hear me?" etc. In an extended conversation, such questions become annoying to the white, and he may exclaim, "Yes, I'm listening, of course, I'm listening, I'm standing right here!" (Daniel and Smitherman 1989, 39)

The previous description of Black-white miscommunication may seem very familiar to sign language interpreters because a similar misunderstanding often happens in Deaf-hearing interactions, minus the confrontation and defensive response at the end. Typically, the Deaf person relates some experience and the hearing person listens attentively, yet impassively. Having not observed evidence of active listening in the form of the back-channeling expressions common to ASL, the Deaf person thinks that the hearing person did not get the point, so repeats the utterance possibly several more times, with increasing intensity. Meanwhile, the hearing person, who did understand the point of the remark the first time, becomes irritated by seemingly unnecessary repetitions. The previous scenario is, of course, mediated by an interpreter. Hearing no words from the hearing person, it would *seem* that there is nothing to interpret. Yet if we view the hearing person's silence as attentive listening, would it not be culturally equivalent in ASL to translate that into the more active form of listening represented by back-channel feedback? (Naturally, if we sense that the hearing person is *not* paying attention through, for example, the sound of rustling papers and sighing, then it would be inaccurate to supply the back-channel feedback in ASL).

Back-channel feedback in ASL is an area ripe for research. Lacking hard data, we can make some tentative observations. There seem to be several distinct types of back-channel feedback (BCF) that are given/expected including, (1) BCF that shows attentiveness and that one is following the story (e.g. nodding and UH-HUH), (2) BCF expressing surprise at something the story teller relates (e.g. REALLY), (3) BCF reacting to or sharing the humor of a remark, (4) BCF that expresses empathy for some misfortune related by the speaker (5). There is also another kind of BCF that the speaker may look for when using a name sign, geographical sign or abbreviation, a BCF that either affirms that the receiver knows the referent or expresses puzzlement that alerts the speaker to the need for more explanation.

As an interactive, high-context language, ASL requires the extensive use of BCF. It is not an optional feature. Many ASL programs include instruction in how to listen appropriately with BCF. When a Deaf person is having a conversation with a hearing person who signs but does not supply the appropriate BCF, it can be a red flag that the hearing person is not getting the signed story but is embarrassed to admit it. Given the importance of BCF in ASL conversations, it is surprising that interpreters are not yet taught to supply this essential conversational element. If the hearing consumer's silent but attentive listening is not translated into the cultural equivalent of attentive listening in ASL, namely back-channel feedback, then it is no wonder that Deaf consumers may repeat their points out of frustration.

CUES

Speaking of silence, is interpreting silences part of our job? After all, what is there to convey? Actually, there can be quite a lot. As discussed in chapter 2, silence in different cultures has many meanings. In American mainstream culture, wherein long pauses are typically avoided, silences perform different functions. There is the silence of respectful attention, the silence of thinking before answering, and the silence that follows an emotionally intense announcement, to name only a few. That we usually have no trouble knowing which is which shows how attuned we are to our own culture. Conveying to our Deaf clients the function of the silence not only prevents them from interrupting an already full moment but also gives them clues to the aural mood.

Besides silences, there are other aspects of a conversation the purposes of which may not be explicit. As a hearing person is getting ready to wrap up a meeting, clues of this intention are clearly present in vocal inflection and body language. For example, if our sign rendition of the hearing person's repeated "Okay . . . okay . . . okay" does not convey the intention of ending the conversation we know to be present from their heavy exhalation of breath and the rustling of papers, we may need to add the sign FINISH to explicitly state that the interview is now concluded.

Although we may feel that conveying information back and forth is the goal of our interpreting, many Deaf people have told me that often they consider cues to the emotional undertones to be of equal or greater importance than the content of the information. In ASL, affect is often conveyed by facial expression, at which we may or may not be natively proficient. Sometimes it may be necessary, therefore, for us to add an explicit comment to make sure that the affect is getting across. Since we are not psychologists, it may be safer to preface this comment with SEEMS (e.g., SEEMS ANGRY, SEEMS UPSET).

When Is Our Responsibility Over?

In keeping with our American tendency to compartmentalize, when we are interpreting for two people and one of them leaves the room, we may feel that our job is done. After all, there is nothing left to interpret. Our Deaf clients may have a different expectation. A frequent occurrence at a medical appointment, for example, is that the doctor exits and the Deaf client asks us clarifying questions about what just took place. One common query is about the affect of the doctor. Did he or she seem to be in a hurry, distracted, or impatient? We may feel it is appropriate to answer this question if we accept the responsibility for having neglected, in the midst of relaying important information, to convey the emotional aspects of its delivery. What about questions regarding the content of the information? Again, if we feel that the lack of clarity in our interpretation was at fault, we may decide to repeat the major points, *but only if we are absolutely certain we remember the information correctly.* If there is the slightest question in our mind whether it was two pills, three times a day or three pills, two times a day, we are obligated to call the doctor or nurse back in to clear up the confusion. Concerning health matters, it is better to err on the safe side, even if we are pretty sure we remember what the doctor or nurse recommended.

Just as our job may begin in the waiting room (before there is anything to interpret), it may not end when the hearing person leaves. Certainly everyone has a right to leave a meeting with a misunderstanding about what took place. It happens every day. Despite our best efforts to the contrary, it will sometimes occur. Often people have their own reasons for "mishearing" even the most lucid explanation. The purpose of our presence, however, is to facilitate communication taking place. Sometimes the Deaf person feels more comfortable asking us to restate the point than the hearing person. To mentally punch the time clock the minute the hearing person leaves the room and refuse to wrap up the transaction with the Deaf client borders on the culturally insensitive, if not the unethical.

Our Responsibility to Educate

The comment has been made that if we do all of this subtle cultural adjustment, the participants will leave the meeting thinking that their own communication strategies were successful. Although it is not clearly defined, part of our job as interpreters is also to educate our consumers.

Therefore, it is sometimes appropriate, after the situation, for us to give our Deaf or hearing consumers information about what cultural adjustments we just made, the cultural expectations that prompted us to do so, and what they themselves might do differently the next time around. There is no general rule. In each situation you must judge which consumers would have the time to listen, would be interested, would understand, and might benefit from your explanations. In my own work, I would say that, unfortunately, most people are too busy or are too involved with their own lives to be open to such discussion. Nevertheless, sometimes it is worth a try, particularly if the two participants intend to have an ongoing relationship or series of meetings. You might begin your discussion with the hearing consumer by reminding him or her about your requests for clarification. "Do you remember how I asked you for examples several times during the interview? Well, in ASL . . ."

The Deaf person may also be interested in a short explanation of hearing cultural expectations. We might explain that hearing doctors usually want to be in control of the interview and therefore prefer short answers, which they can follow up with more questions, or that in hearing job interviews one is supposed to be very positive and try to sell one's skills.

Let us now revisit some of the scenarios from chapter 8 and apply the techniques discussed above.

MEDICAL SCENARIOS

Scenario 1

Hearing Doctor: Hi. How are you?

Deaf Patient: Well, that first pill you gave me last year was awful, made me itch all over, then the blue one made my headache worse, and this one made me feel dizzy in the morning. . . .

Let us use this common situation to go through the nine techniques described earlier and see how each one could be applied. The *waiting room chat* is invaluable for medical appointments. If you learn that this is the patient's first visit to this particular doctor, at least you will find out that you are on equal footing with the doctor in knowing about the events which led up to it. If, on the other hand, the patient and the doctor have a long history together, it may be more difficult for you to catch the context. In the waiting room, however, if the patient doesn't mind giving you a brief overview of what the appointment today is for and what led up to it, you will have a mental picture of the timeline of events and the point of the visit.

Like the interpreter in "It all started when . . . ," you should anticipate how easily this first exchange can turn into a frustrating experience for both doctor and patient. It's a good idea to try to *target the translation* in ASL to focus on the reason for *today's* visit. You may add an *inoculation* by stating that this is not the moment to describe all the events leading up to today, so hold that for a bit later. For example, point-doctor-HE WANT KNOW YOU HERE TODAY FOR-FOR? [HAPPEN++(moving from past till present) THAT HOLD, point-HE WILL ASK-YOU LATER.] WHY HERE? WRONG WHAT?

If that strategy doesn't work, and the patient, like the one in "It all started when . . ." responds with a chronological narration, you can use a *signposting* phrase to clue in the doctor as to the reason the response is not in the form he or she expected.

It is important, in your own mind at least, to *identify the function* of each of these statements. The doctor's question is an attempt to elicit a short statement of what brings the patient in today. The patient's statement is an attempt to give the doctor valuable information connected to the patient's medical history, without which the patient believes the doctor cannot make an enlightened diagnosis. One of my Deaf consultants on this book confided that even though she considers herself to be bilingual and bicultural, for a medical appointment several years ago she wrote out pages and pages explaining her medical history, which the doctor put aside after barely a glance.

Having learned the reasons for the patient's visit during the waiting room chat, the interpreter can use this information to *highlight the point* in the signposting phrase or at the end of the patient's narration (e.g., "So you can see that the reason I'm here today is to try to get another medication for my headaches which won't have such unpleasant side effects").

One way to *balance the context* would be to expand the doctor's question and specify the type of answer the doctor is looking for. On the other side, the interpreter may need to reduce the details of the patient's narrative response, perhaps summarizing it to, "As you know, I have experienced several unpleasant reactions to the medication you have prescribed in the past."

As to what we can do to satisfy the expectations of the Deaf client, if we successfully signposted, the doctor may indeed be listening attentively to the patient's first statement, which we can make more obvious by supplying some *back-channel feedback*. If we pick up some subtle clues of impatience on the doctor's part, however, we can relate those to the client through *cues* as to what kind of silence or restless throat clearing we perceive. Clearly, to use all these techniques in one exchange would be redundant. My effort has been to illustrate the range of possibilities at your disposal. In the remaining scenarios revisited below, only those techniques best suited to the context will be examined.

Scenario 4

Deaf Patient: My friend told me she has glaucoma too and she used a blue bottle of drops that made her vision blurry, but then she got a red bottle of drops that made her eyes feel better. . . .

Hearing Doctor: Never mind about your friend.

"My friend" comments are very common at medical appointments. The most trusted authorities in Deaf culture are other Deaf people's experiences. So if we look under the surface of the statement, its function is to invoke an authority. Some cultures invoke a holy book as the authority; others, like mainstream American, rely on scientific data and the media. The doctor, in dismissing the patient's statement, is reacting to its nonprofessional, almost gossipy tone. If a hearing patient had concerns about his or her medication, yet presented them differently, such as "I read in the *Wall Street Journal*" (or "saw on TV" or "found on the Internet . . .") "that there is a new experimental drug for my condition," the doctor would probably treat the patient's concerns much more seriously.

In interpreting the Deaf patient's comments I am not suggesting that we invent a newspaper article, only that we downplay the chatty tone. Perhaps something like, "Recently, I was made aware of a new medication for my condition . . ." If we have the benefit of the waiting room chat to get a preview of the patient's concerns, identify the function of the statement as invoking an authority, perhaps reduce the context by summarizing the details of the friend's experience, and highlight the request for information as the point, the doctor may be able to satisfy the patient's inquiry after all.

EDUCATIONAL SCENARIO

Scenario 3

Hearing Professor: I am glad you came in to discuss your paper. Hmmm . . . your choice of topic is fine, you have a few good examples . . . but I do have some concerns about your thesis. . . . I'm not sure it is strong enough to support a paper of this length.

Deaf Student: You mean, make the thesis statement longer?

As cited in chapter 8, this scenario went on much longer as misunderstanding compounded misunderstanding. Let's see if highlighting the point early on could have nipped the problem in the bud. Depending on how much lag time we allow ourselves, we may already begin signing before we hear the tip-off phrase, ". . . but I do have some concerns about your thesis." That is the point. We may have gotten a clue that the point was on its way from the "leading-up-to-something" tone of the professor's voice and from our familiarity with the sandwich approach to giving criticism. Once we identify the point and determine that it is a critical comment, it is essential to make that clear in our translation. If we have already signed the comments about the topic and the examples, we may decide to preface the next statement with the sign POINT or POINT WHAT? T-H-E-S-I-S . . . The signs CONCERN or WORRY may not be emphatic enough. Using PROBLEM or TROUBLE with the appropriate facial expression would be more likely to get the student's attention. In the next sentence, "I'm not sure it is strong enough . . . ," the professor again tries to be polite by picking his words carefully. What he is really saying is that the thesis is weak. If we sign something like WEAK or NOT GOOD or NEED CHANGE, it will likely lead to a discussion between the student and professor focused on what specifically needs to be changed in order to make the thesis statement effective.

We can use ourselves as a barometer. If we don't know what the point is ourselves, we cannot convey it in our interpretation. If the professor uses a lot of academic jargon, it may be necessary to ask him or her directly, "Excuse me, but the interpreter wants to make sure she understands clearly. Your point about the paper is what?" Otherwise, it is very possible that real communication will not take place.

JOB INTERVIEW SCENARIOS

It is interesting that notwithstanding our discussion of the cultural set of assumptions in job interviews and the necessity for knowing the rules of the game beforehand, there are still some cultural adjustments we can try in order to make the playing field more level. Remember that it is impossible to generalize. Despite the stressful situation and different set of cultural expectations, some Deaf people give excellent interviews (and some hearing people don't). Novice interpreters should be especially careful about job interviews and realize that there are no hard-and-fast rules about what is most effective.

Scenario 1

Hearing Interviewer: Why do you want this job?

Deaf Applicant: I need the money and you have dental insurance. I have to get a couple of crowns.

Suppose that you interpret the first question straightforwardly and receive this statement in reply. You have several options. One is to increase the register and reduce the amount of context in the answer to make it sound more businesslike, such as the following (which I appropriated from another interpreter): "I believe I am ready for a salary as competitive as what you are offering and would appreciate the type of comprehensive benefits package this company provides." A note of caution: although the elegant phrasing of the above translation would fit in beautifully in a corporate setting, it might not fit the repertoire of the interviewee. We need to walk a tightrope when it comes to selecting a register for our interpretation so that we do not create unwarranted expectations.

Another option is to excuse yourself to the interviewer, saying that you would like to interpret the question again, as you believe you were not

clear the first time around. The second time you could target your translation of the question to emphasize that all jobs pay money but what is it
about working at this particular company in this specific position that
appeals to the applicant?

Scenario 2

**Hearing Interviewer: Why do you feel you are the best qualified
candidate for this position?**

**Deaf Applicant: Well, my first job was as a secretary, my second job
was as a claims adjuster, and my third job was as a supervisor.**

Again, there are several options for cultural adjustments. If you get this
response, you may focus on restructuring the answer by adding an introduction and summary, remembering to pick a register that balances the
expectations of the interviewer with the client's individual style and level
of education. If you have managed a waiting room chat prior to this
moment, you may be able to craft a specific introductory statement to
preface the details. Something like, "My advance from an entry-level
position to supervisor of more than twenty people in a period of only five
years demonstrates my familiarity with and proven responsibilities in this
field," and then use a short conclusion to highlight the connection of the
person's previous experience to the job being interviewed for.

If on the other hand, you did not have a waiting room chat and do not
have an overview, a more general signposting phrase might be used to
preface the details. "I would like to tell you a little about my background
so you can get an appreciation for the breadth of my experience." Then
after you have learned the details, you might use a concluding statement
to sum up the applicant's most striking selling points: "So you can see that
my quick rise to a supervisory position is a clear demonstration of my
aptitude in this field."

Another strategy is to target your translation of the first question into
ASL by figuring out what the interviewer is really looking for. You may
decide that what the interviewer really wants to hear is why this applicant
is unique, what makes him or her different and better than other applicants for this position. Or you could conclude that the point of the question is to elicit the way the applicant sees his or her skills as matching the
requirements of the job. The English question itself is rather vague, so it

may take some familiarity with job interviewing strategies on your part to make it more specific.

Scenario 3

Hearing Interviewer: Do you have any experience with the XYZ software?

Deaf Applicant: No. None at all.

This quick exchange does not seem to give the interpreter much room to maneuver. If you have a lot of experience interpreting job interviews, however, you may realize that this and many other questions are really invitations to the applicant to describe all his or her relevant skills. Therefore, you may safely broaden the question to YOU HAVE EXPERIENCE WITH XYZ SOFTWARE OR OTHER SIMILAR? One option when presented with the answer above is to emphasize the underlying function by interpreting the response as, "To be totally honest, no I do not." At least the applicant may get points for candor.

I hope that you now feel you possess a cultural tool kit for interpreting that contains an appreciation of cultural differences, a set of questions to probe for their presence, and a range of techniques to adjust for them.

12

Interpreting
in a Virtual World

*"The interpreter who agrees to interpret a phone call without an introduction
of what sort of call it will be does so at his or her own peril."*
—DR. NANCY FRISHBERG
Interpreting: An Introduction, 1986

If we agree with the words of Dr. Frishberg, above, those of us who work in
the video relay service environment are in a pretty perilous situation.
Technological advances have completely altered the way sign language
interpretation is delivered, and there is no turning back. More changes are
sure to come. I am writing these words in the summer of 2005 and there is
no doubt they will be out of date by the time you read them. Therefore, in
this chapter, I will not discuss pending legislation, technological specifica-
tions, or even the current shortage of community interpreters following
the mass migration to VRS, as these areas are the most likely to change.
My interest lies in the ongoing challenges of video interpreting, primarily
in the VRS environment. In the context of this book, the focus here will be
how our VRS work relates to cultural issues.

Cultural differences can encompass contrasts between English and
ASL or Deaf and hearing politeness norms, including the expectations
and conventions that have developed around telephone conversations in
American mainstream culture. It can also refer to the situation in which
one or both of the callers are from a different cultural group than the
interpreter.

There is a wide range of subjects in this area that deserve careful study,
but no research has been conducted as yet. At this early stage in the video
interpreting revolution, one cannot expect easy answers, but there are

clearly enough questions for a shelf full of dissertations. My aim is to raise issues and questions so that others can study them further.

In this chapter, we examine VRS from the interpreter's point of view. (It should be noted that different VRS providers have slightly different setups.) Our world now consists of a cubicle in an office suite full of similar cubicles. The interpreter wears a headset and sits alone at a computer desk in front of a large screen and a small camera. When the interpreter is connected to the Deaf caller, they can see each other signing, although the picture quality of the Deaf caller ranges from crystal clear to pixilated and jerky. Calls come in from all over the country from both Deaf and hearing callers (the vast majority originate with Deaf callers). Some last a few seconds, some a few hours. If a call continues for more than twenty minutes, or if the interpreter is having trouble understanding either of the parties, he or she can team up with another interpreter or the call can be handed off to another interpreter.

As we discussed in chapter 7, Deaf people have embraced VRS as the easiest, most comfortable way to make business and personal phone calls, yet it presents one of the most challenging environments for the interpreter.

Challenges for the Interpreter

Some of the reasons that VRS work is so demanding are these:

1. ASL is a three-dimensional language, but it is received through a two-dimensional screen.
2. It is physically taxing to sit in a cubicle and focus on a video screen for hours at a time.
3. Many of the calls have less than perfectly clear images of the Deaf signer, mainly because of technical issues or poor lighting.
4. The sheer number of different callers in a day is overwhelming, especially as the interpreter must adjust to different signing styles and regional signs.
5. Interpreters are continually confronted with names (and name signs) of unfamiliar cities from both hearing and Deaf callers.
6. Calls may be technical, medical, or legal in nature, with specialized vocabulary and interpreters are required to take them all, even though that interpreter might not have the necessary training or background.

7. With calls from all over the country, sometimes callers are from cultural groups with which the interpreter may not be familiar.
8. Many calls to businesses entail tediously navigating through layers of voice-activated menus.
9. Calls to family members can be emotionally intense.
10. Interpreters receive virtually no information about the callers or the subject to be discussed before the call begins.
11. There are many aspects of telephone culture and etiquette that Deaf people have not experienced directly. Interpreters need to make split-second decisions about how to handle any communication breakdowns.

In the recent rush to staff newly opened VRS centers, interpreters are given, at most, a week of training, much of it centered on the technical know-how required to work with this new technology. The FCC views the VRS interpreter as merely a "transparent conduit between two people communicating through different modes" (as cited in RID's draft position paper on VI and VRS). To date not much attention has been paid to the many aspects of VRS work that differ from face-to-face interpreting.

In the next section, we will briefly examine a few of the most challenging aspects of working in the video relay environment: the lack of preparation and context, issues of turn-taking, and silences.

No Context

Interpreter signs: HELLO, THANKS CALL ABC RELAY, ME INTER-PRETER 1165.
Deaf caller signs: HELLO, PLEASE CALL (502) 668-9876.
Interpreter signs: OK. RINGING 1, 2.
Hearing person says: Hello, Pleasant Valley Medical Center.
(Interpreter signs: HELLO, P-L-E-A-S-A-N-T V-A-L-L-E-Y MED-ICAL CENTER)
Interpreter says and sim-coms: Hello, this is ABC Video Relay interpreter 1165 with a video-relay call. Are you familiar with video-relay?
Hearing Person: Yes, I am.
Interpreter says: Fine, I will connect you.
Interpreter signs: YES, GO-AHEAD
Deaf Caller signs: ME F-R-E-D S-M-I-T-H, CALL FOR ASK HOW G-I-N-G-E-R, SURGERY FINISH, HOW?

(Interpreter says: Hello, this is Fred Smith. I am calling to see how Ginger is doing after her surgery.)

Hearing Person: Sure, hold on a moment, I will check. (pause)

(Interpreter signs: SURE, HOLD MINUTE, ME GO CHECK, HOLD)

Hearing Person: I asked the doctor and she seems to be doing fine, no fever, no vomiting . . .

(Interpreter signs: ME FINISH ASK DOCTOR, POINT-HE SAYS G-I-N-G-E-R FINE, FEVER NONE, VOMIT NONE . . .)

Hearing Person: . . . and her *tail* is healing well.

(Interpreter has a "brain freeze" as she throws out the mental picture of Fred's dear old grandmother or sweet little girl that she had in her mind).

Interpreter says and sim-coms: Excuse me, this is the interpreter speaking. Did you say "*tail*"?

Hearing person: Yes, tail.

Deaf caller: YES, G-I-N-G-E-R, MY CAT.

Instances in which the interpreter mentally goes down the wrong path, such as the one above, are common in VRS when no context is provided. One reason for the lack of context in VRS is the imposition of the conduit model with the instruction not to engage in any small talk and to connect the callers as soon as possible. We have already established that ASL and Deaf Culture are on the high-context end of the continuum. What are the implications of interpreting without any knowledge about the speakers, their relationship to each other, and their goals in making their calls?

To shed some light on this question, let us start by comparing VRS calls to "community interpreting" assignments, where we physically travel to a location and interpret in the same room with two or more consumers.

Context in Community Interpreting Assignments

If an interpreting agency called with a job you would probably be given the following information prior to the assignment: the names of the Deaf client, hearing client, and contact person, the address of the assignment, and the type of situation, as well as the date, time, and estimated length of the assignment.

You may happen to know from your own experience in the community the Deaf client's language preference, some previous history about the client(s), as well as names of nearby cities and their name signs and any recent significant events in the community.

By physically traveling to the assignment, you would gain more context (e.g., Is it in a fancy downtown office building or a crowded public hospital?).

When you actually walk into the office or waiting room, you will gain more clues to the upcoming encounter, such as: the demeanor of people in the waiting area (e.g., bored, restless) and information posted on the walls (e.g., posters, doctor's diplomas). You would notice how the staff responds when you introduce yourself (e.g., friendly or nervous about having a Deaf client and interpreter for the first time). The contact person and/or hearing client may supply additional information (e.g., what happened last time, the plan for today). Upon meeting the hearing client(s), the interpreter can observe their age, clothing, attitude, and so on.

When the Deaf client arrives, you may have a "waiting room chat," providing an opportunity to see the client's signing style and assess his or her educational background. You may be given a preview of the upcoming appointment, possibly with information about previous encounters and the client's stated (or unstated) goal. If this is an ongoing assignment, such as a college class or monthly staff meeting, you may have even more background information.

Lack of Context in VRS Calls

Without the benefit of any of the information listed above, VRS interpreters are flying blind, by beginning their interpretations while guessing about language preference, situation, goals, and relationships. This can lead to any of a number of problems. For example, one might begin speaking and signing in a consultative (professional) register and then realize, halfway through the call, that the two callers are related. If the point of the call is eventually figured out (e.g., making a complaint, trying to rent an apartment, informing someone of a death in the family), the interpreter can adjust words and signs to match the callers' intent. It is ironic that most interpreter training programs stress the importance of getting as much information as possible before accepting an assignment in order to do an effective job and yet, when it comes to VRS, we have allowed ourselves to go against our own best advice.

Being a VRS interpreter is the perfect job for mystery fans. Without any direct information about the nature of the call, all one has is a series of clues. The first clue is the phone number and perhaps the state of the incoming call. If you are good with area codes, you might even be able to figure out the city. The next clue is the visual field of the room where the Deaf person has their videophone or web camera. Interpreters get intimate glimpses into tidy living rooms with doilies on the armchairs or messy bedrooms littered with old pizza boxes and beer cans. Then, the main character appears dressed in anything from an impeccable business suit to a ripped motorcycle T-shirt to perhaps nothing at all (at least what we can see from the waist up). The mystery guest, making an auditory appearance, will be the hearing party. We call the number and wait in suspense. Will there be an additional clue when the hearing person answers by announcing the place of business? Not if the bored or overworked receptionist's greeting sounds like: "Goodmorningthankyouforcallingbay-sideserviceshowmayidirectyourcall?"

As Deaf people continue to use VRS, many are becoming sophisticated in their interactions with video interpreters. They realize that in a face-to-face interpreting encounter, the interpreter would have a great deal of information or would ask for it before beginning to interpret. In VRS calls, the interpreter is not allowed to ask any questions (except perhaps, "Is there a specific person or department that you want to ask for?"). Therefore, it behooves Deaf callers to supply at least a few specifics if they want their calls to proceed smoothly. Training by VRS providers or agencies serving the Deaf regarding tips for successful VRS calls would probably result in more satisfied customers who would, in turn, increase their number of calls.

Turn-taking

Turn-taking strategies differ widely between conversations in spoken and signed languages. With spoken languages, people use mostly verbal or paralinguistic indicators to signal that they want a turn to speak. In signed languages, one uses gestural indicators such as waving, increased head nods, or touching the speaker to indicate a desire to speak. What happens in conversations between a Deaf person and a hearing person who do not share the same turn-taking strategies? Research shows it is the interpreter's job to mediate the inevitable overlaps that occur. (See Roy 1989 and 1993; Metzger 1999)

If there is awkwardness in interpreted face-to-face conversations between Deaf and hearing persons, at least speakers have backup visual cues. In interpreted VRS conversations between a Deaf and a hearing person, overlaps are unavoidable. As VRS interpreters describe it, sometimes the callers have two different rhythms that just do not mesh. What is the interpreter's responsibility in this situation?

Telephone Culture

If cultures have their own norms for expected behavior and rules for politeness, speaking on the telephone definitely qualifies. For example, greetings to initiate phone conversations between two hearing Americans consist of a certain number of steps and level of formality, depending on the relationship.

We would no more likely greet our mothers on the phone with: "Good Afternoon, is this Mrs. Bernard? This is your daughter Claudia Lovejoy calling," than we would begin a phone conversation with our physician with: "HEYYYY DOC! It's me, Howie. Whassup?"

Completing the phone call is also governed by a set of unspoken rules and expectations. Ending a call abruptly is seen as rude ("She hung up on me!"). Courteous call closing gives the other person a warning that the end is near and at least one last chance to speak.

Hello and Goodbye in VRS Calls

In the hearing world, there is a unique set of rules for starting and ending phone conversations. Most Deaf callers have not had a great deal of exposure to the expected steps of saying hello and goodbye in spoken phone calls. In a typical VRS call that originates with the Deaf caller, the interpreter handles the opening sequence, often by explaining VRS itself.

Closings on VRS calls are often more problematic. Deaf callers who use TTYs have their own rules for winding up those calls politely by making sure that the other person is finished before hanging up. The convention of typing the phrase "GA to SK" ("go ahead" to "stop keying") basically translates as "I am finished and ready to hang up. If you have something else to say, go ahead, otherwise we can both hang up now." It is followed by either additional conversation, or a series of one or more "Bye SKs."

This polite formula for typed TTY conversations does not transfer to VRS calls. Closing sequences in hearing calls depend greatly on vocal intonation, which is inaccessible to Deaf callers. With VRS calls, there are often awkward pauses, as neither caller is sure if the conversation is winding down. The interpreter may discretely inquire "FINISH?" to the Deaf caller and after receiving an affirmative response, can signal the intent to close the conversation with an appropriate phrase (e.g. "Well, I guess that's all for now . . ."). Or, if the interpreter hears the intonation or verbal message that the hearing caller is getting ready to close, the preparation for closing phrase can be made more explicit so that the Deaf caller can have a chance to add a last comment. Otherwise, it may seem to Deaf callers that hearing callers hang up abruptly when they actually give clear, but unspoken, announcements of their intent to do so.

Silences on the Phone

It may not be surprising to learn that pauses in telephone conversations are shorter than in face-to-face discussions. What might be startling, however, is that in at least one study, fully 95 percent of pauses in telephone conversations were of *less than one second* in duration. Any pause lasting longer than one second prompted comments from one or the other party to restart the conversation (Hopper 1992, 229). Interpreted conversations are riddled with silences caused by time lags. In face-to-face encounters, the reason behind the time lag is more obvious. If the hearing person asks the Deaf person a question and a long silence follows, at least he or she can see that the interpreter has not yet finished signing the question. The hearing person on the phone, however, may have no experience with sign language, Deaf people, or interpreters, so the unexplained silences are even more unsettling.

Experienced VRS interpreters know that innocuous filler phrases can do a lot to smooth out the bumps of otherwise unexplained silences. Some tried and true examples: "Hold on while I get a pen to write that down," "Let me check my calendar," and "Hmmm, let me think about that for a second."

In VRS calls to hearing people, the interpreter can handle long silences on the part of Deaf callers. Unfortunately, automatic voice recognition systems are not as understanding. They seem to be set to expect a very quick response to their demands for an account number or phone number. One of the most frustrating experiences in VRS is to be stuck in an endless loop of interpreting a question, getting the answer, and trying to enter a number while being repeatedly interrupted by an impatient machine voice insisting, "I am sorry, I did not hear your response."

Leaving a Voice Mail Message

Leaving a simple voice mail message is one of the VRS interpreter's most difficult tasks. Many telephone conventions such as when and how to identify oneself, lengths of silences permitted, and getting to the point are squeezed into 30 seconds. What makes the task even more challenging is that the interpreter has had no previous conversation to establish context. Hearing people are so used to the formulaic way one leaves a message; they may never realize there are rules until they get broken. Here are a few of the mishaps that commonly occur in VRS:

1. The Deaf person leaves a message too slowly, and includes pauses for thinking. After some specified number of seconds of silence, the voice mail automatically shuts off. This means the interpreter must call back, perhaps making filler noises or draaaawwwwing out the words to fill the silences.
2. The Deaf person may not realize that one usually summarizes the point quickly in a voice mail message. His story goes on and on until it is cut off midway through.
3. Sometimes Deaf callers walk away in the middle of leaving a message in order to find a piece of paper with an account number or some other information, unaware that the hearing person probably won't wait through a lengthy silence to see if the message will continue.
4. Other messages are too short: "Why are you never home? Call me back!" The Deaf caller forgets to mention her name or number.

The Challenge of Being Transparent

Deaf callers "own" their calls and have control over how they want to be represented. Some callers do not want the hearing person to know that they are Deaf. This request is sometimes made when inquiring about an apartment for rent or a job opening. It is certainly understandable, given continuing discriminatory practices. It is doubtful, however, that Deaf callers realize how tricky it is to pretend that no interpretation is taking place in a two-way phone conversation. Like the voice mail example, this proves how ingrained rules of silence and response time are on the phone. Suppose that the Deaf caller has a job interview over the phone and instructs the interpreter not to announce the call as VRS. When the prospective boss asks an involved question, the interpreter may be tempted to resort to an improvised coughing fit in order to buy some time. After the question and answer is signed back and forth, the interpreter may be able to come up with a natural sounding, enthusiastic response such as, "Oh excuse me, why yes, I have had a great deal of experience with that software!"

Business or Family

After having worked in the VRS environment for a while, one begins to recognize two major categories of calls: business and family, which roughly correspond to weekdays versus weekends. Each has its own special set of challenges.

Business Calls

In addition to the issues that are common to all types of phone calls, (hellos and good-byes, turn-taking, and silences) there are specific expectations in business calls, including

+ When and how to identify yourself by name
+ How long you are given to get to the point of your call
+ How much background information is required and expected
+ How to register a complaint
+ When a "thank you" is expected

Nowadays, calling a business and having the phone answered by a living, breathing human being is the exception rather than the rule. Most businesses employ multilayered automated menu systems (e.g., to check your account balance press 1, to report a theft press 2, to hear these choices again, press 3). It often feels like one is lost in a maze, searching desperately for a way out, getting closer, and closer, only to pick a wrong turn and get thrown back into an endless loop. This frustration is universal. No wonder Deaf callers often greet the VRS interpreter not with HELLO but with a desperate plea for "LIVE PERSON, LIVE PERSON." Ahh, if it were only so easy to achieve.

Family Calls

The hardest thing about interpreting calls between family members is the vast amount of shared information between the callers. The oddest thing about family calls is that it never seems to occur to either party that the interpreter is the only one in the conversation who is completely out of the loop. It usually starts with a list of names. Often the Deaf caller will begin by spelling several relatives' names: "So how is Danny? And Denny? And Donny?" Even if the interpreter does catch the spelling, he or she has no idea of age, relationship, or past history. And if the hearing caller mentions "that trouble he had last year" it could refer to anything from heart trouble, car trouble, or money trouble, to trouble with the law.

Speaking of troubles, some family calls can be intensely emotional. Community interpreting assignments usually occur in professional settings, and it is rare to interpret long conversations between close family members. Yet this is the staple fare of Saturday and Sunday afternoon calls on VRS. Many calls are just to check in and see how everyone is doing and most end happily with a warm exchange of "I love you's." The occasional call, however, demonstrates the power of VRS as grown siblings have their first in-depth conversation (with the help of an interpreter) and long-buried family secrets are unearthed.

Register

Family calls challenge interpreters to master a whole new register, the intimate register. Interpreter training programs usually focus on the casual, consultative, and formal registers because those are the relationships and situations most often found in community interpreting. The intimate register is reserved for discourse between couples, family members, and close friends and is characterized by very high context, where just one word, sign, or facial expression can communicate an entire thought because of the wealth of shared experience. CODAs, who have grown up in Deaf families, probably have the most experience with the intimate register in ASL. There was never a need for interpreting students to practice signing and speaking in the intimate register, as they were never faced with interpreting between a parent and grown child, between siblings, or between lovers—until VRS. It is not unusual to have a two-hour VRS call between a boyfriend and girlfriend, where it seems like nothing is ever said. They just want to share a connection (albeit through the interpreter):

"What are you doing now?"

"Nothing much. What are you doing?"

"Nothin'."

"What are you gonna do later?"

"I dunno, what are you gonna do later?" and so on.

This type of call is challenging because of its tedium. The other end of the spectrum is when a call becomes a heated argument.

Aside from the effort the interpreter expends to "yell" at someone in signs and words for a prolonged period, these emotionally intense calls can push psychological buttons interpreters didn't even know they had. Interpreter training programs instill in students the necessity of being aware of their own limitations. Interpreters are advised to refrain from accepting assignments, for example, a lecture on abortion rights or an NRA meeting, if their feelings about these topics are too strong to remain objective. Being in the unusual position of interpreting intimate details in conversations between family members, however, can tap into long-forgotten or repressed family dramas or traumas of one's own. It is one thing to be aware that a certain political stance will make your blood boil. It is quite another thing when a nagging tone of voice or a contemptuous glance involuntarily triggers an unexpected emotional response in yourself. The best advice is probably to be extra self-aware. If you find you are getting choked up or inexplicably angry interpreting a family call, it is time to ask for a handoff.

Families of Another Culture

Family calls are rife with potential for subjective judgments. What are the implications, for example, when the interpreter and the family members in a VRS call are from different cultural backgrounds? Could a white interpreter wrongly assume that the larger signing space or the vocal expressiveness in an African American family signifies anger? Could a Latino interpreter mistake the reserved facial expressions and neutral vocal quality in an Asian family for indifference when it actually means respect? With no context, preparation, or warm-up before accepting these cross-cultural interpreting assignments, interpreters have even more reason to familiarize themselves with the values and features of the all the cultural communities that they are likely to see on their VRS screens.

Relationship between the Interpreter and the Deaf Caller

When interpreters begin working in the VRS environment, one of the most striking contrasts they discover between their previous community work and VRS is the change in the relationship between the interpreter and the Deaf caller. In VRS calls, there is no warm-up chat to create rapport, no questions about background to establish trust, and no wind-down at the end to solidify the human connection. Efficiency in call handling requires a quick turnaround time between callers so interpreters are directed not to get involved in private conversations. Understandably, too, Deaf callers may just want to find out their bank balance or make that doctor's appointment and get back to their lives as quickly as possible. It is interesting to note, however, that in community interpreting settings, many Deaf consumers previously expressed a strong preference for interpreters to act like "human beings" and not just machines. How do we balance interpersonal skills with competitive, marketplace efficiency? And what does the future hold? How will Deaf people and interpreters relate to each other in face-to-face interpreting encounters? Will it be with the machinelike efficiency of an automated call or the warmth of a human connection?

Video Remote Interpreting

As we have seen, in video relay interpreting, the hearing person, the Deaf person, and the interpreter are in three separate locations. In Video Remote Interpreting (VRI), on the other hand, two of the three parties are in the same location. For example, a Deaf patient is rushed to the emergency room of a hospital in the middle of the night. It is critical to have immediate communication between the patient and the doctor. If the hospital has the necessary technology, an interpreter in a remote location, who ideally has a specialty in medical interpreting, can appear on a video screen a few minutes later and the examination can begin. Other current uses of VRI are in educational settings or for Deaf people who live in remote areas far from most interpreting services.

The experience of VRI is often closer to a real-life interpreting situation than a VRS call. For example, educational interpreters know beforehand what kind of class they will be interpreting and can study course materials prior to the class time, and, in the case of an ongoing class, working with the same clients week after week.

Even though VRI seems like a perfect solution for anytime access to interpreters, there are still problems with this new technology. In a business meeting or college class, for example, how does one get the attention of the person in charge if the remote interpreter or the Deaf person has a question?

Medical settings pose even tougher problems. An interpreter on a video screen will have less flexibility than one who is physically in the same room with the patient. For example, if the patient is lying on his stomach, a live interpreter could make an adjustment and even get down on the floor to make herself visible, but it will be hard to pick up signs and facial expressions from a prone patient via videocamera.

Something else is missing. Although it's hard to measure, it is no less real. Imagine you were ill, in pain, perhaps scared, and you need an interpreter to communicate with your doctor. Would you rather talk to a flickering face on a screen or a live person who is standing near you? It seems that our actual physical presence in the room communicates something too, something that may be impossible to replace. Legal cases, in which patients have sued hospitals for providing a VRI interpreter instead of a live one, have already been filed.

At the time of this writing, VRI has not had as big an impact as VRS, but its untapped potential to revolutionize the interpreting field is tremendous. It is quite possible that in just a few years sign language interpreters will no longer have to worry about traffic jams and parking spaces. They may each have their own video conferencing system set up in their homes. They will position themselves at a mahogany desk, against a lovely blue background. They may virtually travel the world, interpreting a shareholder's meeting in Miami in the morning and a computer conference in Calgary in the afternoon, (all while we are comfortably sitting at home, still wearing pajama bottoms and slippers).

13

Cultural Sensitivity Shouldn't End at Five O'Clock

If we have become sensitized to cultural differences and can effectively manage them while interpreting the messages that pass between our Deaf and hearing clients, we have all our bases covered, right? Probably not. As we saw in chapter 4, our American tendency to compartmentalize our lives is not universally shared. We may feel that when our interpreting assignment is finished, our job is over, but that may not be the way it is viewed by many Deaf people. Most interpreter training programs focus solely on the tasks of interpreting spoken English into ASL and vice versa. Lacking a keen awareness of our relationship to the Deaf community, however, even the most technically proficient interpreter among us may be shunned by the community he or she wishes to serve.

None of the areas we are about to examine have hard-and-fast rules. Nevertheless, they are worthy of thought and discussion among ourselves and with the Deaf people without whom we would not have a profession. In the end, each interpreter will have to make individual decisions about what is appropriate to his or her particular situation. The attention given to these and other related topics, however, is sure to pay off in better working relationships, more open communication, and better feelings between the two communities.

Since this chapter is, in part, about the way that Deaf people see interpreters, I wanted to include some opinions from members of the Deaf community. So I invited two of the Deaf consultants who have been working with me on this book, Daniel Langholtz and Priscilla Moyers, to share their views on the topics covered herein. I believe we can benefit from their wisdom and experience. Of course, they do not speak for all Deaf people, but through their various roles in the Deaf community, they know

Deaf individuals from a variety of backgrounds, ages, and educational levels. Hence, their viewpoints represent not only their individual preferences, but in all likelihood, they reflect those of large sectors of the Deaf community as well.

Personal Issues

ATTITUDE

A common theme underlying the topics in this chapter can be expressed by the ASL sign ATTITUDE (which carries more specific connotations than the English word *attitude*). ATTITUDE seems to hold strong cultural significance, as we saw from some Deaf people's comments in chapter 8. ATTITUDE is frequently the basis for negative judgments or downright rejection of otherwise competent interpreters. For example, "Oh, So-and-so, yes, he is very skilled . . . but I don't want him to interpret for me. Why? Attitude." A written transcription of that remark does not do justice to the facial expression used by the Deaf person when making the final sign. It would be more accurate to translate the last term as BAD-ATTITUDE, in contrast to GOOD-ATTITUDE as in "Oh, Such-and-such, yes, I like her. Her skills are . . . okay, but she has a GOOD ATTITUDE."

Over the years, I have questioned many Deaf people about what they mean by a good or bad attitude. Because it appears to be a key to understanding what Deaf clients appreciate or dislike in an interpreter, I think it is crucial to understand its connotations. One of the central elements of a GOOD ATTITUDE is respect for Deaf people and their language, ASL. Other elements, as they relate to interpreters, are a certain humility regarding our ASL skills and Deaf people's desire to see us act as compassionate human beings, not professional robots who are only doing this job for the money. Deaf people have many stories regarding their experiences with interpreters of varying attitudes. One man told me that he will never forget the interpreter who ruined his presentation by refusing to admit that her skills were inadequate. She made many errors in translating the presenter's ASL into spoken English, which left the hearing audience with an inaccurate impression of the Deaf presenter. At the other pole, a woman confided to me that she fondly remembers how the interpreter's comforting presence made waiting to see if her husband would recover from emergency surgery so much easier to bear. These issues are not specifically addressed in our code of ethics, yet who can deny their significance?

Our Motivation

Two of the most common questions we are asked when we meet a Deaf person for the first time are "Where did you learn sign language?" and "Why did you become an interpreter?" Whatever our answer, the information we offer may not be as important as our underlying attitude. Was it out of respect or pity? One of the possible invitations to launch into our story may be "MOTHER FATHER DEAF?" which subtly anchors the role of interpreter to the tradition that those who had Deaf parents are often led to an almost inevitable calling. Nowadays, when most interpreters have hearing parents but have made the conscious decision to learn sign language and pursue careers as interpreters, we are in essence being asked for our motivation. "We had a Deaf neighbor . . . ," "My best friend in high school had Deaf parents . . . ," "There was an interpreter in one of my college classes . . ." These are typical ways in which one receives an initial exposure to sign language today.

What about the following response: "I learned sign language so I could interpret at church and help save deaf people's souls"? Prior to the establishment of interpreting as a profession, one reason that hearing people learned sign language and became involved in the Deaf community was for religious purposes. Although there are Deaf people today who are strongly religious and may not find anything objectionable in such an answer, to many others it connotes a patronizing attitude, with Deaf people seen as poor unfortunates who are in need of being saved by those who can hear. (A more positive religious connection could be "I learned sign language from a Deaf pastor named . . .")

Another possible motivation might be "I learned SEE signs so I could help show deaf children how to use English." Currently, there is great controversy regarding the best way to educate deaf children. Studies have shown, and a preponderance of culturally Deaf people maintain, that ASL should be the primary language of education for deaf children. Then, using a bilingual approach, teachers apply the medium of ASL to teach written English skills (Lane 1992).

The question of why we learned sign language can be seen as a test of our attitude. Does our answer show respect for ASL and for Deaf people as capable adults? If the phrase "to help deaf people" is part of our response, it may suggest a patronizing attitude, even if the interpreter denies having any such feeling. Although our initial reason for learning sign language may not involve the respect the Deaf community desires, there is always a chance for enlightenment, once we have gotten to know Deaf people individually and collectively. I happen to know two interpreters who, though they learned sign language for the "wrong" reasons, went through a transformation once they became involved with the Deaf community. One, whose initial reason for learning sign language was that he was a member of a church that had a missionary effort aimed at the deaf, later quit that church, became involved with Deaf theater, and eventually became an excellent interpreter. The other initially learned SEE signs because that was the only sign language class offered in his small community college, but later, through a deep involvement with the Deaf community, he acquired native-like fluency in ASL and became a highly respected leader in his field.

Giving Credit to Our Deaf Teachers

After giving our initial reason for learning sign language, the next part of our story usually explains *how* we accomplished that task. Whether or not we began with formal classes at an educational institution in order to become fluent enough to work as interpreters, we must have interacted with members of the Deaf community, trying their patience with our awkward first attempts at signing. Probably there were one or two Deaf individuals who acted as cultural brokers, taking us under their wings, correcting our mistakes, introducing us to their Deaf friends, and sharing their knowledge of Deaf culture. It seems only right that we give them credit. While we may be justly proud of our accomplishment in learning ASL, we probably could not have done it without Deaf people's guidance. By mentioning their names when appropriate, we demonstrate our ties to the community—which may be as close as we can come to the comparing of networks of acquaintances Deaf people share with each other when they first meet.

Name Signs

Many of the points in this chapter are ways of demonstrating respect for the people and culture we have come to know. As discussed in chapter 5, ASL possesses a Traditional Name Sign System by which Deaf people are given one of the two distinct types of name signs, either arbitrary or descriptive. Traditionally, hearing people were not given name signs, since the two cultures had much less contact than they do today; they were referred to by spelling out their English name. The name sign system in ASL is evolving, however, and there are new developments that are viewed negatively by many Deaf people. Some hearing people, mostly novice signers, and even a few Deaf people have a name sign that fits neither into the Arbitrary nor the Descriptive Name Sign Systems. These may be termed "nontraditional" or "blended" name signs, and they typically use a handshape to represent the initial of the person's name but with the sign made in a location and with a movement to suggest a meaning. They may refer to a physical feature (S-WITH LONG WAVY HAIR) or a personal characteristic (D-WHO IS ALWAYS LATE) or even a hobby (M-WHO LIKES MUSIC).

"Deaf people have responded negatively to the increase of nontraditional name signs within their community," warns Sam Supalla in *The Book of Name Signs* (13). He goes on to state:

> The notion of a hearing person possessing a name sign is a much more complex issue. This is especially relevant when considering that the mere possession of a name sign symbolizes membership in the Deaf community. Thus it is necessary for a hearing person to understand the true value of name signs according to the traditions of the Deaf community. (18)

Clearly, we must look at our name sign, if we have one, and consider if it fits the traditional name sign system of ASL. When in doubt, it is always a good idea to consult with a few Deaf community members for their advice. Suppose you examine your name sign and find that it does in fact belong to the nontraditional category. You may be puzzled in recalling that it was made up and given to you by a deaf person, perhaps even your first sign language teacher. There are several theories to explain why this occurs.

> One is that deaf people invented name signs of this kind for hearing people to show that they were outsiders in the community's regard. The other is related to the "reasons" sign language teachers often give their students why signs are made the way they are, perhaps hoping that the (often imagined) etymology will help the memory. Students in the spirit of "every sign must have a reason" may have devised or been encouraged to devise initialized-descriptive name signs. (Mindess, 15)

It may be interesting to learn that it is not only in the United States that novice signers are given "inappropriate" name signs with the thought that if they continue their involvement with the Deaf community, they should later become aware of this fact. I met one of the top sign language interpreters in Paris, whose name is Francis. The first name sign he was given was actually a pun on the fact that phonetically his name sounds like "francs six," so his name sign was the sign for this amount of money. Years later, when he realized the inappropriateness of having a name sign built on a sound pun, he changed it to a more traditional descriptive name sign. (There is no equivalent to arbitrary name signs in LSF, although number name signs were common thirty or more years ago.)

Sharing Personal Information

As discussed in chapter 5, sharing personal information is such a basic value in Deaf culture that to decline to do so can be seen as rude. Whereas to hearing Americans a noncommittal "Fine" or "Okay" may be an acceptable answer to "How are you?" many Deaf people may find such pat answers far too vague. I remember one morning, upon arriving at an all-day assignment, when one of the Deaf participants whom I knew only slightly greeted me with "What's up?" My offered response, "Not much," clearly left him dissatisfied. He pressed me for details, probably in reaction to seeing the circles under my eyes. Grudgingly, I described how my sleep the previous night had been repeatedly interrupted by my feverish toddler. It was not that the information was exceedingly personal or embarrassing, it was just that I was not prepared to disclose it.

This dilemma is not limited to interactions between the deaf and hearing. Priscilla, who works as a Deaf relay interpreter in the courts, reports that she is sometimes taken aback when the Deaf person she is interpreting for inquires about her address or other personal details that she would feel uncomfortable disclosing. Her solution is to "be prepared," to plan ahead of time what she might comfortably answer to questions that could arise. As an example, when I was in my thirties and not yet a mother, I would often get the question "Why don't you have any children?" during the first few minutes after meeting a Deaf person at an assignment. I had a reply ready to use, something like, "We have been trying for a while. Seems like it's taking a long time. Just have to be patient, I guess." This pat explanation steered clear of details that I did not feel like sharing with a stranger, and it was delivered in a way that seemed to imply that I did not wish to discuss the subject any further.

What are some of the questions we might be asked? They can range from inquiries about our marital status or our religion to queries about how much money we earn or how much we paid for our car. Sometimes it may happen that we are not asked a direct question; instead, the Deaf person tells us a long story about his or her marital problems or health problems. At that point, we may wonder if we are expected to reciprocate by relating something equivalent from our own lives. If we notice our companion's lack of eye contact with us, however, and the continuous stream of the narrative, we may reasonably conclude that it is more important for that person to get his or her story out than to hear ours. Showing that we understand and sympathize, if appropriate, can be done with signs such as UH-HUH, REALLY? DIDN'T-KNOW THAT, with appropriate facial expression. Be prepared, however: at the conclusion of the story, he or she may ask if a similar situation ever happened to us. It would be appropriate to make a comment that shows we listened but that also concludes discussion on this topic if we wish to do so (e.g., "I remember a similar thing happening to a friend of mine, but eventually it all worked itself out").

Sticky Issues

"What Do You Think I Should Do?"

One of the clearest tenets of both the old RID Code of Ethics and the new NAD-RID Code of Professional Conduct cautions interpreters to "refrain from providing counsel, advice, or personal opinions" (CPC 2.5). A dilemma can arise because there may be different reasons behind asking our opinion, depending on whether the question comes from a hearing or Deaf client. The hearing nurse, for example, may ask us for our opinion out of ignorance or discomfort with the situation. If she directs a question to us such as "Do you think he would like to sit or lie down for this procedure?" all we need to do is inform her that we are only there to facilitate communication and that she needs to ask the patient directly (and possibly add that we would be happy to interpret her question). Once they get used to the situation, most hearing people accept the fact that we cannot offer our opinions.

When Deaf people ask our advice, on the other hand, it may be with a different rationale. First of all, we can sign—which means instant, easy communication. Second, we are hearing. Sadly, some Deaf people have grown up with the misconception that just because someone is hearing, he or she automatically knows more than Deaf people. (This inaccurate estimation of hearing people's abilities may not only be limited to our greater knowledge. I have had a Deaf person think I could hear a whispered conversation at the far end of a crowded, noisy room or that I could remember what amount of money had been quoted for an insurance policy one year previously.) One more reason we may be asked for our opinion is that, once again, sharing personal experiences and advice is a basic element of Deaf culture. It seems natural to the Deaf person to ask us what we think simply as a human being.

It is the way we decline to give advice or an opinion that demonstrates our cultural sensitivity. Instead of coldly saying "I can't tell you what to do. You have to decide for yourself," we should look for a tactful response that avoids supporting one choice over another. One option, if we are asked "Should I buy that car?" or "Do you think I should have that operation?" is to empathize with the difficulty of making quick decisions. Or we could relate something we do when faced with a similar situation. For example, "I always make a list of pros and cons to help me decide" or "I usually talk with my friends first to find out if they have had a similar experience." Another avenue is to refer them to resources where they may get more information: the Internet, the advice nurse at the local medical center, *Consumer Reports,* the library—and it may be helpful if we offer to interpret a phone call to help them access these services.

A Question of Money

The subject of money can be an extremely sensitive one between Deaf people and interpreters. From our point of view, we should be compensated as professionals. In all likelihood, we have had years of training, have worked our way up in the profession, and still attend workshops and classes and conventions to further improve our skills. What happens when Deaf people ask us outright how much money we make an hour, a day, or a year? Most often, we become defensive. After we get over our shock at being asked a question that is taboo in American hearing culture, we may feel that it is none of their business, since in most cases it is the state, the university, or the hospital that is paying us and not the Deaf person.

The emotionally complicating factor (at least for me and I am assuming for others as well) is that we know that Deaf people as a group have been underemployed (Schein and Delk 1974; Jacobs 1989; Crammate 1987). Furthermore, notwithstanding the ADA, one of the reasons they get turned down for many opportunities is because of the high cost of interpreters.

> Interpreters often "betray" Deaf people simply by "making a living off the community" without contributing to it. It's especially their use of Sign Language . . . the jewel of the culture, for individual, personal gain. It makes no difference that the actual money does not come from Deaf people. Deaf people suffer as a result. Employers are reluctant to hire Deaf people for whom they will have to hire interpreters. Even deeper than this is the distrust of interpreters whose knowledge/skills are for sale. (Smith 1996, 229)

Recently a Deaf person told me with some indignation that interpreters make $90,000 a year! What to do? I could tell her that I certainly don't make that much, nor do most interpreters I know. I could describe the drawbacks of working as an independent contractor—no sick time, no paid vacations, slow periods when there is little work, having to pay one's own medical insurance, and so on—but the facts, I suspect, are not as important as the feelings evoked by this subject. Putting myself in Deaf people's shoes, I can understand the resentment built up from experiences like seeing interpreters getting paid for what looks like "not working" (even more so when an assignment is canceled at the last minute or we are compensated for the entire day though we end up interpreting for only a short period of time) or interpreters with less than a fluent command of ASL still being paid high rates. In the end, it is probably true that interpreters make more money than most Deaf people, and it doesn't seem right to some that we do so through the medium of their language.

An additional factor is that some Deaf people's conception of "work" varies considerably from our own. It may have been inspired by the quintessential Deaf job, printing. Following that template, "work" would be seen as something physically demanding, where you go to the same place every day, get dirty, and sweat. Some Deaf people who work as computer programmers have mentioned to me that other Deaf people chide them for their easy life of "just sitting all day and playing with the computer." Teachers are also viewed as not working very hard—they don't sweat; they spend the day talking; they get to go on those fun field trips; and they take summers off. Interpreting does not fit the mold of "hard work" either.

Interpreters often travel around and meet different people in interesting situations. They sit while interpreting and, when they switch off with their team interpreter, it looks like they get a break every twenty minutes! They also get a double benefit, earning money and learning new information while doing so. Many Deaf people have no idea that interpreting is a difficult mental task. It seems as if we are just talking and using sign language. In this context, it's always interesting to hear the comments of relay interpreters, who admit that they never appreciated what hard work interpreting was until they began to do it themselves.

The sticky question of how much money an interpreter makes will probably not disappear until Deaf people as a group obtain higher salaries. It is up to us, therefore, to handle the issue as tactfully as possible. Here are a few suggestions we may employ as alternatives to "None of your business!" One well-respected interpreter, who is in constant demand by many segments of the Deaf community, explained to me how she uses analogies to illustrate her position on money while avoiding mentioning any actual figures. Sometimes she chooses car mechanics as an example of those who get paid a minimum fee for their time, or plumbers who get paid portal to portal, if that is a parallel to the situation in question. At other times she will point out that doctors, dentists, therapists, and hairdressers usually charge a cancellation fee for missed appointments, as many of us do.

Priscilla recommends that we try educating Deaf consumers on certain points about which they may be unaware, such as the fact that the total bill for interpreting services often includes a sizable sum for the agency that set up the assignment and found the interpreters. Daniel suggests that instead of reacting defensively to the money question, we give a sincere response such as "Yes, it is true that I do get paid for my work. I hope doing my job encourages Deaf and hearing people to better understand each other and work together, so that things will improve and eventually bring about important changes." Other interpreters have suggested that we inform our inquirer if we often donate our services or work pro bono to give back to the Deaf community (see the section titled "The Interpreter as Part of the Reciprocal Pool," 271–72).

The popularity of VRS has led to another tension related to money. "This year [2005] it is estimated that 15 million minutes of video relay will be used" (RIDVIEWS, vol. 22, issue 3, March 2005). Obviously, those are 15 million minutes when interpreters would have previously been out in the community, interpreting doctors' appointments and college classes. Even before the spread of VRS, there existed a shortage of interpreters. As more Deaf people enjoy the ease of video relay and more VRS centers open across the country, the interpreter shortage worsens. Currently, most Deaf people deeply appreciate their quick access to VRS interpreters, and are dismayed about having to wait even a few minutes to get connected to an interpreter. Yet, they are also frustrated as an increasing number of community interpreting assignments go unfilled or are filled by interpreters with less than adequate skills. Those interpreters who do take advantage of the steady work offered by VRS and help fill the around-the-clock need for video interpreters find that when they venture out in the community they are often challenged by the very Deaf people they think they are serving. It is not unusual for an interpreter to be questioned about how many days she devotes to VRS. The underlying (or explicit) message seems to blame interpreters for all the unfilled community assignments and accuse them, once again, of thinking only of money. The irony, of course, is that interpreters would not be working in VRS centers, were it not for the high demand for video relay by Deaf consumers.

At the Assignment

Before the Assignment

In chapter 11 we discussed the "waiting room chat" as a technique to help the interpreter get an idea of what the assignment will be about—main point, timeline, names of the people involved—all in an effort to get a clear picture of the context in order to help us do a better job of conveying the information to the hearing person. In this section we will be focusing on those same moments before the interpreting actually begins, but this time from the Deaf person's perspective.

As the interpreter, when meeting a Deaf client for the first time, you know that there are a few things you need to clearly establish before you can do your job (e.g., language preference, educational level). Suppose, on the other hand, that you are a Deaf person meeting a new interpreter with whom you will have to share intimate details of your life. What would you want to get a sense of first? Probably trust and comfort. For some people that feeling of trust could come from knowing that the interpreter is certified. So, once in a while, we are asked that question directly. We also may be asked if we have had experience with whatever the proceeding will be. For the most part, however, the feeling of trust is based on more intangible factors. Thus, we may be asked for our "story." If we happen to know a relative or friend of our client (only if it is from a noninterpreting context), we might mention this connection. Other personal questions may also be put to us, not to insult us, but to get a sense of us as human beings. If we focus only on the work at hand and refuse to chat or disclose anything more, we may come off coldly businesslike to our Deaf clients.

This kind of chatting does not imply that we need to become personal friends with all those who utilize our services. We may have to find something we feel comfortable discussing (there are always safe topics to fall back on, such as sports, weather, traffic, food). And while we are chatting, we can evaluate the Deaf person's use of language at the same time as the Deaf person is trying to ascertain if we understand his or her signing, and if not, whether we are honest enough to admit it and ask for the statements to be repeated until we do. They may be trying to see if the interpreter feels like "one of us" or is just a member of the hearing world who happens to know how to sign.

Daniel, who gives lectures or presentations in various cities around the country, relates that in the opening chat he is judging the receptive skills of his soon-to-be voice interpreter. If he notices that the interpreter is missing a lot of his signing, he concludes with a sinking heart that he will have to "take care of this interpreter" as well as give his lecture. He wants interpreters to honestly admit when they don't get all of it. Faking it never works. In Daniel's mind interpreters earn "bonus points" if they ask questions pertinent to the upcoming interpreting service (e.g., What is this situation about? Is this your first meeting with the doctor? Do you have any material I could read to catch me up?).

My recommendation, therefore, is that you put yourself in the Deaf person's shoes and try to think what would make you feel at ease if you had to have a third party present when discussing your divorce settlement or the results of your biopsy. But be prepared for surprises. Sometimes you may find, when you arrive fifteen minutes early for an assignment ready to chat, that the Deaf person does not want to say anything at all. He or she may be emotionally upset and worried about the upcoming appointment or may be relating to you as the hearing professional who keeps business in a separate compartment from social interaction. In the end, therefore, you will need to use your sensitivity and take your cues from the Deaf consumer.

Lunchtime

Suppose you and your team interpreter have just worked strenuously for three or four hours; your arms are tired and your brain is mush. Finally, it's time for the lunch break at your all-day assignment! All you want to do is fill your stomach, empty your head, and perhaps catch up on what's happening with your team interpreter's love life. So what do you do when the Deaf person you've been interpreting for inquires, "Mind if I join you two for lunch?"

There are several factors to keep in mind in deciding how to respond. First, are you being paid for the lunch hour? In a job that goes from nine to five, for example, where we get paid for eight hours of work, we might consider the lunch hour to be part of the job and not our free time. Second, are we interpreters the only people who sign at this event? If there are other Deaf participants or others who can sign, it might be easier to decline the invitation, knowing that the person who asked us can find someone else with whom to converse during lunch. If there are no others who can sign, we may feel we must make a small declaration of our allegiance. In this situation, do we feel more a part of the Deaf world because of our ability to sign and accept the responsibilities that entails? Or do we identify more with the hearing world and thereby assert our individual right to take a break from signing?

In some cases, no decision on our part will be required. Sometimes, the Deaf person prefers to eat alone in order to rest his or her eyes and prepare for the next session or says thoughtfully, "You two go ahead and chat [without signing] and have a good lunch. See you back at one o'clock." Other times it is clear that this will be a working lunch for the whole group, and you and your team must juggle eating and signing. It is a nice bonus when you and your team interpreter are sensitive enough to each other's needs to be able to work this out smoothly. For example, my teammate knows that I am always starving at noon, so he lets me have the first turn at eating while he interprets. I know he really likes to enjoy his coffee and dessert, so I take over and let him finish his dessert as slowly as possible. At yet other times you may be looking forward to having lunch with your Deaf consumer, who may be a friend with whom you like spending time.

If there are no clear protocols, however, the moment can be awkward. The Deaf person asks, "Where are you going for lunch?" You and your partner glance at each other, realizing that the hour of gabbing you had planned may not happen. The pause lasts too long and the Deaf person, sensing that you two want to be alone, lets the subject drop and walks off. Is he or she offended? Should you change your plans and resign yourselves to having a different lunch break than you had hoped for? From his perspective as a social worker, Daniel cautions interpreters who feel it is always their *duty* to have lunch with the Deaf person to examine themselves for possible feelings of codependency. Perhaps there are those, on the other hand, who feel "the more the merrier" at lunchtime.

Priscilla advocates honesty as the best policy. If you can foresee that there is no way you will be able to effectively interpret the afternoon session without a mental break, you may want to inform the Deaf client ahead of time that during the lunch break you will need to close your eyes because you are exhausted, have to run an errand, or need to be alone. Another diplomatic way of handling the situation is to tell the Deaf person that she or he is welcome to have lunch with you, but that you and the other interpreter had planned to discuss a topic in which you share a common interest (an upcoming camping trip, dog breeding, potty training, or whatever). That leaves it up to the Deaf person to decide whether he or she finds your proposed discussion boring or is as interested in it as you are.

In situations such as these, it seems we need to have command of polite ways to decline an offer in ASL. Make use of appropriate facial expression with signs such as DON'T-MIND, as in "If you don't mind, I have something I need to do during lunch." In the end, you must make your own decision for each situation, balancing your needs and the good or bad feelings they may engender. Of course, the solution might arise spontaneously if, when comparing restaurant plans, you find that one of you longs for sushi and the other for a fast-food burger. Groaning and laughing at each other's choice of nourishment, you may each go your own way with no hard feelings at all.

After the Assignment

One of the most common complaints I have heard from Deaf people about interpreters is that we rush off too quickly after the interpreting job is finished. In chapter 11, we discussed the question of what is the interpreter's responsibility if he or she discovers there was an incomplete understanding of the interpreted situation. In this section we will focus on what is culturally appropriate behavior after the assignment is completed from the Deaf perspective and what to do if we cannot fulfill this expectation. As was mentioned earlier, Deaf culture follows a longer, more elaborate leave-taking process than does hearing American culture. At a party, good-byes, last bits of news, and hugs can easily last more than half an hour. A work assignment is not a party, but the cultural tendencies remain.

We should not be surprised if, after completing the interpreting assignment, as we walk out of the building with the Deaf person, he or she asks us what we think about what just took place. It does not violate the Code of Professional Conduct to cultivate a few neutral yet human responses to this type of question. Daniel says that if he has just given a lecture or a presentation, he appreciates a comment from the interpreter such as "Nice working with you" or "That was a tough audience." If, on the other hand, as is more often the case, the Deaf person has been on the receiving end of the services and is worried about what has transpired, the interpreter can give a noncommittal response such as "Just have to wait and see what happens." Sometimes we can make use of our knowledge of having been in these situations many times. For example, if after a job interview the Deaf person asks if he or she appeared to be overly anxious, we could remark that everyone, deaf and hearing, is nervous in job interviews.

In general, it is not hard for us to learn to assume a slower pace as we say good-bye, restate when the next meeting will be, perhaps accept thanks from the Deaf person or even a hug. A problem most often arises, however, because of the nature of our work lives as freelance interpreters. In order to earn a living, we must predict how long an assignment will take so that we can plan when we may accept our next one. Sometimes it is not even up to us. When we work through agencies, they give us the estimate (or guarantee) that such and such an assignment will last one hour. It is not unusual, therefore, to have three or four assignments in one day, each of which we must leave at the anticipated ending time or risk arriving late to the next one. Although we may not schedule every appointment back-to-back, we unfortunately do not have the luxury of adding one or two hours between assignments in case these happen to run over their predicted time slots. Human events being what they are, quite often appointments run longer than expected. This puts us in the uncomfortable position of not only having to run to our car after a hasty good-bye but also sometimes actually deciding that we must leave an assignment before it is officially over.

What can we do when this awkward situation arises? The best way to minimize antagonism is to warn all parties involved upon our arrival that we have to leave at a preestablished time. We hope that information can help them tailor their conversation to end accordingly. Commonly, however, people get so involved in their communication that they, like Cinderella, forget that time will soon run out. It is helpful, therefore, to give them a few advance warnings: "Remember, the interpreter has to leave at three," "Just to remind you, the interpreter is leaving in ten minutes." If you give the last warning ten minutes or so before you must leave, the parties have a chance to wrap things up, reiterate their most significant points, or ask one last question. Although it may not need mentioning, I would suggest that conveying an air of regret about leaving prematurely may also be appreciated. "Sorry I have to go now. Wish I could stay longer" can go a long way toward smoothing what might otherwise seem like insensitivity on your part.

Asking for Feedback

Interpreting can be a lonely profession. Often we want so much to do a good job, but without a team interpreter we have no one to give us feedback on our work. In interpreter preparation programs, we may never enjoy the critiques of our interpreting, yet we value the information we receive from the instructor and fellow students to help us improve our skills. Once we are out working, we may feel the need to get a sense of our effectiveness as interpreters, so we ask the people who have been watching our signing, our Deaf consumers. Common solicitations for feedback (especially from novice interpreters) are "Was that okay?" or "Anything you want to tell me about my work?" These questions seem to be open invitations for any and all comments, but what happens when the Deaf person honestly replies like this: "I don't think you are ready to work as an interpreter," "You are not as clear as the interpreter I had last week," "You stood in the wrong place," "You used the wrong sign"? Probably we rush out of the room, hide in our cars, and cry.

We have already discussed the sandwich approach to giving criticism in American hearing culture. I suspect, however, that there is more going on in these situations than merely failing to introduce a criticism with a positive comment. We must take a look inside and ask ourselves what we are really trying to elicit with our questions. If we are honest with ourselves, I believe we will often admit that what we really want is reassurance, compliments, and even a short diagnostic evaluation.

The vast majority of our Deaf consumers are not trained in the specific vocabulary and techniques of doing diagnostic evaluations of sign language interpreters. (Even experienced interpreter trainers often go through weeks of intensive training to attain such skills.) When we ask "Was that okay?" we might get the response, "Yeah, I understood you," which is the Deaf consumer's basic criterion for making a judgment. Such an answer, however, might not feel satisfactory to us.

Suppose we get a more detailed response from the Deaf consumer that points out several weaknesses. We may feel hurt or insulted or that we ought to give up the field altogether. We need to remember, however, that even though it might have stung, criticism in this case can be taken as a compliment, because it means that the Deaf person cares enough to want us to improve and stay involved with the Deaf community.

One way to get what we are asking for is to ask a specific question such as "Was my spelling clear today?" But the best alternative might be to continue to attend workshops or depend on other interpreters for feedback, because we must remember that the Deaf person is focusing on his or her transactions. Is it really fair to expect someone who is going through a tax audit or a tonsillectomy to pay attention to our use of classifiers or nonmanual markers?

Community Involvement

One effective way to counter the negative image of the interpreter as someone who appears to be only interested in making money from the Deaf community is to support the Deaf community by becoming involved to some degree. It is also essential to our proficiency in ASL to see the language and culture operating in everyday contexts outside of our interpreting assignments. In order to become connected in this fashion, we need to find out what opportunities exist. There are many avenues to involvement; we can subscribe to one or more Deaf-related newsletters or chat with Deaf friends to learn about upcoming events. It may be as simple as going to a sports or cultural event, or we may pursue some deeper involvement such as working for a Deaf cause with members of the Deaf community.

One factor that may inhibit our seeking this type of involvement could be a fear of bumping into someone for whom we have interpreted previously in an emotional situation. We might worry that it would be awkward to see this person again. As Priscilla points out, however, Deaf people are more used to switching hats, as they often see each other in different roles

and capacities within the Deaf community. She and Daniel both appreciate interpreters who come to Deaf events, take part in the community, and
master the art of switching hats.

Daniel has some caveats, however. If you want to be in a position of
power, such as on an advisory board or in a Deaf theater production, he
says, wait to be invited by a Deaf person with the appropriate authority.
Be a peer. Support, without taking over. Sometimes it helps to offer your
expertise by enumerating skills that you think may be of use to the community. Examine your motives to see if you are interested as a voyeur,
because of a savior complex, or because it lets you feel like a "big fish in a
small pond." Other Deaf people have expressed resentment at hearing
people who come into the community to learn about its ways, and when
they feel they have learned enough, just seem to leave without a word.

Convinced that there is no end to learning, Priscilla suggests that we
become involved in different types of activities within the Deaf community. For example, if a recreational club's event is over, try looking into an
organization with social or political goals. In this way, she says, you will
meet a variety of Deaf people and become more aware of the complexity
and diversity of the culture.

Signing All the Time at a Mixed Event

There is one simple thing we can do to broadcast a message of inclusive-
ness: when there are Deaf people in the room, sign all the time, even if you
are talking to another hearing person. It goes without saying that if no
Deaf people are paying attention to your conversation, your signing need
not be as clear as if you were interpreting on stage. In fact it will probably
be pretty murky, because we all know as native English speakers that when
we speak and sign at the same time, it is the signing that suffers. The point
I would like to make, however, is that hearing people can access several
conversations simultaneously by catching a word here or a phrase there,
and can then move closer to join one of them. Since we can sign, we possess the means to make the situation equally accessible to Deaf people. If a
Deaf person, glancing around the room, glimpses something you signed
and is interested enough to come over and join your conversation, you can
decide if you want to switch to ASL or pay more attention to clarifying
your signed English as you continue speaking.

This polite behavior may come more naturally at a party where there
are both Deaf and hearing people present. At a work assignment, however,

it is easy to forget to sign during breaks, when we grab a few minutes to catch up with our team interpreter. Even though we have no intention of slighting the Deaf people for whom we are working, their seeing the two interpreters chatting and giggling in a corner can give an impression of exclusion. I suggest, therefore, that if you need to communicate something personal, perhaps about the very assignment at hand, find a private space where you can talk alone and unobserved.

Priscilla advocates frankness. She says that during a break, she would prefer it if, when absolutely necessary, the interpreters tell her they are tired and ask if she would mind if they chatted for a few minutes without signing. "That way," she explains, "I will know that it's not that they are trying to keep something from me, they just want to take a break from signing."

The Interpreter as Part of the Reciprocal Pool

As we discussed in chapter 5, an informal yet important system of reciprocity operates within the Deaf community. As "visiting members" of that community, are we expected to contribute to the pool of resources from which all may benefit? The answer, I believe, is yes—if we want to show our respect for Deaf culture and express gratitude to the community that shares its language with us and thereby enables us to follow our profession. What can we contribute? There is a great range of possibilities, limited only by our talents and imagination. If we do not happen to possess the ability to repair a car or sew a costume, we can always give someone a ride or help someone move.

There is one special skill, however, that as interpreters we all possess—the ability to interpret between ASL and English. When, therefore, is it appropriate for us to donate our services and interpret for free? Here are a few possibilities. One is interpreting informally for our friends at a social gathering. Specifically, at emotionally laden occasions such as a funeral or wedding, it may feel more appropriate to donate our services than to haggle over a fee. (Some agencies have a policy of not charging a fee to the Deaf consumer for a funeral, while absorbing the cost and still paying the interpreter). Also, interpreting at fund-raising events for the Deaf community can be seen as part of our contribution, which would also hold true for political or social causes that we may strongly support.

Sometimes, however, working out the details is tougher than the decision to donate our services. For example, in order not to endanger the livelihood of interpreters in general, it may be better that the organization officially pay you a fee (so that the line item for interpreters can remain in their budget) with the understanding that you will give them back a check, fully or partially equivalent to the one you received. Or you might say that you would be willing to volunteer your services but would like a letter for tax purposes documenting your donation. If you know that Deaf people would have to pay you out of their own pockets (instead of the hospital, school, state agency, or employer), you might tell them you have a sliding scale and charge them less than your normal fee, or nothing at all.

It would be difficult to list all the possible situations where one could comfortably work for free, since it depends on many factors specific to each person and each event. Sometimes your "donation" may not take place at a formally structured occasion. It could happen on the spur of the moment, such as a phone call you don't mind interpreting after your paid assignment is over. Whenever you decide to offer your services gratis, however, you are repaid in the knowledge that you are giving back something to the community that affords you your livelihood.

Conclusion

My aim has been to demonstrate the pervasive impact of culture, not only on our work as sign language interpreters, but in our own lives as well. We now know that we are not alone in dealing with people from different cultures. The field of intercultural communication has much insight to share about the challenges posed by alternate worldviews, values, and communication styles. I hope you are now able to see your work from a new perspective, or better yet, several new perspectives. We have examined aspects of mainstream American Deaf and hearing cultures and also begun to explore the perspectives of multicultural groups. I encourage you to continue your own investigation of culture by reading more about American culture, world cultures, and the other cultures we have begun to describe.

We have also seen that far from being static collections of antiquated behaviors, cultures are living, evolving organisms. It will be fascinating to see what the future holds for Deaf culture. Our own interpreting profession is going through similar shifts thanks to new developments in technology. We will undoubtedly keep refining and redefining our role as we keep up with these changes.

Perhaps the material in this book has led you to conclude that interpreting in a culturally sensitive manner is a far more complex task than you initially thought. We have seen how interpretations that fail to take cultural differences into account can lead to misjudgments and stereotypes on all sides. We must keep in mind, however, that our appreciation of the cultural aspects of our clients' communication can lead to successful, mutually respectful, interpretations.

Afterword

If you are reading this book for the first time, you are probably overwhelmed by all the complexities associated with bridging the gaps between the Deaf world and society at large. If you have already read the first edition before enjoying this edition, you were probably amazed at the number of changes that have occurred since 1999 that have impacted the Deaf community and the interpreting world. While these transformations have made the interpreter's job more stimulating and exciting, they have added even more complications.

With a severe shortage of interpreters throughout the nation, interpreters are expected to take on increasingly challenging jobs for which they may or may not be fully prepared. In addition, many of the most skilled interpreters are abandoning traditional assignments in favor of more stable and perhaps more lucrative settings such as video interpreting and legal interpreting. The implications for the Deaf community are far reaching and may have reached a crisis proportion.

In addition to experiencing the frustrations of not having interpreters available to fill requests and not having fully qualified interpreters doing assignments, Deaf individuals have had to deal with the new style that is required of video relay interpreters—straight interpreting, minus the personal connection. This means no waiting room chat, no exchange of personal information about their connection to the Deaf community, no empathy expressed, nothing except for a cold, straight relay of voice-to-sign and sign-to-voice communication. This new style of interpreting has not been confined to the video relay setting. It has spilled over to a wide variety of situations outside the video relay context, where both interpreters and Deaf consumers have begun to accept this kind of interpreting model when dealing with each other. In my mind, this has created yet another wall between the Deaf community and the interpreting community.

I'm a strong proponent of maintaining a healthy link between the Deaf community and professional interpreters. I believe that interpreters should attempt to be members of the Deaf community and have a deep desire to be allies of Deaf people. I also believe that the interpreters should embrace the culture of Deaf people. This includes forging a personal connectedness between themselves and the Deaf people involved. I also believe interpreters should make themselves available to support the Deaf community, whether it be in the role of interpreter or in other roles, such as cooking at a Deaf community fundraising event, teaching crafts at a summer program for Deaf children, or working as a crew member in a local Deaf drama production. All these activities support the image of the interpreter as someone who is not in the business just to make money but rather as someone who believes in the goals of and supports the Deaf community.

Furthermore, this second edition highlights the need to be concerned about meeting the needs of all segments of the Deaf community. While ASL is usually the unifying factor, the members of the Deaf community are just as diverse as their hearing counterparts. For this reason, you, as the interpreter, need to have the motivation, determination, and the right attitude to take on this challenge of removing the barriers between yourself and others who do not share your ethnic, religious, and cultural backgrounds.

Where does this leave you as a working interpreter or as a future interpreter? I believe you will do well if you continue to remind yourself that interpreting is a service profession and that your role is to provide support to individuals who are in situations where language barriers exist. More important to me as a Deaf consumer, your loyalty should remain with Deaf people even though you are providing services to both the ASL users and English-speaking, non-signing individuals.

Developing the right attitude is clearly the way to go and perhaps the most ambiguous aspect of becoming the best interpreter possible. Too often, I see working interpreters who still do not "get it." They forget or neglect to sign in the presence of Deaf people when they are talking with hearing people in a social context. They don't show much empathy to Deaf people who need to deal with a playing field that is not level. They don't understand the hunger for information among many Deaf people and do not take that into account in their work. In a nutshell, they don't fully understand or appreciate Deaf culture.

For this reason, you will do well to incorporate specific suggestions and ideas from the second part of this book on how to successfully mediate the cultural and language divide between the Deaf and hearing communities in both your professional and personal interactions with Deaf people.

More important, this section provides clues on how you can develop the right attitude and becoming effective in supporting Deaf people in various interpreting situations. Adopting this kind of attitude and behavior will set you on the road to becoming one of those interpreters who is much loved and well respected by the majority of the Deaf community. I hope it is your goal to be in that category.

Dr. Thomas K. Holcomb

Bibliography

Akamatsu, C. Tane. "Teaching Deaf Asian and Pacific Island American Children." In *Multicultural Issues in Deafness*, edited by Kathee M. Christensen and Gilbert L. Delgado. White Plains, NY: Longman Publishing Group, 1993.

Akinnaso, F. Niyi, and Cheryl Seabrook Ajirotutu. "Performance and Ethnic Style in Job Interviews." In *Language and Social Identity*, edited by John J. Gumperz. Cambridge, England: Cambridge University Press, 1982.

Althen, Gary. *American Ways: A Guide for Foreigners in the United States*. Boston, MA: Intercultural Press, 1988.

Alvord, Lori, and Elizabeth Cohen Van Pelt. *The Scalpel and the Silver Bear*. New York: Bantam Books, 1999.

Aramburo, Anthony J. "Sociolinguistic Aspects of the Black Deaf Community." In *The Sociolinguistics of the Deaf Community*, edited by Ceil Lucas. San Diego, CA: Academic Press, 1989.

Azodeh, Emmanuel. "A Sign of African-American Pride." *Silent News*. March 1994.

Baker, Charlotte, and Robbin Battison, eds. *Sign Language and the Deaf Community: Essays in Honor of William C. Stokoe*. Silver Spring, MD: National Association of the Deaf, 1980.

Baker-Shenk, Charlotte. "Characteristics of Oppressed and Oppressor Peoples: Their Effect on the Interpreting Context." In *Interpreting: The Art of Cross-Cultural Mediation*, edited by Marina McIntire. Silver Spring, MD: RID Publications, 1986.

Barnlund, Dean C. *Public and Private Self in Japan and the United States: Communicative Styles of Two Cultures*. Boston, MA: Intercultural Press, 1989.

Bellah, Robert N., Richard Madsen, William M. Sullivan, Ann Swindler, and Steven M. Tipton. *Habits of the Heart*. New York: Harper and Row, 1985.

Bennett, Milton J. "Towards Ethnorelativism: A Developmental Model of Intercultural Sensitivity." In *Education for the Intercultural Experience*, 2d ed., edited by R. Michael Paige. Boston, MA: Intercultural Press, 1993.

Bienvenu, M. J. "Reflections of American Deaf Culture in Deaf Humor." In *TBC News, The Bicultural Center*, September 1989, no. 17.

Bohannan, Paul. *We, the Alien.* Prospect Heights, IL: Waveland Press, 1992.

Bragg, Bernard, and Eugene Bergman. *Tales from a Clubroom.* Washington, DC: Gallaudet University Press, 1981.

Carmel, Simon. "American Folklore in the Deaf Community," videotape, Washington, DC, Gallaudet University, 1981.

———. "Deaf Folklore and Culture," videotape, Fremont, CA: Ohlone College, 1982.

Carroll, Jerry. "Carrying the Torch for Politeness," *San Francisco Chronicle,* 1 June 1997.

Carroll, Raymonde. *Cultural Misunderstandings: The French-American Experience.* Chicago, IL: University of Chicago Press, 1988.

Chong, Nilda. *The Latino Patient.* Boston, MA: Intercultural Press, 2002.

Chough, Steven. "The Fascinating Asian/Deaf Cultures in America." In *Deaf Studies V—Towards 2000 Unity and Diversity.* Washington, DC: Gallaudet University Press, 1998.

Condon, E. C. "Cross-Cultural Interference affecting Teacher-Pupil Communication in American Schools." In *Intercultural Communication: A Reader,* 3d ed., edited by Larry A. Samovar and Richard E. Porter. Belmont, CA: Wadsworth, 1982.

Condon, John C., and Fathi Yousef. *An Introduction to Intercultural Communication.* New York: Macmillan, 1975.

Crammate, Alan. *Meeting the Challenge: Hearing Impaired Professionals in the Workplace.* Washington, DC: Gallaudet University Press, 1987.

Dahlen, Tommy. *Among the Interculturalists.* Stockholm, Sweden: Stockholm University, 1997.

Davis, Jeffrey and Samuel Supalla. "A Sociolinguistic Description of Language Use in a Navajo Family." In *Sociolinguistics in Deaf Communities,* edited by Ceil Lucas. Washington, DC: Gallaudet University Press, 1995.

DeVita, Philip R., and James D. Armstrong, eds. *Distant Mirrors: America as a Foreign Culture.* Belmont, CA: Wadsworth, 1993.

Dolnick, Edward. "Deafness as Culture." *Atlantic Monthly* 273 (September 1993).

Fant, Lou. *Silver Threads.* Silver Spring, MD: RID Publications, 1990.

Farnell, Brenda. "Sign Language." *Houghton Mifflin Encyclopedia of North American Indians.* http://college.hmco.com/history/readerscomp/naind/html/na_036000_signlanguage.html (accessed May 18, 2005).

Finkle, Joshua. "Life in ASL." In *ASL PAH!,* edited by Clayton Valli et al., Burtonsville, MD: Linstok Press, 1992.

Fisher, Glen. *International Negotiation: A Cross-Cultural Perspective.* Boston, MA: Intercultural Press, 1980.

Forestal, Eileen. "Understanding the Dynamics of Deaf Consumer-Interpreter Relations." Telecourse. Westminster, CO: Front Range Community College, 1994.

Frishberg, Nancy. *Interpreting: An Introduction.* Silver Spring, MD: RID Publications, 1986.

Fromkin, Victoria, and Robert Rodman. *An Introduction to Language.* New York: Holt Rinehart and Winston, 1983.

Galanti, Geri-Ann. *Caring for Patients from Different Cultures.* Philadelphia, PA: University of Pennsylvania Press, 1997.

Gannon, Jack. *Deaf Heritage.* Silver Spring, MD: National Association for the Deaf, 1981.

Gerner de Garcia, Barbara. "Addressing the Needs of Hispanic Deaf Children." In *Multicultural Issues in Deafness,* edited by Kathee M. Christensen and Gilbert L. Delgado. White Plains, NY: Longman Publishing Group, 1993.

———. "Meeting the Needs of Hispanic/Latino Deaf Students." In *Deaf Plus: A Multicultural Perspective,* edited by Kathee Christensen. San Diego, CA: Dawn Sign Press, 2003.

Gochenour, Theodore. *Considering Filipinos.* Boston, MA: Intercultural Press, 1990.

Gropper, Rena C. *Culture and the Clinical Encounter: An Intercultural Sensitizer for the Health Professions.* Boston, MA: Intercultural Press, 1996.

Gumperz, John J., and Jenny Cook-Gumperz. "Introduction: Language and the Communication of Social Identity." In *Language and Social Identity,* edited by John J. Gumperz. Cambridge, England: Cambridge University Press, 1982.

———. *Beyond Culture.* 1976. Reprint, New York: Anchor/Doubleday, 1981.

———. "The Anthropology of Manners." *Scientific American* 192 (1955): 89.

Hall, Edward T. *The Dance of Life.* Garden City: Anchor/Doubleday, 1983.

———. *The Hidden Dimension.* 1966. Reprint, New York: Anchor/Doubleday, 1982.

———. *The Silent Language.* 1959. Reprint, New York: Anchor/Doubleday, 1981.

Hall, Edward T., and Mildred Reed Hall. *Understanding Cultural Differences: Germans, French and Americans.* Boston, MA: Intercultural Press, 1989.

Hall, James. "Communications: Mobile Phones in Vogue in Africa" *Interpress News Service,* 2003. http://ipsnews.net (Accessed March 7, 2005).

Hall, Stephanie. "Train Gone Sorry." In *American Deaf Culture,* edited by Sherman Wilcox. Burtonsville, MD: Linstok Press, 1989.

Hammond, Sue Anne, and Linda Hagar Meiners. "American Indian Deaf Children and Youth." In *Multicultural Issues in Deafness,* edited by Kathee M. Christensen and Gilbert L. Delgado. White Plains, NY: Longman Publishing Group, 1993.

Harris, Philip R., and Robert T. Moran. "Understanding Cultural Differences." In *Intercultural Communication: A Reader,* 3d ed., edited by Larry A. Samovar and Richard E. Porter. Belmont, CA: Wadsworth, 1982.

Henley, John. "Finns Answer to Call of Mobile." *Guardian Newspapers.* 11 November 2002.

Hermida, Alfred. "Asia Plays with Hi-tech Visions." *BBC News Online.* 10 October 2003. http: //news.bbc.co.uk/go/pr/fr/-/1/hi/technology/3177348.stm (Accessed March 6, 2005).

Highwater, Jamake. *The Primal Mind.* New York: Meridian, 1981.

Holcomb, Thomas K. "Develoment of Deaf Bicultural Identity." *American Annals of the Deaf* 142, no. 2 (1997).

Hopper, Robert. *Telephone Conversation.* Bloomington, IN: Indiana University Press, 1992.

Hoza, Jack. *It's Not What You Say, Its How You Say It,* Washington, DC: Gallaudet University Press, (forthcoming).

Jacobs, Leo M. *A Deaf Adult Speaks Out.* 3d ed. Washington, DC: Gallaudet University Press, 1989.

Jensen, J. Vernon. "Perspective on Non-Verbal Intercultural Communication." In *Intercultural Communication: A Reader* 3d ed., edited by Larry A. Samovar and Richard E. Porter. Belmont, CA: Wadsworth, 1982.

Jones, Phillip. "Issues Involving Black Interpreters and Black Deaf." In *Interpreting: The Art of Cross-Cultural Mediation,* edited by Marina McIntire. Silver Spring, MD: RID Publications, 1986.

Kannapell, Barbara. "Inside the Deaf Community." In *American Deaf Culture: An Anthology,* edited by Sherman Wilcox. Burtonsville, MD: Linstok Press, 1989.

Kapp, Robert A., ed. *Communicating with China.* Boston, MA: Intercultural Press, 1983.

Katriel, Tamar. *Talking Straight: Dugri Speech in Israeli Sabra Culture.* Cambridge, England: Cambridge University Press, 1986.

Kennedy, Joyce Lain. *Job Interviews for Dummies.* Foster City, CA: IDG Books Worldwide, 1996.

Kluckhohn, Florence R., and Fred L Strodtbeck. *Variations in Value Orientations.* 1961. Reprint, Westport, CT: Greenwood Press, 1973.

Kochman, Thomas. *Black and White Styles in Conflict.* Chicago, IL: University of Chicago Press, 1981.

Krannich, Caryl Rae, and Ronald L. Krannich. *Interview for Success.* Manassas Park, VA: Impact Publications, 1982.

Kunerth, Jeff. "Deaf Culture Fades." *Orlando Sentinel,* 27 January 2005.

Lane, Harlan. *The Mask of Benevolence: Disabling the Deaf Community.* New York: Knopf, 1992.

———. *When the Mind Hears.* New York: Random House, 1984.

Lane, Harlan, Robert Hoffmeister, and Ben Bahan. *A Journey into the Deaf-World.* San Diego, CA: Dawn Sign Press, 1996.

Lang, Harry G. *A Phone of Our Own.* Washington, DC: Gallaudet University Press, 2002.

Lederer, William J. *The Ugly American.* New York: Norton, 1958.

Leeds-Hurwitz, Wendy. "Notes in the History of Intercultural Communication: The Foreign Service Institute and the Mandate for Intercultural Training." *Quarterly Journal of Speech* 76, no. 3 (1990): 262–81.

Lewis, John G. "Ebonics in American Sign Language: Stylistic Variation in African American Signers." In *Deaf Studies V — Towards 2000 Unity and Diversity.* Washington, DC: Gallaudet University Press, 1998.

Lopez, John R. "Hispanic Americans: Roots of Oppression and Seeds of Change." In *A Kaleidoscope of Deaf America.* Silver Spring, MD: National Association of the Deaf, 1989.

Lovejoy, Elijah. "Negative Red Flags." In *Experiential Activities for Intercultural Learning,* vol. 1, edited by H. Ned Seelye. Boston, MA: Intercultural Press, 1996.

Lovenheim, Peter. *How to Mediate Your Dispute.* Berkeley, CA: Nolo Press, 1996.

Luce, Louise Fiber. *The French-Speaking World.* Lincolnwood, IL: National Textbook, 1991.

MacKinnon, Ian. "Kosher Phone Taps into New Market for Mobiles." *Times Online.* 3 March, 2005. http://www.timesonline.co.uk

McIntire, Marina, and Gary Sanderson. "Who's in Charge Here?: Perceptions of Empowerment and Role in the Interpreting Setting." *RID Journal of Interpretation* 7, no. 1 (1995).

Metzger, Melanie. *Sign Language Interpreting: Deconstructing the Myth of Neutrality.* Washington, DC: Gallaudet University Press, 1999.

Meyer, Marcella. "Marcella's Musings." *GLAD News,* 1994.

Miller, Stuart. *Understanding Europeans.* Santa Fe, NM: John Muir, 1987.

Mindess, Anna. "What Name Signs Can Tell Us about Deaf Culture." *Sign Language Studies* 66 (1990): 1–24.

Moore, Julie. "Looking at RID and NAD Interpreter Evaluations through an Intercultural Lens." *RID Journal of Interpretation* (1997).

Moore, Matthew S., and Linda Levitan. *For Hearing People Only,* 3d ed., Rochester, NY: Deaf Life Press, 2003.

———. *For Hearing People Only.* Rochester, NY: Deaf Little Press, 1992.

Morris, Desmond, Peter Collet, Peter Marsh, and Marie O'Shaughnessy. *Gestures.* New York: Stein and Day, 1979.

Morsbach, Helmut. "Aspects of Nonverbal Communication in Japan." In *Intercultural Communication: A Reader,* 3d ed., edited by Larry A. Samovar and Richard E. Porter. Belmont, CA: Wadsworth, 1982.

Mutti, Sheri Farinha. "Sign Language Interpreters: Something Positive," *NorCal Newsline* (Spring 1996).

Natadecha-Sponsel, Porance. "The Young, the Rich, and the Famous: Individualism as an American Cultural Value." In *Distant Mirrors,* edited by Philip R. DeVita and James D. Armstrong. Belmont, CA: Wadsworth, 1993.

National Multicultural Interpreter Project. "A Curriculum for Enhancing Competencies for Working within Culturally and Linguistically Diverse Communities." El Paso, TX: El Paso Community College, 2000. www .epcc.edu/Community/NMIP/Welcome.html

National Multicultural Interpreter Project. "Cultural and Linguistic Diversity Series: Life Experiences of Donnette Reins, Muskogee Creek, videotape. El Paso, TX: El Paso Community College, 2000.

National Multicultural Interpreter Project. "Multicultural Interpreter Issues: From the Deaf Multicultural Perspective," videotape. El Paso, TX: El Paso Community College, 2000.

National Multicultural Interpreter Project. "Multicultural Interpreter Issues: From the Multicultural Interpreter Perspective," videotape. El Paso, TX: El Paso Community College, 2000.

Nydell, Margaret K. *Understanding Arabs: A Guide for Modern Times*, 4th ed. Boston, MA: Intercultural Press, 2006.

Odunfa, Sola. "Ruder by the Day." *BBC Focus on Africa Magazine*. London, England. January–March, 2004. p. 24–25 (SIRS Researcher Data Base).

Ogden, Paul W. *The Silent Garden*. Washington, DC: Gallaudet University Press, 1996.

Padden, Carol. "The Deaf Community and the Culture of Deaf People." In *Sign Language and the Deaf Community: Essays in Honor of William C. Stokoe*, edited by Charlotte Baker and Robbin Battison. Silver Spring, MD: National Association of the Deaf, 1980.

Padden, Carol, and Tom Humphries. *Deaf in America*. Cambridge, MA: Harvard University Press, 1988.

————. *Inside Deaf Culture*. Cambridge, MA: Harvard University Press, 2005.

Paige, R. Michael, ed. *Education for the Intercultural Experience*, 2d ed. Boston, MA: Intercultural Press, 1993.

Parasnis, Ila, ed. *Cultural and Language Diversity and the Deaf Experience*. New York: Cambridge University Press, 1996.

Philip, Marie. "Cross-Cultural Comparisons: American Deaf Culture and American Majority Culture." Telecourse. Westminster, CO: Front Range Community College, 1993.

Plant, Sadie. "On the Mobile." Report commissioned by Motorola, 2001. http:www.motorola.com/mot/doc/0/234/_MotDoc.pdf-1327.SKB (Accessed March 16, 2005).

Plant, Sadie. "A World of Difference." *New Statesman*. London: 15 September 2003. 16: 774, R9–R10.

Preston, Paul. *Mother Father Deaf*. Cambridge, MA: Harvard University Press, 1994.

Ramsey, Claire L. "On the Border: Cultures, Families, and Schooling in a Transnational Region." In *Deaf Plus: A Multicultural Perspective*, edited by Kathee Christensen. San Diego, CA: Dawn Sign Press, 2003.

Rexroat, Nikki. "The Colonization of the Deaf Community." *Social Work Perspectives* 7, no. 1 (Spring 1997): 18–26.

Rheingold, Howard. *Smart Mobs.* Cambridge, MA: Perseus Publishing, 2002.

Rousch, Daniel. *Indirectness Strategies in American Sign Language.* Unpublished Master's thesis, Gallaudet University, 1999.

Rowland, Michael. "Michelin's *Guide Vert Touristique:* A Guide to the French Inner Landscape." In *The French-Speaking World,* edited by Louise Fiber Luce. Lincolnwood, IL: National Textbook, 1991.

Roy, Cynthia. "Features of Discourse in an American Sign Language Lecture." In *The Sociolinguistics of the Deaf Community,* edited by Ceil Lucas. San Diego, CA: Academic Press, 1989.

———. *A Sociolinguistic Analysis of the Interpreter's Role in the Turn Exchanges of an Interpreted Event.* Ph.D. dissertation, Georgetown University, Washington, DC, 1989.

———. "A Sociolinguistic Analysis of the Interpreter's Role in Simultaneous Talk in Interpreted Interaction." In *Multilingua* 12 (4), 1993.

Ruben, Brent D. "Human Communication and Cross-Cultural Effectiveness." In *Intercultural Communication: A Reader,* 3d ed., edited by Larry A. Samovar and Richard E. Porter. Belmont, CA: Wadsworth, 1982.

Rutherford, Susan. *A Study of American Deaf Folklore.* Burtonsville, MD: Linstok Press, 1993.

Sacks, Oliver. *Seeing Voices.* Berkeley, CA: University of California Press, 1989.

Samovar, Larry A., and Richard E. Porter. *Intercultural Communication: A Reader,* 3d ed. Belmont, CA: Wadsworth Publishing, 1982.

Samovar, Larry A., Richard E. Porter, and Lisa A. Stefani. *Communication Between Cultures.* Belmont, CA: Wadsworth Publishing, 1997.

Schein, Jerome D. *At Home among Strangers.* Washington, DC: Gallaudet University Press, 1989.

Schein, Jerome D., and Marcus T. Delk Jr. *The Deaf Population of the United States.* Silver Spring, MD: National Association of the Deaf, 1974

Schragle, Peter S., and Gerald C. Bateman. "Impact of Captioning." In *Deaf American Monograph.* Silver Spring, MD: National Association of the Deaf, 1994.

Schuchman, John. *Hollywood Speaks.* Urbana, IL: University of Illinois Press, 1988.

Schwartz, Michael A. "Demand on Interpreters to 'Open Up' is Misguided," *Silent News,* January 1996.

Seelye, H. Ned, ed. *Experiential Activities for Intercultural Learning,* vol. 1. Boston, MA: Intercultural Press, 1996.

Shahar, Lucy, and David Kurz. *Border Crossings: American Interactions with Israelis.* Boston, MA: Intercultural Press, 1995.

Smith, Cheri, Ella Mae Lentz, and Ken Mikos. *Signing Naturally—Level One.* Berkeley, CA: Dawn Sign Press, 1988.

Smith, Theresa B. *Deaf People in Context.* Ph.D. dissertation, University of Washington, 1996.

Sontag, Deborah. "Poor, Deaf and Mexican, Betrayed in Their Hope." *New York Times.* 25 July 1997.

Storti, Craig. *Cross-Cultural Dialogues.* Boston, MA: Intercultural Press, 1994.

———. *Old World/New World: Bridging Cultural Differences –Britain, France, Germany and the U.S.* Boston, MA: Intercultural Press, 2001.

———. *The Art of Crossing Cultures.* Yarmouth, ME: Intercultural Press, 1990.

Stewart, Edward C., and Milton J. Bennett. *American Cultural Patterns: A Cross-Cultural Perspective,* 2d ed. Boston, MA: Intercultural Press, 1991.

Sue, Derald Wing, and David Sue. *Counseling the Culturally Different.* New York: John Wiley & Sons, 1990.

Supalla, Samuel J. *The Book of Name Signs.* San Diego: Dawn Sign Press, 1992.

Teuber, Harmut. "Free Enterprise: A Euphemism for Greed?" *RID Views* 14, no. 3 (March 1997).

Triandis, Harry C. *Individualism and Collectivism.* Boulder, CO: Westview Press, 1995.

Triandis, Harry C., Richard Brislin, and C. Harry Hui. "Cross-Cultural Training across the Individualism-Collectivism Divide." *International Journal of Intercultural Relations* 12 (1988): 26–89.

Tucker, James. "The Impact of ASL Research on the American Deaf Community." In *Deaf Way,* edited by Carol Erting et al. Washington, DC: Gallaudet University Press, 1994.

Turner, Craig. "For Canada's Jailed Indians, Justice Is Going Traditional." *San Francisco Chronicle,* 14 May 1996.

Tylor, Edward B. *Primitive Culture.* 1871. Reprint, Harper and Row, 1958.

Valli, Clayton, Ceil Lucas, Esmé Farb, and Paul Kulick, eds. *ASL PAH!* Burtonsville, MD: Linstok Press, 1992.

Van Cleve, John V., ed. *Gallaudet Encyclopedia of Deafness and Deaf People.* vol. 3. New York: McGraw-Hill Book Co., 1987.

Wanning, Esther. *Culture Shock! USA.* Portland, OR: Graphic Art Center Publishing, 1991.

Weaver, Gary. *Culture, Communication and Conflict.* 2d ed. Needham Heights, MA: Simon and Schuster, 1998.

Wei, Yao. "The Importance of Being KEQI." In *Communicating with China,* edited by Robert A. Kapp. Boston, MA: Intercultural Press, 1983.

Whorf, Benjamin Lee. In *Language, Thought and Reality: Selected Writings of Benjamin Lee Whorf,* edited by John B. Carroll. Cambridge: MIT Press, 1956.

Wilcox, Sherman, ed. *American Deaf Culture: An Anthology.* Burtonsville, MD: Linstock Press, 1989.

Witter-Merithew, Anna. "The Socio-Political Context of Interpreting as Mediation." Telecourse. Dayton, OH: Sinclair College, 1996.

Young, Linda Wai Ying. "Inscrutability Revisited." In *Language and Social Identity,* edited by John J. Gumperz. Cambridge, England: Cambridge University Press, 1982.

Zaharna, R.S. "Understanding Cultural Preferences of Arab Communication Patterns." *Public Relations Review* 21: 241–55, 1995.

About the Author and Contributors

$\blacklozenge$

Anna Mindess has worked as a sign language interpreter for over twenty-five years in business, legal, educational, medical, video relay, and performing arts settings. She holds a Comprehensive Skills Certificate and a Specialist Certificate: Legal from the Registry of Interpreters for the Deaf. Her M.A., from San Francisco State University, in a special interdisciplinary major she designed is called language and culture with a focus on sign language. Anna has lectured and led workshops across the U.S. and Europe. Her articles have appeared in American, French, and German publications. She is the author of *Reading Between the Signs Workbook*. Anna and Thomas Holcomb have collaborated on several projects, including the video *See What I Mean: Differences Between Deaf and Hearing Cultures* and *Cultural Detective®: Deaf Culture* for the CulturalDetective.com series.

Thomas K. Holcomb comes from a multigenerational Deaf family. He, his parents, grandparents, and children are all Deaf. Tom is Professor of Deaf Studies at Ohlone College in Fremont, California, where he teaches courses related to Deaf Culture, Deaf Education, and Interpreting. Previously, he taught at San Jose State University and Rochester Institute of Technology/National Technical Institute for the Deaf in Rochester, New York. Tom is considered a leading authority on Deaf Culture. He was awarded the Teacher of the Year Award by American Sign Language Teacher Association (ASLTA) in 2002. He is also an accomplished storyteller and is the featured performer in the Boys Town Press videotape series, *Read with Me: Stories for Your Deaf Child*. His recent collaborations with Anna Mindess include a DVD entitled *See What I Mean: Differences Between Deaf and Hearing Cultures* and an upcoming DVD entitled *A Sign of Respect: Strategies for Effective Deaf/Hearing Interactions*. His academic preparation includes a B.A. in psychology from Gallaudet University, an M.S. in career development from Rochester Institute of Technology, and a Ph.D.

in Curriculum and Instruction from the University of Rochester. He is frequently invited to present at conferences and has published widely on topics related to Deaf culture, Deaf identity, student development, and mainstreaming.

Daniel Langholtz is a longtime colleague, consumer, friend, and fan of interpreters. He holds a B.A. in social work from NTID/RIT, an M.A. in social work from New York University, and is a licensed social worker. Dan has worked for many years at the University of California Center on Deafness in San Francisco, doing both clinical work and training in the area of mental health and deafness. He is a consultant in the fields of mental health, interpreting, HIV/AIDS, accessibility, and relationships between Deaf and non-deaf people. Dan also works at multiple rural school sites providing counseling services to Deaf and Hard of Hearing students from pre-kindergarten through high school. Dan is a Certified Deaf Interpreter. He is involved with training and mentoring Deaf community members striving to become Deaf interpreters. Dan has long been an active member of RID, having worked on numerous committees for the Ethical Practices System, mediation, certificate testing, and the revision of the Code of Professional Conduct.

Priscilla Moyers grew up in a Deaf family and graduated from the California School for the Deaf at Fremont. She attended CSUN and Gallaudet University before receiving a B. A. in English literature with a minor in English as a Second Language from San Francisco State University. Priscilla has worked as a research assistant with the ASL Literacy Research Project at San Francisco State University. She has also interpreted for Deaf persons and in medical, mental health, and platform settings. She has taught ASL for more than fifteen years, both privately and at educational institutions including California State University Northridge and Vista College in Berkeley. After completing an intensive program in legal interpreting in 1993, she began freelancing in the courts, enhancing access to the judicial system for Deaf consumers. Now a Certified Deaf Interpreter (CDI), Priscilla continues to serve as a legal intermediary interpreter. She provides seminars and workshops on interpreting and how to become a CDI and also does consulting work on American Sign Language and its cultural issues.

Index

"n" refers to in-text notes.